IMPROVING
COLLEGE
READING

Third Edition

IMPROVING COLLEGE READING

Third Edition

Lee A. Jacobus

University of Connecticut

HARCOURT BRACE JOVANOVICH, INC.

New York   San Diego   Chicago   San Francisco   Atlanta

ISBN: 0-15-540930-1
Library of Congress Catalog Card Number: 77-90202
Printed in the United States of America

Preface

Improving College Reading, Third Edition, is a collection of forty new selections that is designed to stimulate a serious interest in reading. In this edition I have preserved the qualities of the earlier editions that made them useful for both classroom work and self-instruction. New to this edition are vocabulary previews introducing each of the five sections, which familiarize readers with some of the words used in the subsequent selections. In response to observed student needs and to suggestions from instructors who have used the book in their courses, I have emphasized vocabulary development to a far greater degree in this edition than I did in the previous ones.

I have tried to include material that would interest young adults. The development of skills like the ability to recognize vocabulary, to retain details and important information, to derive inferences from the text, and to generalize and recognize the principal purpose of reading materials can be taught most efficiently when readers are indeed engaged in the act of reading.

The range of subject matter is broad—from law to education, from television to literature, from adventure to history, from racing to cloning. Selections discuss the Hamilton–Burr duel, the Nobel Prizes, earthquakes, the strange fate of J. Edgar Hoover's fortune, building an igloo, the way wolves choose their prey. Each selection is in its own way rewarding and informative. Taken in totality, they offer an insight into the culture we all share.

The selections are grouped in five sections of increasing difficulty. Within each section, most passages are of approximately the same difficulty, so they may be read in any order. For this edition, I used the most current research and relied on my own experience to arrange the selections by grade. And although it was taken into consideration, the length of a passage is not a guide to its level of difficulty.

The exercise material in each section is carefully matched in difficulty to the selections in the section. As the selections become more difficult, so do the exercises. Throughout, there is an emphasis on retention and on vocabulary development. The exercises focus readers' attention to the passage in such a way as to help them develop a sense of what to look for, how to hold on to what has been read. Inferential skills become more important as the passages become more difficult.

The exercises retain the kinds of question that appeared in the second edition. Students are generally familiar with these kinds of question. The question patterns remain uniform from the beginning to the end of the book, so that no artificial barriers will block readers' measured progress. The 100-point total is maintained for convenience of scoring and ease of measuring individual progress. Students can keep track of their reading speed and their progress in maintaining speed levels by means of scoring graphs and a progress chart found at the end of the book. Since the passages increase in difficulty, it is important to emphasize that any reader who maintains a constant score from the beginning to the end of the book has made measurable progress.

I would like to thank users of the two previous editions whose suggestions helped me to improve this edition. The UConn Summer Program has been the source of a number of suggestions that I used. The Northeast Association of Two-Year College Teachers of Reading, through its annual meetings and its individual members, has been very helpful to me. I would also like to thank Maryanne Twaronite for her help with the manuscript. Finally, I owe a debt of real gratitude to Matthew Milan, Jr., whose expertise in this area is considerable, and whose faith in all these editions was unwavering. His advice was essential to all editions of the book.

Finally, I want to dedicate this book to the instructors and the students who will use it, with the hope that it will do them the good service that any worthwhile book can do in the pursuit of learning.

Lee A. Jacobus

Contents

SECTION I

Vocabulary Preview

The following words come from the nine reading selections in Section I. Study the list carefully, pronouncing the words aloud if possible. Conceal the definitions with a card or your hand and test your command of the meanings of the words.

ambience, *noun*   atmosphere; general feel of a place or situation
anthropoid, *noun*   manlike animal
apprehension, *noun*   arrest, having been caught; uncertainty, fear
astonishing, *adj.*   surprising; amazing
awesome, *adj.*   amazing; inspiring fear or dread
colossal, *adj.*   huge
contorted, *adj.*   twisted out of shape
distraught, *adj.*   worried, upset
ecstatic, *adj.*   delighted, very happy
eerie, *adj.*   weird; scary
eloquent, *adj.*   effective in speaking
emerge, *verb*   to come out; to leave
erudite, *adj.*   intelligent; educated
figment, *noun*   something imaginary
giddy, *adj.*   dizzy; silly
gimmicky, *adj.*   deceptive, tricky, false
guile, *noun*   trickery; deceit
hexagonal, *adj.*   having six sides
hoax, *noun*   trick; fake
immobilized, *adj.*   unable to move
indulgent, *adj.*   tolerant; lenient
ingenious, *adj.*   clever; inventive
interminable, *adj.*   without end, endless

intrigued, *adj.* curious; interested

legitimate, *adj.* authentic; legal

maneuver, *verb or noun* to change strategy, shift; move, change in strategy

manipulate, *verb* to control; to manage

meticulous, *adj.* extreme attentiveness to detail; great care

phenomenon, *noun* occurrence; event

polygraph, *noun* lie detector machine

precept, *noun* teaching; rule for living

prowess, *noun* strength; skill

psychic, *adj.* mental; extrasensory

purportedly, *adv.* supposedly

redoubtable, *adj.* formidable, strong; commanding respect

serenity, *noun* peacefulness; calmness

skeptically, *adv.* with suspicion or disbelief

sleuth, *noun* detective

specimen, *noun* example

spectacle, *noun* sight; exhibition

spew, *verb* to vomit forth; to throw up

stygian, *adj.* relating to hell; dark and hellish

Styx, *noun* in Greek mythology, the river running between the world and Hades

tedious, *adj.* tiring; dull

vie, vied, *verb* to compete for; to match against someone

vivid, *adj.* clear; intense; lively

Complete the following sentences, using the correct words from the list.

1. Because Stephen was always in the library, we considered him to

   be _____.

2. We always gave Billy the _____ jobs because he did not seem to mind monotony or repetition.

3. Luis and Marjy _____ with each other for control of the student senate.

4. Manny's coming to class was a _____ we were not prepared to deal with.

5. Helen's skill on the skateboard was truly _____.

6. Sid _____ from the building with a happy look on his face.

7. The professor was _____ while we explained our absence.

8. Casino night was not a fake. It featured a _____ roulette table.

9. Nothing could have been more _____ than Mildred's speech.

10. Leonie's _____ with a racing bike was well known everywhere.

11. The bottom of my clothes closet is dark, dank, and almost

_____ .

12. The language he _____ forth was intolerable.

13. Jimmie was _____ by the weight of the car.

14. Nothing really happened. It was all a _____ experience.

15. Hector was not just bothered, he was really _____ .

1 *PAULA TAYLOR*

Coretta King Carries On

The widow of one of America's most important civil-rights leaders has carried on her husband's work since his assassination. She had helped in the movement while he lived. The inner strength Martin Luther King gave her remains to help her now that he is dead.

Over the years Coretta's courage was tested time and again. Once she got a phone call telling her Martin had been rushed to the hospital in New York. A mentally disturbed woman had stabbed him in the chest with a letter opener. Three hours of surgery were needed to remove the weapon. Afterwards doctors told Coretta that its point had been touching Martin's heart. If he had panicked and moved suddenly or even sneezed, he would have died instantly. Even after the successful surgery, he remained on the critical list for several days.

Though terribly worried, Coretta remained calm. When Martin began to recover, she took his place at meetings and gave speeches from his notes. Many people credit her with holding the movement together during this critical time.

Shortly before Dexter was born, Coretta again feared for her husband's life. He was arrested for leading a sit-in at a lunch counter in Atlanta. For this minor offense, the judge handed down a harsh sentence of 6 months hard labor at the State Penitentiary.

Coretta was terribly upset. The penitentiary was 300 miles from the Kings' home in Atlanta. Pregnant and with 2 small children, she could rarely make the 8-hour trip to visit her husband. She knew how black prisoners were treated in southern jails. Martin might be beaten—or worse.

Before lawyers had time to appeal the judge's decision, Martin was roughly dragged from his Atlanta jail cell. He was chained and handcuffed. In the middle of the night, he was taken to the penitentiary.

When Coretta heard what had happened, she was distraught. Just as she was about to give up hope, the telephone rang. "Just a moment, Mrs. King," the long-distance operator said, "Senator John F. Kennedy wants to speak to you."

"How are you, Mrs. King?" a warm voice inquired. After chatting a few minutes about her family and the new baby they were expecting, Senator Kennedy told Coretta he was concerned about Martin's arrest. "Let me know if there's anything I can do to help," he told her. The next day, Martin was released.

Two years later, Coretta had another talk with John Kennedy. By then he was President. Martin had been jailed in Birmingham. Coretta was not allowed to see or even phone him. Fearing the worst, she called the White House. Once again, Kennedy came to the rescue, and Martin was freed.

Through all the dark moments of her life, Coretta never doubted that the cause to which she and Martin had dedicated their lives was right. Even on April 4, 1968, when she faced the supreme test—the death of her husband—her faith never wavered. She had suffered much. A lesser woman might have withdrawn from the world in grief. Coretta did not.

The day after Martin was shot, Coretta made an eloquent statement to the press. She said that both she and Martin had accepted the fact that his life might suddenly be cut short. They both felt it wasn't how long one lived that was important, but how well. Martin Luther King had given his life trying to help people find a better way to solve their problems than by hatred and violence. Coretta urged those who had loved and admired her husband to help carry on the work he had begun.

The day before his funeral, Coretta took Martin's place in the march he was to lead in Memphis. From all over the country thousands of people came to march with her. Thousands more stood along the route in silent tribute to the memory of their leader and the bravery of his widow.

Coretta's faith carried her heroically through the ordeal of Martin's funeral. Throughout the long hours of speeches and television coverage, she never broke down. All who saw her marveled at her serenity and inner strength.

LENGTH: 640 WORDS

1 Coretta King Carries On

SCORING: Reading time: _____ Rate from chart: _____ W.P.M.

RETENTION	number right_____ × 4 equals_____ points
INFERENCES	number right_____ × 3 equals _____ points
COMPLETION	number right_____ × 4 equals _____ points
DEFINITIONS	number right_____ × 3 equals _____ points

(Total points: 100) **total**_____ points

RETENTION   Based on the passage, which of the following statements are True (T), False (F), or Not answerable (N)?

1. _____ Once, Martin Luther King was in a hospital in New York.

2. _____ Dexter is Coretta King's brother.

3. _____ Martin Luther King was arrested at a lunch counter in Atlanta.

4. _____ Coretta King had a hard time calling John F. Kennedy on the telephone.

5. _____ Once Kennedy was president, he turned his back on Martin Luther King.

6. _____ Martin Luther King was arrested, but not handcuffed.

7. _____ Coretta King was often arrested herself.

8. _____ Martin Luther King died in 1974.

9. _____ Coretta King did not really understand the dangers her husband faced.

10. _____ Both Coretta and Martin believed fervently in their cause.

INFERENCES

1. _____ Which of the following statements is probably most accurate?
   (a) The White House was involved in ordering Martin's arrest.
   (b) Coretta was influential in carrying on Martin's work after his death.
   (c) Coretta and Martin vied with each other for power in the movement.

2. _____ Which of the following statements is probably inaccurate?
   (a) Both Coretta and Martin favored violence on a controlled basis.
   (b) John F. Kennedy seems to have admired Martin King.
   (c) Martin Luther King's work was threatened by his sudden death.

COMPLETION   Choose the best answer for each question.

1. _____ Over the years, Coretta's courage: (a) dwindled. (b) was eloquent. (c) grew enormously. (d) was tested often.

2. _____ Martin Luther King was stabbed by: (a) a sheriff in Georgia. (b) one of his own followers. (c) an unstable woman. (d) a hated enemy.

3. _____ After Martin's death, people marveled at Coretta's: (a) inner strength. (b) fiery speeches. (c) lack of resentment. (d) organizational skills.

4. _____ When Martin was jailed in Birmingham, Coretta: (a) gave him up for dead. (b) could not even phone him. (c) informed her lawyers immediately. (d) asked him if there was anything she could do to help.

5. _____ On April 5, 1968, the day after Martin was shot, Coretta: (a) withdrew in grief. (b) refused to speak to anyone but Kennedy. (c) made the eight-hour trip to Atlanta. (d) made an eloquent statement to the press.

6. _____ Martin was arrested in Atlanta for leading a: (a) parade. (b) sit-in. (c) strike. (d) radical movement.

DEFINITIONS   Choose the definition from Column B that best matches each italicized word in Column A.

Column A	Column B
1. they had *dedicated* their lives	_____ a. most important
2. she could *rarely* make the trip	_____ b. got frightened
	_____ c. contended
3. she was *eloquent*	_____ d. committed
4. if he *panicked*	_____ e. calmness
5. amazed at her *serenity*	_____ f. soon
	_____ g. not often
6. a warm voice *inquired*	_____ h. effective in speech

7. the *supreme* test

8. he was *concerned* about Martin

9. she did not *waver*

10. *solve* their problems

_____ i.   asked

_____ j.   find the answer to

_____ k.   the most

_____ l.   worried

_____ m. remain steadfast

_____ n.   change

2 *ALEXANDER B. KLOTS AND ELSIE B. KLOTS*

Tarantula Hunters

We do not often think that such awesome animals as tarantulas are sometimes defenseless against predators. Yet, there is one redoubtable insect that uses tarantulas as a long-term food supply.

We might well expect the big powerful and poisonous tarantulas to be relatively free from enemies, at least of their own size. But there is a group of wasps, smaller than the giant spiders, which regularly seek them out, defeat them in combat, and use them as food for their young. These wasps are members of a world-wide family, the *Pepsidae,* which specialize on spiders, large or small according to their own size. In our deserts there are some large enough to cope with even the largest tarantulas.

The tarantula hawks, as they are commonly called, are quite beautiful; they are dark, metallic blue with clear or salmon colored wings. The females, which are larger than the males and may be three inches or more long, do the hunting. Running nervously over the ground, a female tarantula hawk may encounter a tarantula; or, if she finds a tarantula's burrow, she does not hesitate but dives into it and grapples with its occupant. Eventually she manages to curl her abdomen beneath the body of the tarantula and to sting it in the big nerve centers (ganglia) which control its actions. The tarantula goes limp. It is, however, merely paralyzed and may live for weeks, completely immobilized.

The wasp then drags its bulky prey to a suitable crevice or hole. There it glues an egg to it and leaves it. Shortly the wasp egg hatches and then the young wasp, a grub-like creature called a *larva,* has a plentiful supply of fresh food. It will eventually grow and transform to an adult wasp, to take up the task of tarantula hunting as food for its own offspring.

LENGTH: 240 WORDS

TARANTULA HUNTERS   From *The Community of Living Things in the Desert* by Alexander B. Klots and Elsie B. Klots. Copyright © 1967 by Creative Education, Inc. Reprinted by permission.

2 Tarantula Hunters

SCORING: Reading time: _____ Rate from chart: _____ W.P.M.

RETENTION   number right_____ × 4 equals _____ points

INFERENCES   number right_____ × 3 equals _____ points

COMPLETION   number right_____ × 4 equals _____ points

DEFINITIONS   number right_____ × 3 equals _____ points

(Total points: 100) **total**_____ points

RETENTION   Based on the passage, which of the following statements are True (T), False (F), or Not answerable (N)?

1. _____ The male wasp is somewhat larger than the female.

2. _____ The young wasp is called a larva.

3. _____ The tarantula, not the wasp, is immobilized.

4. _____ Tarantulas live underground.

5. _____ The wasp buries the tarantula fairly deep in the ground.

6. _____ The tarantula hawk is a relatively small bird.

7. _____ Many lizards live on tarantulas, too.

8. _____ The tarantula-hunting wasp lives only in American deserts.

9. _____ Desert tarantulas are usually fairly small.

10. _____ The wasps prey on spiders that are their own size.

INFERENCES

1. _____ Which of the following statements is probably most accurate?
   (a) The tarantula hunters kill tarantulas only during certain months.
   (b) Tarantulas kill a goodly number of wasps during the struggle.
   (c) The wasps do not actually kill the tarantulas in the struggle.

2. _____ Which of the following statements is probably inaccurate?
   (a) The wasps and the tarantulas apparently have a tough struggle.
   (b) One tarantula can feed a whole brood of infant wasps.
   (c) Each wasp has three or four offspring.

Choose the best answer for each question.

1. _____ Actually, the tarantula hawks are: (a) deadly. (b) rather shy in their way. (c) quite beautiful. (d) remarkably sharp-sighted.

2. _____ One thing is clear: the wasp is: (a) unafraid of the tarantula. (b) very skittery. (c) easily panicked. (d) alert to the ambiance of the morning.

3. _____ The tarantula hunter attaches an egg to the spider and then: (a) flies overhead. (b) runs nervously along the ground. (c) leaves. (d) goes off to die.

4. _____ A tarantula-hunting wasp will hunt: (a) as many spiders as it has eggs for. (b) when threatened. (c) spiders smaller than it. (d) salmon-colored spiders.

5. _____ The wasp deposits the immobilized spider in: (a) the sand. (b) a suitable crevice or hole. (c) a barrow. (d) its own home.

6. _____ The wasp stings the tarantula in its: (a) eyes. (b) nerve center. (c) neck. (d) larval cavity.

DEFINITIONS Choose the definition from Column B that best matches each italicized word in Column A.

Column A	Column B
1. it is *merely* paralyzed	_____ a. after a while
2. a *plentiful* supply	_____ b. struggle
3. it may *encounter* a spider	_____ c. testy
	_____ d. abundant, sufficient
4. she does not *hesitate*	_5_ e. unable to move
5. completely *immobilized*	_____ f. mainly
6. to be *relatively* free	_____ g. comparatively
7. it will *eventually* grow	_____ h. meet
8. regularly *seek* them out	_____ i. change
	_____ j. awesomely
9. grow and *transform*	_____ k. wait
10. *grapple* with its occupant	_____ l. effectively
	_____ m. hunt
	_____ n. only

3 *PEGGY FISHER*

The Shoplifting Rite of Passage

Shoplifting is probably as old as shops. But in today's shopping malls, shoplifters exhibit some new twists and some new approaches. The newest may be in the attitude of the shoplifter: moving from humiliation to pride.

Shoplifting. It used to be considered a harmless rite of passage. A child moved from babyhood into the "gang" by stealing a Batman comic from the local paper store. Friends listened with indulgent smiles at cocktail parties as adults entertained one another with their "harmless" childhood adventures. Occasionally, someone would admit he/she had been caught and brought to the local police station "for a scare." But generally the stories ended as lightly as they began, not being caught, and for the most part, never stealing anything again.

Perhaps that was a more innocent time to be growing up, 10 or 15 years ago. And being caught meant more. One 26-year-old woman said it was five years before she dared return to the store where she had been caught stealing a record when she was 14.

It is the middle of the pre-Christmas rush when Marsha Feller, manager of Casual Corner at South Portland's Maine Mall, takes a few minutes to talk about shoplifting. "They are so brazen," says Feller angrily of the teenagers who steal from her store. "I prosecute everybody. I'm in court with four or five right now."

Feller gives this account of a recent incident that took place in Casual Corner: A 14-year-old high school girl with a stolen corduroy vest concealed

---

THE SHOPLIFTING RITE OF PASSAGE   *Maine Times,* December 17, 1976. Reprinted by permission of Peggy Fisher.

under her coat tried to get past the inventory control device situated by the only entrance to the shop. The alarm rang and Feller apprehended the youngster and sat her down in her small office behind the shop. "I asked her why she took it," says Feller. "She said, 'It was too much money but I wanted it so I took it.' "

Feller told the girl it was store policy to prosecute and the girl replied, "What a bummer!" Soon, several of the girl's friends appeared in the office, including the girl's sister. The young shoplifter said to her sister, "Hey, when you got caught were you prosecuted?" The sister said no, she wasn't. "Far out," said the 14-year-old. Then of her own situation, "What a bummer."

As is her policy with all juveniles, Feller called the girl's mother. The mother arrived, apologetic and humiliated, but the girl showed little remorse. "The girl cried a little . . . they all cry," says Feller. "Not because they did something wrong . . . because they got caught." As it turned out, the youngster had shoplifted in the past but this was her first apprehension.

Feller was amazed the next day when the same girl—now released in her parents' custody until her court date—came back to the store with her boyfriend to show him the alarm system and describe how she had taken the vest. "She's a hero to her friends," says Feller.

LENGTH: 465 WORDS

3   The Shoplifting Rite of Passage

SCORING: Reading time: _____ Rate from chart: _____ W.P.M.

RETENTION	number right _____ × 4 equals _____ points	
INFERENCES	number right _____ × 3 equals _____ points	
COMPLETION	number right _____ × 4 equals _____ points	
DEFINITIONS	number right _____ × 3 equals _____ points	

(Total points: 100) **total** _____ points

RETENTION   Based on the passage, which of the following statements are True (T), False (F), or Not answerable (N)?

1. _____ Shoplifting was once thought to be a harmless rite of passage.

2. _____ Marsha Feller prosecutes shoplifters who are particularly brazen.

3. _____ One woman waited twenty-six years to go back to a shop she had stolen from.

4. _____ Variety stores have the worst shoplifting problem.

5. _____ The girl in the article tried to steal a coat.

6. _____ The incident cited occurred in Casual Corner.

7. _____ The shoplifter had a sister who had also stolen merchandise.

8. _____ Shoplifters used to be taken to the police station "for a scare."

9. _____ Statistics show that the number of shoplifters is on the rise everywhere.

10. _____ The shoplifter was caught when an alarm rang.

INFERENCES

1. _____ Which of the following statements is probably most accurate?
(a) Marsha Feller believes that people's attitudes toward shoplifting have changed.
(b) Marsha Feller believes American life may have seemed different in the old days, but only on the surface.
(c) Marsha Feller believes that shoplifting is simply a rite of passage.

2. _____ Which of the following statements is probably inaccurate?
   (a) Most shoplifters are likely to go to court on charges if they are caught.
   (b) Marsha Feller was surprised to see the thief back in the store the next day.
   (c) The thief was really ashamed of what she had done.

COMPLETION   Choose the best answer for each question.

1. _____ The girl was released: (a) on the spot. (b) two weeks later. (c) at the jailhouse. (d) in her parents' custody.

2. _____ The girl's mother was: (a) hard to reach. (b) humiliated. (c) defiant. (d) much too indulgent.

3. _____ After it was all over, the girl came back to the store with her: (a) father. (b) boyfriend. (c) sister. (d) lawyer.

4. _____ Marsha Feller thinks that, to her friends, the girl is a: (a) heroine. (b) thief. (c) problem child. (d) snob.

5. _____ The incident in question happened: (a) in July. (b) three years ago. (c) before the pre-Christmas rush. (d) only yesterday.

6. _____ Stealing a Batman comic is mentioned as a requirement for: (a) hitting the big time. (b) understanding shoplifting. (c) joining the gang. (d) life.

DEFINITIONS   Choose the definition from Column B that best matches each italicized word in Column A.

Column A	Column B
1. Feller *apprehended* her	_____ a. surprised
2. they are so *brazen*	_____ b. intimidated
3. a recent *incident*	_____ c. shame
	_10_ d. explain
4. listen with *indulgent* smiles	_____ e. amused
5. adults *entertained* one another	_____ f. fresh, surly
6. policy with all *juveniles*	_8_ g. sorry
7. Feller was *amazed*	_1_ h. caught
8. the mother arrived, *apologetic*	_5_ i. occurrence
9. showing little *remorse*	_4_ j. tolerant
10. *describe* how it happened	_____ k. eerie
	_6_ l. youths
	_____ m. ingenious
	_____ n. suspicious

4 *ROBERT McCULLOUGH*

The Southwest's Enduring Indian

American Indians are part of the natural landscape of the Southwest. Some tourists notice the Indians, and some do not. But the real miracle is that the Indians have survived the changes of the white world around them.

When you visit the southwest, it's no real problem to ignore its Indians. Redoubtable and often invisible to tourists, they endure as one of this country's last natural resources. Visible or invisible, depending on whether your interest is genuine, they exist out there still as exciting and beautiful and exasperating as the real estate they inhabit and protect from us.

The Pimas. The Papagos. The Hopis. The Navahos, Havasupais, Hualapais. The Jicarillas. The Mescareros. The Zunis and the Chemeheavis. The Isletas. The Labunas. The Nambes. The Humas and the Yaquis. Merely stringing their names together sounds like poetry.

We pave our landscapes, choke in our smogs, and poison our water, and with a bewildered backward glance at their reverence for the earth and straightforward way of life it dawns on us that their civilization is less uncivilized than we'd been taught to believe. Any Cub or Brownie could tell us the facts about Indians, of course, since it takes a third grader's eyes and ears (and purity of heart) to really understand.

That the southwestern Indians have survived at all is a miracle. And that they're still civil enough to suffer out the Compleat American Tourist with his Polaroid poking into their sacred rituals and ceremonies is an even greater miracle. Reverse the roles. Can you imagine a horde of Instamatic equipped

THE SOUTHWEST'S ENDURING INDIAN   *The Kiwanis Magazine,* May 1974. Reprinted by permission of *The Kiwanis Magazine* and Robert McCullough.

Hopi Indians spewing out of a tour bus into a New England village "to snap the natives in their natural habitat?"

It's a phenomenon worth noting, too, that you can still buy an authentic Papago basket or a Katchina doll in the art and craft centers out there and not get fleeced. This rather quaint merchandising approach, called "giving the customer his money's worth," is based on an old Indian religious precept—something about not cheating. There are indications that they are getting a bit testy about always holding the queen of spades in this game of hearts with the white man, and it's rumored that the Navahos are driving steely hard bargains out there at Window Rock. It's no longer possible, for instance, to buy for peanuts an exquisite Navaho rug that it took an Indian lady over a year to weave. Nor is it a simple maneuver to rip open Black Mesa, transform the coal underneath it into electricity on the spot, and not pay the tribe a handsome premium for the privilege.

Like the song goes, "Times, they are a changin'." A big bunch of Indian young folks, fed up with the cities, have drifted back to the reservations with interesting ideas. They've even hired lawyers—young Indian lawyers. It seems that all that worthless property they've been sitting on for so long has veins of uranium ore under it. And coal. And oil. And Lord knows what else is under that desert. So before progress gets out of hand I'd suggest you get your business straight and visit these southwestern Indian folks on their home territory while the old ambience is still above ground. It sure isn't ever going to be the same again.

When I talked with an Acoma Indian filling station operator near Grants, New Mexico, last summer he admitted he kept the house up there on the "Sky City" butte just for a "place to get away to on the weekends." During the rest of the week he lived in town near the superhighway. Later that same day while the Indian community crowded into the spare little church at Acomita for their yearly San Lorenzo Day ceremonies an overzealous Indian trooper ticketed every pickup truck parked a trifle too far into the road bordering the church property. Shaking her head sadly, an old Indian lady standing in the overflow crowd of worshippers uttered what I sensed to be an unmentionable discouraging word.

There are still wondrous, unsullied, mystical sights and sounds and smells to be stored in one's memory bank labelled "Southwest." I can close my eyes and it's no trouble conjuring up unparalleled dawns. I remember waiting one out, heart pounding, last summer in the Acoma valley. At first the mesa bathed in a silky blue-violet, only to be transformed (and you're never really ready for it) by that exploding fireball into a miracle of red and then another miracle of orange and yellow. Then the awareness that the shadows were still an intense complementary blue-violet.

The absolute fact of Mesa Verde, experiencing for the first time those twenty skyline-skimming miles from the park entrance to the cliff dwellings and inside knowledge about a place the geography books and atlases never prepare you for. The quietness of Canyon de Chelly at dusk.

Shrieking sunsets in the desert.

The sense of the continuum and the beehive activity at the Taos pueblos.

An Indian family walking together into an oblivion of red earth and sagebrush.

"Traditionalist" diehards may howl about the rape of Black Mesa but the spiritual and cultural erosion in the southwest is more alarming to me. As the years slip by and the old ones die, fewer Indian youngsters embrace the old traditions and somehow forget to memorize the litanies and the songs of their forebears. Much of the lore has disappeared already, and the loss is stunning.

LENGTH: 875 WORDS

4   The Southwest's Enduring Indian

SCORING: Reading time: _____ Rate from chart: _____ W.P.M.	

RETENTION   number right _____ × 4 equals _____ points

INFERENCES   number right _____ × 3 equals _____ points

COMPLETION   number right _____ × 4 equals _____ points

DEFINITIONS   number right _____ × 3 equals _____ points

(Total points: 100) **total** _____ points

RETENTION   Based on the passage, which of the following statements are True (T), False (F), or Not answerable (N)?

1. _____   The Indian is playing cards with white tourists.

2. _____   Once it was possible to buy Navaho rugs for very little money.

3. _____   The Indians do not approve of cheating in business deals.

4. _____   Reservation land is as worthless today as ever.

5. _____   There is coal under Black Mesa.

6. _____   It is no longer possible to buy authentic Papago baskets.

7. _____   The Navaho has long since gone from Window Rock.

8. _____   Some Indians have become lawyers.

9. _____   Apparently there are tourists poking into sacred rituals.

10. _____   The tourists cannot miss the Indians no matter what.

INFERENCES

1. _____   Which of the following statements is probably most accurate?
(a) In a generation the Indian will be in much the same situation as now.
(b) Chances are, the Indian will grow wealthier in a generation.
(c) Poverty seems the certain lot of most Indians a generation from now.

2. _____   Which of the following statements is probably inaccurate?
(a) Dealings between Indians and whites have always been pretty fair.

(b) The Indians have tended not to cheat the whites over the years.
(c) New Englanders would not like to see Indian tourists each summer.

COMPLETION   Choose the best answer for each question.

1. _____ If there is coal under Black Mesa, the Indians will: (a) do a coal dance.   (b) make money.   (c) be sorry.   (d) not be able to touch it.

2. _____ Third graders are supposed to: (a) have keen eyes and ears.   (b) be Brownies.   (c) study Indians.   (d) have purity of heart.

3. _____ We have been taught that the Indians' civilization is: (a) brilliant, but marred.   (b) raw.   (c) basically sound.   (d) uncivilized.

4. _____ If you buy art objects in Indian shops you will not: (a) get fleeced.   (b) get the real thing anymore.   (c) want to come home.   (d) have good luck.

5. _____ An Indian woman weaves a rug in: (a) an adobe.   (b) over a year.   (c) the back of a shop.   (d) her natural habitat.

6. _____ That the southwest Indians have survived at all is: (a) curious.   (b) a tribute to Washington.   (c) a miracle.   (d) because of the Hopis.

DEFINITIONS   Choose the definition from Column B that best matches each italicized word in Column A.

Column A	*Column B*
1. *Reverse* the roles	_____ a. general feel of the place
2. a *phenomenon* worth noting	_____ b. bothersome
	_____ c. inventive
3. a *bewildered* backward glance	_____ d. occurrence
4. natural *habitat*	_____ e. suggestive
5. beautiful and *exasperating*	_____ f. switch around
	_____ g. beautiful
6. they *endure*	_____ h. living space
7. an *exquisite* Navaho rug	_____ i. live on
	_____ j. honest, real
8. the old *ambience* is still there	_____ k. teaching
9. an old Indian *precept*	_____ l. habitual
10. there are *indications* that	_____ m. signs
	_____ n. confused

5 *ARLENE FRANCIS*

TV's Oldest Game Show

"What's My Line?" was a pioneer on the airwaves. No one thought that the program would attract the interest of the entire nation as much as it did. But, being rooted in our curiosity about what other people do for a living, it became the longest-running game show on television. Arlene Francis, one of its stars, tells us about it.

When television moved into the living room along with the couch, the easy chair and the potato chips, a little over a quarter of a century ago, I was starring in a radio drama. It was all about the adventures of a gorgeous (what-the-hell, they couldn't see me on radio) girl detective called Anne of Scotland Yard. A sort of sexy private eyelash, who got her man with guile instead of guns. To give you an idea of the blessings of radio, I played this part up to two weeks before my son was born! A tribute to my deception came from my dear friend Claire Trevor. She wired me, "You don't sound the least bit pregnant but you sound as though you might be any minute!"

In radio you had to do everything with your voice. Your body was in fantasy land. You could be cross-eyed, fat and flabby but as long as you knew how to manipulate speech you could play anything from a pig to a princess. Who knew? . . . But television was moving in and I was sure I was moving out. After all, I didn't look like Jean Harlow. Mind you, I didn't resemble Boris Karloff either, but I wasn't Miss Universe and I felt sure movie-starlet looks were what the home screen would demand. But I hadn't figured on the war and the turnabout it would give to the world of entertainment. I became the moderator (or matchmaker) of a wildly successful program called "Blind Date," in which the Army, the Navy and the Marines vied over a telephone for an evening of

TV'S OLDEST GAME SHOW   "I Was There from First to Last." Reprinted with permission from *The Saturday Evening Post* © 1976 The Curtis Publishing Company.

dining and dancing with three beautiful girls. Then followed "Soldier Parade," "Talent Patrol," "Home" and shining through all those years, the super structure, "What's My Line?," that never changed its reasonable query or reward.

It looks like an innocent child alongside of today's gimmicked, greedy gobbledygook. Nowadays what you hear goes something like this:

"You have just won $22,500 and a trip to the moon on gossamer wings in this terrific C-130, which will fly you to Egypt where you will float down the Nile on Cleopatra's barge, fully equipped with this fantastic Wurlitzer organ and Westinghouse kitchen," cries the ecstatic announcer to the bikini-clad overweight lady wearing a baby bonnet. She had guessed who was buried in Grant's tomb.

What a long way the game show has traveled since "What's My Line?" got underway in 1950. Twenty-five years later (January 1st, 1975), when it left the airwaves, the Goodson-Todman early achiever was still giving away to the contestant the same amount of money it always gave, upwards to $50.

How explain its remarkable survival? I've always thought it was because the first question anyone asks of another in the USA, after "How do you do?" is "*What* do you do?" Most of us are curious about how our fellowman makes a living. And on WML we had a chance to meet them all. Over a twenty-five-year period (I was there from first to last) I don't think we missed a legitimate business. I recall even being mixed up in an illegitimate one in the very early days before all contestants were double-checked on their occupation. A very attractive young woman signed in as a plumber's assistant. What Goodson-Todman didn't know was the *manner* in which she assisted! At any rate, the switchboard lighted up during the show and informed the operators the lovely creature didn't know as much about plumbing as she did about prostitution. . . . After that giddy incident every contestant was researched thoroughly. After all, TV was quite new in 1950 and a baby industry had to make a few baby mistakes. I'll admit, ours was a beaut! Nevertheless, for seventeen years of Sunday nights, under the administration of the erudite and gracious John Daly, WML was the ritual habit of millions of satisfied customers.

We dressed in evening clothes for the occasion and the only changes over the years were the varieties in style and coiffure. My hair advanced from brown to blonde, John's receded just a little, and darling Bennett Cerf acquired some salt in the pepper. All in all it was quite a proper program. Belly dancers? Nudist colonists? Slapstick comics? John Daly would have none of it, and Mark Goodson, who handles all of his own productions with the meticulous care of a drill sergeant, was able to give it the kind of distinction that set it apart. It was a far cry from our syndicated program, which like most recent productions was oriented toward the young and zany.

LENGTH: 770 WORDS

5   TV's Oldest Game Show

SCORING: Reading time: _____ Rate from chart: _____ W.P.M.

RETENTION	number right _____ × 4 equals _____ points	
INFERENCES	number right _____ × 3 equals _____ points	
COMPLETION	number right _____ × 4 equals _____ points	
DEFINITIONS	number right _____ × 3 equals _____ points	

(Total points: 100) **total** _____ points

RETENTION   Based on the passage, which of the following statements are True (T), False (F), or Not answerable (N)?

1. _____ Arlene Francis got her first break in show business on television.

2. _____ Miss Francis seems quite self-conscious about her appearance.

3. _____ The producers of "What's My Line?" had been successful in movies.

4. _____ Arlene Francis was a star on radio more than twenty-five years ago.

5. _____ "What's My Line?" awarded a top prize of $50.

6. _____ One plumber's helper on the show turned out to be a prostitute.

7. _____ The show actually survived because of its off-color comedy.

8. _____ "What's My Line?" was a steady performer on Friday nights.

9. _____ Bennett Cerf was frequently on the show.

10. _____ Arlene Francis was on the show from its beginnings to its ending.

INFERENCES

1. _____ Which of the following statements is probably most accurate?
   (a) The point of the show was to promote Arlene Francis and John Daly.
   (b) The game was to guess the occupations of various contestants.

(c) Fifty dollars was a great deal of money for any game show to give away.

2. _____ Which of the following statements is probably inaccurate?
(a) Contemporary shows seem rather gimmicky compared with "What's My Line?"
(b) People thought the movie starlet "look" was not appropriate for early television.
(c) The producers double-checked all contestants after the "accident."

COMPLETION Choose the best answer for each question.

1. _____ One role Arlene Francis played on radio was a: (a) plumber. (b) nudist colonist. (c) drill sergeant. (d) detective.

2. _____ One show that Miss Francis moderated was: (a) "Blind Date." (b) "Big Deal." (c) "Some Luck!" (d) "How Do You Do?"

3. _____ The contestant who won the "trip" in the C-130 guessed: (a) a song title. (b) who was buried in Grant's Tomb. (c) her own name. (d) which way was up.

4. _____ In radio you had to do everything with your: (a) friends. (b) producers. (c) voice. (d) imagination.

5. _____ John Daly would have on the show no: (a) zanies. (b) corporals. (c) belly dancers. (d) soldiers, sailors, or Marines.

6. _____ In 1950, television was: (a) dull. (b) silly. (c) quite new. (d) impossible.

DEFINITIONS Choose the definition from Column B that best matches each italicized word in Column A.

Column A	Column B
1. the *erudite* John Daly	_____ a. delighted
2. its remarkable *survival*	_____ b. intelligent
	_____ c. reliability
3. with *meticulous* care	_____ d. considerable
4. the Marines *vied* over a telephone	_____ e. extremely attentive
5. the kind of *distinction* it had	_____ f. interested
	_____ g. long life
6. under his *administration*	_____ h. competed

7. the *ecstatic* announcer

8. most of us are *curious*

9. *illegitimate* businesses

10. after that *incident*

_____ i. dishonest

_____ j. special style

_____ k. lied

_____ l. leadership

_____ m. occurrence

_____ n. zany

6 SUZANNE HILTON

Stress Testing a Golf Ball

The lowly golf ball is a product of modern scientific engineering. It has suffered pounding, ripping, and wind-testing in an attempt to perfect the game that many people have called the silliest form of frustration ever invented. Golf may be silly, but science has helped to refine it.

Golf can be traced back to the days of the Romans. They used a bent stick to hit a leather ball stuffed with feathers. By 1457, a Scottish king found that his people had been spending so much time playing "golfe and futeball" that they had been neglecting their archery. Since he was counting on their prowess with bows and arrows to keep enemies from invading Scotland, he had no choice but to declare both games illegal. But soon after, gunpowder became popular for wars, and archery was no longer of much use. Golf came back to stay.

The golf balls used then were called "featheries." They had been made by wrapping leather tightly around wet goose feathers. But after the feathers had dried out, the balls often burst when hit and showered the course with feathers. A Scottish minister invented "gutties." They were made of gutta-percha, a gum from a Malaysian tree. They did hold together, but they also had a disadvantage. They flew far out when hit and then suddenly plummeted straight down to the ground. Golfers soon found that after the "gutties" had been nicked a few times, they traveled farther than new ones. Soon golf ball makers began putting the little nicks on when they made them. Such balls did travel farther—so much farther that golf courses had to be made larger. But there had to be a limit. The space on the earth for golf courses is not endless. So the ball was limited in size

STRESS TESTING A GOLF BALL   From *Beat It, Burn It, and Drown It,* by Suzanne Hilton. Copyright © 1974, Suzanne Hilton. Published by The Westminster Press. Used by permission.

and weight. Now the only things that could be changed were the materials used to make the balls—and, of course, the dimples on it.

One company asked an aerospace professor how it could make its ball fly farther than any other. He tested many old balls in a subsonic wind tunnel so he could make comparisons. Some had round dimples, some had diamond shapes, squares, or cones. It was impossible to tell with the eye which balls had the best lift and the least drag. But by using over-sized balls in the wind tunnel, the professor could see there was a lot of difference in action between balls—mostly caused by the shape of the dimples.

The professor took some newly designed golf balls out onto a golf course. He built a machine that, unlike a person, would hit each golf ball exactly the same way. After many hours of testing and using a computer, the ball with the hexagonal-shaped dimples beat all the others.

LENGTH: 450 WORDS

6   Stress Testing a Golf Ball

SCORING: Reading time: _____ Rate from chart: _____ W.P.M.

RETENTION	number right _____ × 4 equals _____ points
INFERENCES	number right _____ × 3 equals _____ points
COMPLETION	number right _____ × 4 equals _____ points
DEFINITIONS	number right _____ × 3 equals _____ points

(Total points: 100) **total** _____ points

RETENTION   Based on the passage, which of the following statements are True (T), False (F), or Not answerable (N)?

1. _____ One of the problems was minimizing drag on the golf ball.

2. _____ The Manned Space Center kept some of the research secret.

3. _____ Early golf games were played near Malaysian trees.

4. _____ In the 1400s, Scots practiced archery.

5. _____ The Romans could prepare leather.

6. _____ "Gutties" were invented by a minister.

7. _____ Nick Percha first "dimpled" the golf ball.

8. _____ The aerospace professor used extra large golf balls for testing.

9. _____ The professor's machine actually hit the golf balls.

10. _____ None of the dimples tested were cone shaped.

INFERENCES

1. _____ Which of the following statements is probably most accurate?
   (a) Golf balls do not fly at supersonic speeds.
   (b) Golf balls have always been a standard size and weight.
   (c) Oversize golf balls really travel.

2. _____ Which of the following statements is probably inaccurate?
   (a) The dimples keep the golf ball in the air longer.
   (b) The professor worked pretty much on intuition and good guessing.

(c) Wind tunnels help people see the maneuvering of the golf ball in flight.

COMPLETION   Choose the best answer for each question.

1. _____ Among other things, the professor used a: (a) bent stick.   (b) computer.   (c) gut nicker.   (d) Malaysian tree.

2. _____ Romans stuffed their golf balls with: (a) geese.   (b) leather.   (c) prowess.   (d) feathers.

3. _____ The dimple shape that was best was the: (a) soft.   (b) square.   (c) hexagonal.   (d) round.

4. _____ Many of the golf balls the professor tested were: (a) old.   (b) green.   (c) extra heavy.   (d) too feathery.

5. _____ Golf was back to stay when: (a) the Romans left Britain.   (b) the Scots gave up.   (c) gunpowder became popular.   (d) Malaysia became a colony.

6. _____ The ball was limited in size and weight because: (a) the lift was better.   (b) golf courses must be limited in size.   (c) feathers are scarce.   (d) of a declaration of a fifteenth-century Scottish king.

DEFINITIONS   Choose the definition from Column B that best matches each italicized word in Column A.

Column A	Column B
1. an *aerospace professor*	_____ a. precisely
2. he was counting on their *prowess*	_____ b. fault
3. enemies *invading* Scotland	_____ c. different from
4. *shower* the course	_____ d. intact
5. they had a *disadvantage*	_____ e. skill
6. the balls often *burst*	_____ f. scientist
7. hit each ball *exactly*	_____ g. reign
8. he *invented* "gutties"	_____ h. impressively
9. *unlike* a person	_____ i. explode
10. he *declared* the game illegal	_____ j. entering
	_____ k. sprinkle
	_____ l. pronounced
	_____ m. developed
	_____ n. destroying

Alex Haley: From the Brink of Suicide to the Best-Seller List

It is difficult to believe that the man who wrote the book on which televi-sion's most popular drama was based should have come close to suicide. The search for his family's roots—roots that began in the hold of a slave ship—was an emotionally exhausting experience. Roots *is more than a good story; it is a man's search for personal meaning.*

Only two years ago, Alex Haley was a man in the depths of despair. At one point, he was considering suicide. Now, he is this season's hottest writer—his book, *Roots,* is a record-breaking best seller, and ABC aired a $6-million, 12-hour drama based on the book. A slight, scholarly-looking man with a slow grin and a voice touched with a Tennessee-bred softness, Haley is the last person you'd expect to have created the most brutally dramatic book of the year.

But much of what is best in *Roots*—the story of his family traced back over seven generations—was written out of this man's own agony and despair. His voice is low-pitched, and faraway, and he is close to tears as he tells the story.

"I had already put in 10 years of work on my book when I ran into a complete dead end. Writing about my first ancestor, Kunta Kinte, on his voyage to America aboard a slave ship had become impossible for me. I had tried and failed many, many times. Finally, in desperation, I booked passage on a freighter bound for Africa. Every night I went down into the hold of the ship, stripped to my underwear and lay all night on a wooden plank, trying to imagine what it

ALEX HALEY: FROM THE BRINK OF SUICIDE TO THE BEST-SELLER LIST   Reprint by permission of *Family Weekly,* copyright © 1977 for "Alex Haley: From the Brink of Suicide to the Best-Seller List" by Mary Long.

would be like for a young man to lie there in chains, hearing the cries of men screaming, praying and dying all around him.

"I began to worry that I might be losing my mind" he says quietly. "One night, standing out on the stern deck, watching the freighter's wake, I felt overwhelmed by my burden. I was about $50,000 in debt. My publisher and my agent were at me constantly, asking when I would finish this interminable book. I had told them six months, even though I knew I still had several years of work ahead of me. Inside my head I was suffering the horrors of what happened to Kunta Kinte in the ship hold. Then, I thought how easy it would be just to slip over the rail into the sea. I was almost joyful at the idea."

But at that moment Haley says he had the most vivid psychic experience of his life. "I heard the soft voices of my dead family talking to me, encouraging me. They were saying, 'You must finish. Go on with your book.' It took a tremendous physical effort to push my body away from the rail. I scuttled on my hands and knees, back over the hatch covers to my room. I lay on my bed, sobbing for hours. That night, I knew I finally would be able to find the words to tell my family's story."

The turmoil and labor that went into *Roots* is just about unheard of—nearly 10 years of tedious detective work, over two years of writing. The work was so complex that Haley used to separate his research into manila folders and spread them out, row upon row, in his room. "I planted them like seeds," the writer says, his fingers jabbing the air as though nailing up the words one by one, "and I plowed through them on hands and knees."

What he harvested was a 600-page book that's both a record-breaking best seller and the fulfillment of a personal mission.

LENGTH: 555 WORDS

7 Alex Haley: From the Brink of Suicide to the Best-Seller List

SCORING: Reading time: _____ Rate from chart: _____ W.P.M.

RETENTION	number right _____ × 4 equals _____ points	
INFERENCES	number right _____ × 3 equals _____ points	
COMPLETION	number right _____ × 4 equals _____ points	.
DEFINITIONS	number right _____ × 3 equals _____ points	

(Total points: 100) **total** _____ points

RETENTION Based on the passage, which of the following statements are True (T), False (F), or Not answerable (N)?

1. _____ The television dramatization of *Roots* was twelve hours long.

2. _____ Each night, Haley slept on an actual slave ship.

3. _____ Haley is a big, burly man.

4. _____ Kunta Kinte came from Africa in a slaver.

5. _____ The entire project took Haley about twelve years to complete.

6. _____ Haley's publisher and agent were not worried about the book's completion.

7. _____ After a psychic experience, Haley knew he would finish the book.

8. _____ The manila folders had previously been his publisher's.

9. _____ Haley actually crawled on his hands and knees back from the rail.

10. _____ When he booked passage for Africa, Haley was desperate.

INFERENCES

1. _____ Which of the following statements is probably most accurate?
   (a) Most writers have little trouble writing their books.
   (b) Haley's despair was unusual even for most writers.
   (c) Because of their moodiness, writers often think of suicide.

2. _____ Which of the following statements is probably inaccurate?
   (a) *Roots* involved complex research even though it was a novel.

(b) *Roots* was basically a family novel.

(c) Understanding a slave's feelings was fairly easy.

COMPLETION   Choose the best answer for each question.

1. _____ Haley apparently comes from: (a) Africa.   (b) Manila.   (c) Tennessee.   (d) Chicago.

2. _____ *Roots* traces a family over: (a) and over.   (b) its entire history.   (c) the ocean.   (d) seven generations.

3. _____ Much of preparing for the book was: (a) detective work.   (b) slow and dull.   (c) seed work.   (d) a matter of shrewd bargaining.

4. _____ Haley thought of suicide on the ship's stern: (a) at night.   (b) only once or twice.   (c) because of the wake.   (d) after a storm.

5. _____ To feel what Kunta Kinte felt, Haley: (a) wrote the book.   (b) saw a ghost.   (c) slept on a board.   (d) went deep into debt.

6. _____ *Roots* is described as: (a) family fare.   (b) long, but not tedious.   (c) quite vivid.   (d) brutally dramatic.

DEFINITIONS   Choose the definition from Column B that best matches each italicized word in Column A.

Column A	Column B
1. *tremendous* physical effort	_____ a. sturdy
2. this *interminable* book	_____ b. tiring
3. such a *vivid* image	_____ c. a hopeless situation
4. I felt *overwhelmed*	_____ d. indefinable
5. years of *tedious* work	_____ e. great
6. voices *encouraged* him	_____ f. intense
7. in *desperation*	_____ g. serious
8. the *depths* of despair	_____ h. endless
9. a *psychic* experience	_____ i. lowest points
10. my first *ancestor*	_____ j. gave hope
	_____ k. sensitized
	_____ l. early relative
	_____ m. extrasensory
	_____ n. defeated

8

HENRY N. FERGUSON

The Devil's Caverns

The great Carlsbad Caverns National Park is now one of the jewels in our national park system. However, the caves were discovered only a short time ago, and their character was mysterious and frightening for many years. Today we no longer think of them as devilish, although they are indeed awesome.

One afternoon in late summer, some seventy years ago, a lone cowboy slowly loped across a Western prairie looking for strays. Suddenly he pulled back on the reins. In the distance he could see a cloud of heavy black smoke belching from a low-lying range of hills in the nearby Guadalupes. The cowboy touched spurs to his mount and headed in the direction of this peculiar phenomenon.

As he approached the eerie spectacle he could see the mouth of a yawning pit; his ears caught the ceaseless beat of countless wings. The "black smoke" turned out to be a tremendous flight of bats, pouring out of a cave. The cowboy watched the flight emerge for three hours, and when it had ended, he built a great bonfire, dropped flaming torches into the cave and saw them vanish into the darkness hundreds of feet below. He had discovered Carlsbad Caverns, an astonishing underground world hidden deep beneath the scorching desert of New Mexico.

Jim White was the cowboy who spotted this big hole in 1901. Almost immediately he began exploring it with the aid of kerosene torches, at first alone and then with a Mexican boy, searching out nearly all of its major marvels.

Once, Jim's torch became extinguished and the explorer almost went mad with fear as contorted limestone monsters seemed to leap at him in the last flicker of lights before darkness closed in.

THE DEVIL'S CAVERNS   From "Nature's Big Tunnel in the Guadalupes" by Henry N. Ferguson. *Gracious Living,* 1976. Reprinted by permission of Henry N. Ferguson.

"I heard strange noises," he told friends later. "Sounds like sleigh bells, chimes, streetcar gongs; once I thought I heard someone playing a piano." Finally he found the string he had used to mark his route, and made his way out.

Later, White learned that the "music" he had heard was no dream symphony at all. It came from the slender stalactites as bats brushed them with their wing tips. Each formation gives off a different note, from the tiniest tinkle to the deepest bass, when it is struck with the fingernail.

Jim and his wife moved to the cave, and curious people started coming to see it. Jim would lower the more daring of his guests down into the Stygian blackness in a huge iron bucket which is still on display at the caverns. Finally the Government investigated the place, liked what it saw, and bought the cave and 55,000 surrounding acres for a National Park site.

The story of Carlsbad Caverns goes back some 250,000,000 years into the Permian period of earth's history, when the desert was a shallow inland sea. Then, about 60,000,000 years ago, an upheaval of the earth created the Rocky Mountains and formed the great caverns that exist today.

Three-quarters of a million people come each year to gape at the awesome marvels of this desert garden of unearthly delights. Every day battalions of tourists file along an ingenious switch-back trail into the vast maw—down some 850 feet to an underground world that some describe as the "devil's country." And, indeed, it is easy to imagine that one is walking on the far side of the River Styx. There is an immediate awareness, too, that here God has given man great wonders, but has not supplied the vocabulary to describe them.

No one knows when the caverns' natural entrance appeared; it probably resulted from the collapsing of the roof over a long corridor. But the bats, according to radio-carbon dating on bottom-layer guano and fossil bat skeletons in the bat cave, prove that the entrance has existed for at least 17,000 years. There is no evidence that Indians were ever tempted to probe the mysteries of the cavern's depths. However, ancient peoples did know of the entrance; they left drawings on its walls and cooked mescal in nearby rock pits. Carbon dating of human remains and artifacts places occupants in the area as long ago as 12,000 years. A group of desert people comparable to the Basketmakers is believed to have moved in some 4,000 years ago, and remained until the Apaches ran them off in the Thirteenth Century.

LENGTH: 640 WORDS

8   The Devil's Caverns

+--+
| SCORING: Reading time: _____ Rate from chart: _____ W.P.M.|
+--+
| |
| RETENTION   number right _____ × 4 equals _____ points |
| |
| INFERENCES   number right _____ × 3 equals _____ points |
| |
| COMPLETION   number right _____ × 4 equals _____ points |
| |
| DEFINITIONS   number right _____ × 3 equals _____ points |
| |
| (Total points: 100) total _____ points |
+--+

RETENTION   Based on the passage, which of the following statements are True (T), False (F), or Not answerable (N)?

1. _____ The Carlsbad Caverns are in hills near the Guadalupes.

2. _____ The "black smoke" came from a kerosene torch.

3. _____ Jim White was so scared he never married.

4. _____ The caverns' entrance goes back some 60,000 years.

5. _____ Bats have lived in the cave at least 17,000 years.

6. _____ Most of the caverns are beneath an inland sea.

7. _____ One Indian group comparable to the Basketmakers moved in four thousand years ago.

8. _____ Jim White was heading into town when he discovered the caverns.

9. _____ Actually, Jim White was on foot when he found the caverns.

10. _____ People went to see the caverns even before they became part of a national park.

INFERENCES

1. _____ Which of the following statements is probably most accurate?
    (a) The Apaches used the caverns as a hideout.
    (b) Jim saw the commercial possibilities at once.
    (c) Jim combined curiosity with unusual courage.

2. _____ Which of the following statements is probably inaccurate?
    (a) Bats thrive in deep underground caverns.

(b) The caverns were useless for Indian survival years ago.

(c) Tourists still visit the caverns despite their devilish qualities.

COMPLETION   Choose the best answer for each question.

1. _____ Soon after his discovery, Jim went to the caverns with: (a) a mule. (b) more supplies. (c) a Mexican boy. (d) a sense of adventure.

2. _____ The Indians who knew about the caverns left: (a) promptly. (b) drawings. (c) strange legends. (d) because of the bats.

3. _____ The caverns actually go down: (a) 850 feet. (b) almost a mile. (c) only 250 feet. (d) further than a man knows.

4. _____ Apparently the stalactites can make: (a) music. (b) people sick. (c) men quaver. (d) a ghostly glow.

5. _____ Once the desert area was a: (a) mountain range. (b) Permian period. (c) shallow inland sea. (d) broad western prairie.

6. _____ If one were on the far side of the River Styx, one would be in: (a) Arizona. (b) a cavern. (c) heaven. (d) devil's country.

DEFINITIONS   Choose the definition from Column B that best matches each italicized word in Column A.

Column A	Column B
1. *probe* the mysteries	_____ a. courageous
2. watch the flight *emerge*	_____ b. lenient
3. an *astonishing* underground world	_____ c. weird
4. the *eerie* spectacle	_____ d. search into
5. the eerie *spectacle*	_____ e. occurrence
6. this peculiar *phenomenon*	_____ f. surprising
7. *ancient* peoples survived	_____ g. distinguish
8. an *immediate* awareness	_____ h. sight
9. he *discovered* Carlsbad Caverns	_____ i. leave from
10. the more *daring* guests	_____ j. instantaneous
	_____ k. historic, old
	_____ l. found
	_____ m. say, respond
	_____ n. disturbed

9 GEORGE H. HARRISON

On the Trail of Bigfoot

No one knows if there is such a creature as Bigfoot, but signs of a humanoid have been appearing for some time in the Pacific Northwest. One skeptical investigator, George Harrison, had an experience that made him pause for thought.

There it was . . . a Bigfoot track . . . six inches wide and very fresh.

As I dropped to my knees for a closer look, exciting thoughts raced through my head. Was this for real? Or was someone playing a colossal joke on us?

Skeptically testing the stream bank near the footprint, first with my thumb, and then by jumping on the ground with treaded boots, I realized that whatever made this track an inch deep had to weigh far more than my 170 pounds.

Again I looked at the track—each toe well defined; the ball of the foot behind the big toe typical of anthropoids. Then I quickly pulled off my boot and sock and placed my 10½ B foot next to the track . . . only half as wide. This must have been Bigfoot!

Whatever it was had stepped from the bank to a log, walked down the log and into the water and proceeded down the stream bed. The tracks were there, clearly visible under the water.

Off came my boots again and into the water . . . Cold! . . . Too cold and too remote for any sensible person to be wading for fun.

I wouldn't have believed this could happen last June when *National Wildlife* agreed to co-sponsor the American Yeti Expedition, led by Robert W. Morgan of Miami, Florida.

In June when I headed for the Pacific Northwest to join in the search for "Bigfoot," "Sasquatch," "Yeti," "America's Abominable Snowman"— or whatever you want to call it—I privately thought that our quarry was the figment of someone's imagination. The idea of such creatures, nine feet tall, covered with hair and living in the U.S. wilderness in 1970, seemed pretty ridiculous.

Two years before, *National Wildlife* had printed what was purportedly the first photograph ever taken of Bigfoot. Roger Patterson shot this remarkable color sequence with a 16mm movie camera near Bluff Creek in the wilderness of northern California in October 1967. Patterson and a companion told us they had flushed the creature along a logging trail. Thrown from his horse, Patterson recovered in time to shoot about 12 seconds of jerky footage showing what appeared to be a hairy anthropoid walking away and disappearing into the woods.

Before printing the story and photographs, a *National Wildlife* editor flew to the West Coast to interview Patterson, who believed so strongly in Bigfoot and the photographs he had made that he instantly agreed to take a lie detector test. The results convinced the experienced polygraph operator that Patterson was *not* lying.

The creature in Patterson's film is enormous. Based on its 17-inch long footprints and 41-inch stride, estimates put Bigfoot about seven feet tall and between 350 and 400 pounds. Compared to many other reported sightings and footprints, this was not a particularly large specimen. In the movie it walked with a very human stride, swinging its long arms, and its large pendulous breasts indicated it was female.

Nonetheless, many people called Patterson a "nut" and the creature in his photograph a big man dressed in an ape suit. But careful examination of the footage by a score of experts failed to prove it a hoax. Additional reported sightings of a large hairy anthropoid—37 sightings in 1969 alone—plus constant nudging from our readers, kept *National Wildlife* editors interested in a possible follow-up expedition and story.

If you have ever seen the magnificent scenic beauty of the Pacific Northwest, you know why I was intrigued by the chance to go there, whether we found Bigfoot or not. Admittedly, the expedition was not strictly "scientific" in the sense that purists use the word, implying many people, large financial backing, and months of exploration. But its purpose was serious, based on honest curiosity, and there was certainly more than enough mystery for any enthusiastic outdoor sleuth.

The first phase of the expedition was designed to look for signs of Bigfoot, test various devices for attracting it, and bring back enough evidence in the way of photographs, droppings, hair, and anything else that would help launch Phase Two—which hopefully will be climaxed by a Bigfoot capture.

Robert Morgan, expedition leader, was employed by the Federal Aviation Administration until, after much reading and research, he became hooked on Bigfoot. In 1969, he led a three-man team into the same remote Cascade

Mountain area on a fact-finding hunt. With deep snow still on the ground, Morgan's team found a set of clearly defined barefoot tracks in a snowbank, and a second set in the bottom of an icy mountain stream.

Further intrigued, Morgan organized the current expedition with better equipment and more qualified observers, and invited me to go along. Joining us were Allen S. Facemire, cinematographer-reporter, who was to make a documentary film to gain backing for Phase Two, and Robert Carr, an archeologist studying at the University of Miami. The key scientific adviser to our group was Laymond M. Hardy, a biologist and zoologist, who did not accompany us but who subsequently examined all the materials gathered on the trip.

I did not know what to expect as our heavily loaded micro-bus headed for our base camp in the Cascades. I soon learned, however, that we were already in Bigfoot country when we stopped in Stevenson, Washington, a quiet one-stoplight town on the north bank of the mighty Columbia River. More than anywhere else, Stevenson has been a nerve center for Bigfoot sightings. Nearly everyone in town and half of Skamania County believes, at least a little, in Bigfoot—or in something that lives in the nearby mountains and looks like a huge hairy human being.

LENGTH: 900 WORDS

9   On the Trail of Bigfoot

SCORING: Reading time: _____ Rate from chart: _____ W.P.M.

RETENTION   number right _____ × 4 equals _____ points

INFERENCES   number right _____ × 3 equals _____ points

COMPLETION   number right _____ × 4 equals _____ points

DEFINITIONS   number right _____ × 3 equals _____ points

(Total points: 100) **total** _____ points

RETENTION   Based on the passage, which of the following statements are True (T), False (F), or Not answerable (N)?

1. _____ The incident described happened in Miami, Florida.

2. _____ The first track George Harrison saw was one foot deep.

3. _____ The first tracks Harrison saw were on the bank of a cold stream.

4. _____ Harrison felt the expedition was not really "scientific."

5. _____ The creature that Patterson filmed waved at him.

6. _____ Many sightings were recorded in 1969.

7. _____ The expedition was led by a cameraman.

8. _____ The first phase of the expedition was to find signs of Bigfoot.

9. _____ The base camp was in the Cascades.

10. _____ People in Skamania would be likely to believe such a myth.

INFERENCES

1. _____ Which of the following statements is probably most accurate?
(a) When he started out, Harrison was very skeptical about the existence of Bigfoot.
(b) Robert Morgan felt he was indebted to the Skamanians.
(c) There are no Skamanians.

2. _____ Which of the following statements is probably inaccurate?
(a) The films of Bigfoot are unreliable, but still very interesting.

(b) The expedition that Harrison joined was well financed.

(c) Morgan and his men were fairly confident of catching Bigfoot.

COMPLETION   Choose the best answer for each question.

1. _____ The expedition was in Bigfoot country when it stopped in: (a) the icy stream.   (b) the valley.   (c) Stevenson, Washington.   (d) Columbia.

2. _____ Careful examination of Patterson's film did not: (a) prove it a hoax.   (b) help.   (c) convince Morgan.   (d) alarm the sheriff.

3. _____ Phase Two of the expedition was designed to: (a) last for a month.   (b) include people from Miami.   (c) scare Bigfoot.   (d) capture Bigfoot.

4. _____ Another name for Bigfoot is: (a) Skamany.   (b) Yeti.   (c) Sammy.   (d) Morgan.

5. _____ Apparently the footprints lasted even: (a) though it was cold.   (b) through several seasons.   (c) until today.   (d) under running water.

6. _____ Patterson apparently survived a successful: (a) expedition.   (b) lie detector test.   (c) flight through the woods.   (d) motorcycle chase.

DEFINITIONS   Choose the definition from Column B that best matches each italicized word in Column A.

Column A	Column B
1. test various *devices*	_____ a. unlikely, preposterous
2. *experienced* polygraph operator	_____ b. trying
	_____ c. instruments
3. a *colossal* joke	_____ d. investigator
4. tracks clearly *visible*	_____ e. huge
5. the *figment* of imagination	_____ f. interested
	_____ g. observable
6. a large *specimen*	_____ h. example
7. outdoor *sleuth*	_____ i. having known
8. further *intrigued*	_____ j. sudden, instant
	_____ k. surprising
9. a *remarkable* color sequence	_____ l. spied on
10. seemed pretty *ridiculous*	_____ m. knowledgeable, veteran
	_____ n. a fiction

SECTION II

Vocabulary Preview

The following words come from the ten reading selections in Section II. Study the list carefully, pronouncing the words aloud if possible. Conceal the definitions with a card or your hand and test your command of the meanings of the words.

acquired, *verb*   gotten; purchased; possessed

adverse, *adj.*   bad; unfavorable; opposed

affirmatively, *adv.*   positively, agreeing in a positive manner

alleged, *verb* or *adj.*   stated without proof; said, supposed

amateur, *noun*   not a professional

amid, *prep.*   in the middle of, in

anecdotal, *adj.*   like a story; like a joke

artifact, *noun*   object created for effect; piece of art

asexual, *adj.*   without sex; without sexual intent or concern

assertedly, *adv.*   supposedly; stated positively

austerely, *adv.*   economically; severely; soberly

benefactor, *noun*   person who helps; person who donates things

blare, *verb*   to make a loud noise

candidly, *adv.*   openly; honestly; fairly

chromosome, *noun*   part of a cell containing the genes

clandestine, *adj.*   secret

cloning, *verb*   reproducing genetic copies

concede, *verb*   to give in; to admit

conjectural, *adj.*   possible; pertaining to a guess

cringe, *verb*   to wince; to shrink away in fear

demise, *noun*   death

dirge, *noun*   funeral music

dispel, *verb* to scatter; to chase away

diversity, *noun* variety

eclectic, *adj.* taking from many sources; not pure

elite, *adj.* select; special

emits, *verb* sends out; lets out

excruciating, *adj.* very painful

extermination, *noun* the killing off

extraterrestrial, *noun* being from a planet other than Earth

extricate, *verb* to free from difficulty; to get out of a jam

finesse, *noun* smooth style; skill

flourish, *verb* to thrive; to do well; to survive

fratricide, *noun* the killing of one's brother

genetic, *adj.* relating to the genes; inherited

homing, *verb* returning home; aiming in

hostile, *adj.* unfriendly

infectious, *adj.* catching

infiltration, *noun* the filtering in, usually where it is unexpected

inhibit, *verb* to forbid; to restrain

invariably, *adv.* always, without exception

magnificent, *adj.* great

merger, *noun* the joining together of things, usually businesses

nucleus, *noun* heart or center of something

obliterated, *verb* destroyed without a trace

ominously, *adv.* threateningly

ordination, *noun* official acceptance into an order

partition, *noun* the separation into parts, usually political

persists, *verb* continues; remains

plaguey, *adj.* annoying

posthumous, *adj.* after death

prevalent, *adj.* widespread; existing generally

primate, *noun* manlike; of the class of monkeys and apes

pseudo-science, *noun* fake science

rational *adj.* reasonable; thoughtful; unemotional

refuge, *noun* hideout; secure place

refugee, *noun* person dispossessed, usually from another country

regime, *noun* government

replica, *noun* reproduction; imitation

repository, *noun* museum; place of collection

severed, *adj.* separated from; cut off from

sophisticated, *adj.* highly developed; fully experienced

technological, *adj.* scientific; of high technical development

torrential, *adj.* intense

ultimatum, *noun* final warning

unencumbered, *adj.* without burden; light for travel

virtually, *adv.* essentially; just about

Complete the following sentences, using the correct words from the list.

1. Because of his sophistication and social _____ he was a perfect host.

2. Whenever I wash my car it _____ rains.

3. Alfonso's mean look would _____ anyone from having a good time.

4. I like genuine antique cars, but the _____ leave me cold.

5. Even though we all knew about it, the operation was thought to be

   _____.

6. The explosion _____ the entire town square.

7. We do not know if extraterrestrials could _____

   on earth.

8. I like a lively tune, but that music sounds like a _____.

9. Prejudice against the Irish was _____ in Boston in the 1870s.

10. By setting things straight, Hilda can _____ any nasty rumors.

11. A & P Company and Stop and Shop once contemplated a _____

    _____.

12. The police gave the bandits an _____.

13. The Storm Troopers were Hitler's _____ guard.

14. If we _____ our mistakes, will you change your own demands?

15. With his arm almost _____ Ron crawled back out of the canal.

16. It was incredible because the pain must have been_____ .

17. The crowd turned mean and suddenly behaved in a very _____ _____ manner toward me.

18. Tina's grin was so _____ that we all began smiling.

19. Hilary seems to have _____ an English accent on her vacation.

20. I didn't know it, but apparently the judge was speaking _____ when he recommended a guilty plea.

The Military Porpoise

A debate has arisen over the Navy's training of the docile porpoise for secret-mission work. Another creature of the sea has become our servant, but whether for good or evil remains to be seen.

You remember "Flipper," of course, television's lovable performing porpoise. But "killer porpoises"?

Well, he may or may not be a killer, but there is today a new breed of porpoise—the warrior. He has that same infectious smile on his face, but his is a deadly, secret mission that is a source of growing controversy.

Here at the tip of Point Loma along the Pacific Ocean is the U.S. Navy's Undersea Research and Development Center, the training facility for the nation's military porpoises.

Some of the activities conducted here are known but most are secret.

The Navy freely discusses some missions of its porpoises. They are known to be trained to detect enemy mines and frogmen. Whales or sea lions get similar assignments.

The sea mammals also have been taught to detect and retrieve military hardware from the ocean, saving thousands of dollars and aiding in weapons research. They also are taught to rescue frogmen and to protect divers from sharks.

If, as has been reported, the porpoises are being trained in more aggressive assignments, little is being said about it.

The porpoises' "sonar system"—much like manmade radar—is so well developed that it is highly accurate in distinguishing between types of metals, sizes of objects and even types of submarines.

THE MILITARY PORPOISE "Porpoise Studies Stir Debate," *The Hartford Courant,* May 30, 1973. Reprinted by permission of United Press International.

Tests here have shown the porpoises nearly 100 per cent accurate in selecting between the smaller of two steel balls both barely two inches in diameter. (And that was with the porpoise blindfolded.)

In short, the porpoise is highly intelligent and has a brain as large and as complicated as that of man. Porpoises learn quickly, can communicate well with man and lend themselves to sophisticated military uses.

Although the Navy has generally refused comment on military missions of its mammals, published reports in recent years have hinted at some types of training military porpoises are receiving, including the "Kamikaze" porpoise. He allegedly is trained to carry explosives and blow up enemy submarines—and himself as well.

Others are reported to be trained to detect and attack enemy frogmen by pulling off their face masks, tearing their regulator hoses and pulling off their swim fins.

Although the Navy won't discuss the mission, a team of porpoises trained here reportedly spent a year in Vietnam guarding Cam Ranh Bay against Communist frogman infiltration. Rumors said several Communist guerrillas were killed by porpoises armed with switch-blade devices on their snouts. The porpoises assertedly were controlled by radios operated by sailors from patrol boats.

A British scientific publication suggested last year that a "man to dolphin" translator has been developed that transforms human speech into pitch modulated whistles understood by the porpoises. According to his report porpoises—naturally friendly to man—were being taught aggressive behavior by the implantation of electrodes in the pleasure and pain centers of their brains.

In reply to the various reports of hostile activities by the porpoises, the Navy's last official comment on the matter was: "In spite of science fiction, conjectural and sensational so-called news stories to the contrary, the Navy has never, is not and has no plans to train any animal to injure itself in any way in connection with any alleged military mission or tactic."

LENGTH: 713 WORDS

10   The Military Porpoise

| SCORING: | Reading time: _____ Rate from chart: _____ W.P.M. |

RETENTION	number right ____ × 4 equals ____ points
INFERENCES	number right ____ × 3 equals ____ points
COMPLETION	number right ____ × 4 equals ____ points
DEFINITIONS	number right ____ × 3 equals ____ points

(Total points: 100) **total** ____ points

RETENTION   Based on the passage, which of the following statements are True (T), False (F), or Not answerable (N)?

1. _____ It is rumored that porpoises have already been used for military missions in Vietnam.

2. _____ Porpoises are naturally friendly to humans.

3. _____ None of the porpoise research is actually done in America.

4. _____ Porpoises are the only sea beasts used in Navy experiments.

5. _____ The IQ of porpoises is higher than that of humans.

6. _____ The British assert that there is no way to communicate with the porpoise.

7. _____ Some published reports have hinted at a self-destructive porpoise bomb.

8. _____ Porpoises are intelligent, but they are relatively slow learners.

9. _____ Generally, the Navy has refused comment on porpoise military missions.

10. _____ The Russians have even more trained porpoises than we do.

INFERENCES

1. _____ Which of the following statements is probably most accurate?
    (a) There is not much future in such porpoise studies.

(b) The experiments are secret because the public might grow alarmed.

(c) The porpoises seem to be enjoying themselves, despite their missions.

2. _____ Which of the following statements is probably inaccurate?

(a) The Navy statements seem to be contradictory.

(b) The Navy would have informed the public if rumors had not leaked out.

(c) The scientific value of these experiments is a low priority for the Navy.

COMPLETION   Choose the best answer for each question.

1. _____ The porpoise is apparently a: (a) mammal.   (b) form of aspidistra.   (c) good sport.   (d) controversial species.

2. _____ Porpoises could accurately distinguish between two: (a) naval officers.   (b) frogmen.   (c) steel balls.   (d) electrodes.

3. _____ A British scientific publication commented on a "man to dolphin":   (a) sign system.   (b) translator.   (c) agreement.   (d) hardware development.

4. _____ One function of sea lions is to: (a) detect frogmen.   (b) kill whales.   (c) go on "kamikaze" missions.   (d) develop sea tactics.

5. _____ The porpoises seem to have to be taught: (a) sonar systems.   (b) the meaning of research.   (c) computer language.   (d) aggressiveness.

6. _____ The porpoises can understand different kinds of: (a) visual signs.   (b) whistles.   (c) fish.   (d) words.

DEFINITIONS   Choose the definition from Column B that best matches each italicized word in Column A.

Column A	Column B
1. it is highly *accurate*	_____ a. supersensitive
2. *sophisticated* military missions	_____ b. disagreement
	_____ c. catching
3. *transform* speech	_____ d. supposed
4. the *training facility*	_____ e. damaging
5. source of *controversy*	_____ f. convert

6. the same *infectious* smile

7. *distinguishing* between types

8. taught to *detect*

9. *hostile* activities

10. any *alleged* mission

_____ g. exact
_____ h. research center
_____ i. choosing
_____ j. unfriendly
_____ k. complex
_____ l. search
_____ m. find
_____ n. anecdotal

11 *JAMES ROSS*

Concentration Camp Music

There was nothing to sing about in the Nazi concentration camps. So it comes as a surprise to learn that there was, indeed, music in at least one of them. Concentration camp music shows that the human spirit, even when it is as thoroughly crushed as it was at Terezin, finds a way to express itself.

Life in the Terezin, Czechoslovakia, concentration camp under the Nazi regime was a startling mixture of tragedy and optimism. The community of Jews daily faced torture or execution, but in the midst of the hate and fear the Jews created music of high artistic quality.

Joza Karas, a violin instructor at the Hartt College of Music of the University of Hartford, recently was awarded $250 by the Connecticut Arts Commission to continue a project designed to preserve the music written by Terezin inmates. Karas, a non-Jew and a native of Czechoslovakia, has been searching for the music and survivors of Terezin for more than three years.

"The creation of this music is a moving human story," Karas said. "We hear of the tragedy of the camps but until recently the other side of life had not shown up." He said much of the music has artistic value. "But the historical value is more important—this work should be known to mankind."

Before the German occupation of Czechoslovakia in World War II, Terezin was a quiet community of 6,000, although it had been built as a garrison and a fortress inside. The Nazis used the inner fortress as a prison and execution center for political prisoners of all nationalities.

The townspeople in the outer part of the city were moved out and by November 1942 the first of 140,000 Jewish inmates passed through the gates of

CONCENTRATION CAMP MUSIC   From "Czech Camp Music of Jews Preserved" by James Ross. *The Hartford Courant,* October 23, 1976. Reprinted by permission.

Terezin. The town held up to 60,000 Jews at one time and the massive over-crowding led to poor sanitary conditions and the spread of disease.

About 30,000 Jews died there from malnutrition and disease and tens of thousands more were shipped from Terezin to the gas chambers of Auschwitz.

Most of the Jews sent to Terezin were from Bohemia and Moravia, but a number of prominent Jews from Germany also arrived. Among the first group of 200 inmates was a German pianist who found and repaired a piano left in the town and formed a singing group.

The group developed into a chorus and several choruses were added as more people arrived. "It started as a clandestine operation," Karas said, "and the groups held concerts in attics while someone stood guard." The Jews were allowed to bring only 50 kilos of belongings into the camp and musical instru-ments were forbidden. But the instruments were smuggled in, wrapped in blankets or taken apart into strips of wood.

The Nazis eventually discovered the musical activity, Karas said, and they decided to use the musicians to their own advantage. Terezin became a showplace and the International Red Cross was invited to the camp to dispel the prevalent rumors of German torture and murder of Jews.

The Jews were forced to scrub the streets and paint the houses in preparation for the visit. To cut down on the overcrowding, the Nazis shipped several thousand Jews to Auschwitz.

The musical community performed concerts and operas for the visitors. The symphony orchestra members were given new clothes for a concert in the town square, but the Nazis were unable to provide the Jews with new shoes. Flower pots were put up in front of the stage, hiding their tattered shoes.

In most of the German-occupied areas, everything Jewish was forbidden. The music of Jewish composers, such as Mendelssohn, was included in the ban. But in Terezin, Karas suggested, the Nazi attitude was "to hell with them."

The Terezin community included a number of well-known Jewish compos-ers and singers. The elders of the community attempted to place the artists in less menial jobs where they could find time to practice. The Jewish elders also were given the task of selecting those who were to be sent "to the east"—to the extermination camps.

The musical community formed string trios and quartets and opera com-panies in the three year period. The groups performed the works written in the camp by the noted composers. The compositions, Karas said, "are often hard to identify as concentration camp music."

"Many of the texts express a longing for home," Karas said, "but they encouraged people to optimism." The amateur musicians, however, "expressed more of the sense of life there."

A woman poet who eventually died in the gas chambers with her son put some of her poems to music, he said. "They have low musical value," Karas added, "but they are poetical folk songs which explain the mood of the camps."

Karas left Czechoslovakia in 1950 as a political refugee. Several years ago he read about the music of Terezin in a Czech musical magazine and in the past three years he has collected all the known music from the camp.

He visited his homeland in August 1970 for two weeks after months of planning his research through correspondence and study. He acquired copies of works, photos, slides, books and first-hand information from former inmates.

Karas has been getting in touch with some of the camp's musicians who live in this country. He recently met a violinist living in Louisville, Ky., who was lost to family and friends since he survived Terezin. Another survivor is a conductor of the Toronto Symphony.

The Czech-born violin instructor, who also performs for the Hartford Symphony Orchestra, has presented lectures on the music of Terezin to various groups. In November 1970 he was invited to Israel as a guest of the government in recognition of his research. In the fall of 1971 the camp's music was the subject of an American television documentary.

The $250 grant from the arts commission, Karas said, will cover some of the cost of printing the negatives of documents. But there is more research to be done. Karas hopes to record some of the music and eventually complete a book on the subject from the documents and taped interviews.

LENGTH: 814 WORDS

11   Concentration Camp Music

SCORING: Reading time: _____ Rate from chart: _____ W.P.M.

RETENTION	number right _____ × 4 equals _____ points	
INFERENCES	number right _____ × 3 equals _____ points	
COMPLETION	number right _____ × 4 equals _____ points	
DEFINITIONS	number right _____ × 3 equals _____ points	

(Total points: 100) **total** _____ points

RETENTION   Based on the passage, which of the following statements are True (T), False (F), or Not answerable (N)?

1. _____ The first Jews arrived at Terezin in 1942.

2. _____ It was easy to smuggle musical instruments into the camp.

3. _____ None of the musicians survived the Terezin concentration camp.

4. _____ Joza Karas was a young Jew imprisoned in the camp.

5. _____ Most of the Jews at Terezin were from Germany.

6. _____ The Nazis disliked classical music.

7. _____ The camp musicians performed operas, but no string music.

8. _____ Music by Jewish composers was banned in most of the German-occupied lands.

9. _____ Karas is not the only person in the United States who knows the truth about Terezin.

10. _____ The camp at Terezin was very overcrowded.

INFERENCES

1. _____ Which of the following statements is probably most accurate?
   (a) The Nazis tolerated the music because of its propaganda value.
   (b) The Bohemians and Moravians were naturally musical anyway.
   (c) The Nazis were particularly interested in Bohemian propaganda.

2. _____ Which of the following statements is probably inaccurate?
   (a) More Jews died in the gas chambers than from disease.
   (b) The musical groups were sparked by some gifted individuals.
   (c) The music composed at Terezin was of uniformly high quality.

COMPLETION   Choose the best answer for each question.

1. _____ The things the Germans could not provide for the concerts were: (a) a Czech soprano.   (b) ties.   (c) shoes.   (d) music stands.

2. _____ One country that honored Karas for his research was: (a) Czecho-slovakia.   (b) Israel.   (c) Germany.   (d) Bohemia.

3. _____ The Jewish elders were given the job of choosing: (a) who should die.   (b) what should be played.   (c) the soloists.   (d) concert times.

4. _____ The groups performed some works: (a) of the German masters.   (b) actually written in the camps.   (c) improperly.   (d) clandestinely.

5. _____ One of the first musicians at the camp was: (a) a Moravian carpenter.   (b) soon killed.   (c) Mendelssohn.   (d) a German pianist.

6. _____ Joza Karas is himself: (a) a Jewish refugee.   (b) now frightened.   (c) a violinist.   (d) in the Red Cross.

DEFINITIONS   Choose the definition from Column B that best matches each italicized word in Column A.

Column A	*Column B*
1. a project *designed* to save	_____ a. nonprofessional
2. the *massive* crowding	_____ b. adverse
3. a *clandestine* operation	_____ c. as a reward for
4. to *dispel* the rumor	_____ d. full view of
5. in less *menial* jobs	_____ e. finally became
6. encourage people to *optimism*	_____ f. obtained
7. the *amateur* musicians	_____ g. colossal
8. he *acquired* materials	_____ h. planned out
9. *in recognition of* research	_____ i. secret
10. the group *developed* into a chorus	_____ j. being in a good position
	_____ k. looking on the bright side
	_____ l. chase away
	_____ m. ordinary, lowly
	_____ n. insisted on

12   *ISAAC ASIMOV*

UFOs

With our probes into outer space reaching farther and farther from Earth, we can hardly help but wonder if we are alone in the universe. If we are not alone, is it possible that other beings are reaching out to us and already may have begun exploring our planet.

When most people think about flying saucers or, as they are more austerely called, "unidentified flying objects" (UFOs), they think of them as spaceships coming from outside Earth, and manned by intelligent beings.

Is there any chance of this? Do the "little green men" really exist? There are arguments pro and con.

Pro.   There is, according to the best astronomical thinking today, a strong chance that life is very common in the universe. Our own galaxy, containing over a hundred billion stars, is only one of perhaps a hundred billion galaxies.

Current theories about how stars are formed make it seem likely that planets are formed also, so that every star may have planets about it. Surely *some* of those planets would be like our Earth in chemistry and temperature.

Current theories about how life got its start make it seem that any planet with something like Earth's chemistry and temperature would be sure to develop life. One reasonable estimate advanced by an astronomer was that there might be as many as 640,000,000 planets in our galaxy alone that are Earthlike and that bear life.

But on how many of these planets is there *intelligent* life? We can't say, but suppose that only one out of a million life-bearing planets develops intelligent life forms and that only one out of ten of these develops a technological civilization more advanced than our own. There might still be as many as 100

UFOS "UFOs: Are They Visitors from Space—or Unreliable False Observations?" by Isaac Asimov. *TV Guide,* December 14, 1974. Reprinted with permission from *TV Guide®* Magazine. Copyright © 1974 by Triangle Publications, Inc. Radnor, Pennsylvania.

different advanced civilizations in our galaxy, and perhaps a hundred more in every other galaxy. Why shouldn't some of them have reached us?

Con. Assuming there are 100 advanced civilizations in our own galaxy and that they are evenly spread throughout the galaxy, the nearest one would be about 10,000 light-years away. Even assuming coverage of that distance at the fastest speed we know of—the speed of light—the trip would take at least 10,000 years. Why should anyone make such long journeys just to poke around curiously?

Pro. It is wrong to try to estimate the abilities of a far-advanced civilization, or their motives either. For one thing, the situation may not be average. The nearest advanced civilization may just happen to be only 100 light-years away, rather than 10,000.

Furthermore, because *we* know of no practical way of traveling faster than light doesn't mean an advanced civilization may not know of one. To an advanced civilization a distance of 100 light-years or even 10,000 light-years may be very little. They may be delighted to explore over long distances just for the sake of exploring.

Con. But even if that were the case, it would make no sense to send so many spaceships so often (judging by the many UFO reports). Surely we are not *that* interesting. And if we *are* interesting, why not land and greet us? Or communicate without landing? They can't be afraid of us, since if they are so far advanced beyond us, they can surely defend themselves against any puny threats we can offer.

On the other hand, if they want to be merely observers, and not interfere with the development of our civilization in any way, they could surely so handle their observations that we would not be continually aware of them.

Pro. Again, we can't try to guess what the motives of these explorers might be. What might seem logical to us, might not seem so logical to them. They may not care if we see them, and they also may not care to say hello. Besides, there are many reports of people who have seen the ships and have even been aboard. Surely some of these reports must have something to them.

Con. Eyewitness reports of actual spaceships and actual extraterrestrials are, in themselves, totally unreliable. There have been innumerable eyewitness reports of almost everything that most rational people do not care to accept—of ghosts, angels, levitation, zombies, werewolves, and so on.

What we really want, in this case, is something *material;* some object or artifact that is clearly not of human manufacture or Earthly origin. These people who claim to have seen or entered a spaceship never end up with any button, rag, or other *object* that would substantiate their story.

Pro. But how else can you account for all the UFO reports? Even after you exclude the mistaken, the gags and hoaxes—there remain many sightings that can't be explained by scientists within the present limits of knowledge. Aren't we forced to suppose these sightings are extraterrestrial spaceships?

Con.   No, because we don't know that the extraterrestrial spaceship is the *only* remaining explanation. If we can't think of any other, that may simply be a defect in our imagination. If an answer is unknown, then it is simply unknown. An Unidentified Flying Object is just that—unidentified.

The most serious and levelheaded investigator of UFOs I know is J. Allen Hynek, a logical astronomer who is convinced that some UFO reports are worth serious investigation. He doesn't think they represent extraterrestrial space-ships, but he does suggest that they represent phenomena that lie outside the present structure of science, and that understanding them will help us expand our knowledge and build a greatly enlarged structure of science.

The trouble is that whatever the UFO phenomenon is, it comes and goes unexpectedly. There is no way of examining it systematically. It appears suddenly and accidentally, is partially seen, and then is more or less inaccurately reported. We remain dependent on occasional anecdotal accounts.

Dr. Hynek, after a quarter of a century of devoted and honest research, so far ends with nothing. He not only has no solution, but he has no real idea of any possible solution. He has only his belief that when the solution comes it will be important.

He may be right, but there are at least equal grounds for believing that the solution may never come, or that when it comes, it will be unimportant.

LENGTH: 816 WORDS

12   UFOs

SCORING: Reading time: _____ Rate from chart: _____ W.P.M.

RETENTION	number right _____ × 4 equals _____ points	
INFERENCES	number right _____ × 3 equals _____ points	
COMPLETION	number right _____ × 4 equals _____ points	
DEFINITIONS	number right _____ × 3 equals _____ points	

(Total points: 100) **total** _____ points

RETENTION   Based on the passage, which of the following statements are True (T), False (F), or Not answerable (N)?

1. _____ The UFO appearances seem to have been systematic.

2. _____ J. Allen Hynek has been aboard a spacecraft.

3. _____ An advanced civilization may be only 100 light-years away from Earth.

4. _____ There may be millions of planets like ours in the universe.

5. _____ Most stars are likely to have planets around them.

6. _____ We have more than anecdotal accounts of UFO sightings.

7. _____ Hynek believes that UFOs lie outside the present structure of science.

8. _____ There have been eyewitness reports of ghosts and werewolves.

9. _____ After twenty-five years of research, Hynek has come up with important findings.

10. _____ Hynek has a definite solution for the UFO controversy.

INFERENCES

1. _____ Which of the following statements is probably most accurate?
   (a) Whatever UFOs are, they do not concern life on Earth very much.
   (b) UFOs are the most significant "news" of the twentieth century.
   (c) Whatever UFOs turn out to be, they may be very important for us.

2. _____ Which of the following statements is probably inaccurate?
   (a) There seem to be many UFO sightings.
   (b) The motives of an advanced civilization may be quite like ours.
   (c) Eyewitness reports of UFOs are not totally reliable by themselves.

COMPLETION   Choose the best answer for each question.

1. _____ Some of the UFO sightings may be: (a) spaceships from Mars.   (b) unintentional.   (c) hoaxes.   (d) a gift of the gods.

2. _____ What we really want for verification of UFOs is: (a) tape recordings.   (b) films.   (c) detailed interviews.   (d) some material object.

3. _____ UFOs are: (a) balloons.   (b) frisbees.   (c) serious.   (d) unidentified.

4. _____ The fastest speed we know of is: (a) not enough.   (b) the speed of light.   (c) five times the speed of sound.   (d) puny by comparison.

5. _____ Current theories suggest that any planet like Earth will: (a) exist in space.   (b) host UFOs.   (c) develop life.   (d) be explored.

6. _____ Our galaxy may be one: (a) of a hundred billion.   (b) hundred light-years away.   (c) of the best.   (d) of the hundred most interesting.

DEFINITIONS   Choose the definition from Column B that best matches each italicized word in Column A.

Column A	Column B
1. of Earthly *origin*	_____ a. bounds
2. a *technological* civilization	_____ b. many
3. to *estimate* the abilities	_____ c. brought forth
	_____ d. relegate
4. *substantiate* their story	_____ e. science
5. the present *limits* of knowledge	_____ f. infrequent; sporadic
6. dependent on *occasional* accounts	_____ g. uncertain
7. there have been *innumerable* sightings	_____ h. scientifically advanced
	_____ i. extricate
8. defend against *puny* threats	_____ j. guess
	_____ k. verify; uphold
9. theory *advanced* by Hynek	_____ l. source; beginning
10. *unreliable* reports	_____ m. preposterous; insane
	_____ n. weak; flimsy

13 *MICHAEL J. CONNOR*

Flying with Your Tuba

For those musicians who do not play either the flute or another portable instrument, traveling is a serious problem. One musician solved the problem by pretending his instrument was a passenger: he bought an extra airline ticket and propped up his "friend" in the seat next to his.

His overcoat bulging ominously, Claus Adam managed to board an airline flight at a New York airport not long ago without arousing suspicion. Partly that was a credit to his tactical finesse. He had one of his three traveling companions scout the way to skirt potentially curious airline employees, while the other two huddled close to Mr. Adam to hide the bulge.

No, marshal, Mr. Adam's not a bomber or a hijacker. He's a musician, and the mysterious object under his coat was his cello. Mr. Adam's maneuverings just show how bad things are getting all over. While the dollar falters in European currency markets, and 18-year-olds get the right to buy booze in Tennessee, and earthquakes wrack Turkey, and postage stamps are going up, musicians are having a tough time hauling instruments to their engagements.

Transporting your instrument has become, one musician says, "the curse of the profession." Like other people, musicians have to depend on airplanes for long-distance trips and taxis and crowded buses and subways in cities. But other people generally are relatively unencumbered, and to hear the tuba players and the bassists tell it, its a wise student who stakes his career on, say, the flute.

Safety is one big rub. Most large instruments are breakable or dentable, and all of them are expensive. For example, a modestly priced cello for professional use may cost $5,000 and up; cellist Jacqueline du Pre's may be worth as much as $90,000. Musicians are reluctant to ship their instruments as baggage out of fear that baggage handlers and cold temperatures in baggage areas will damage them.

"To let your bass go in the hold of an airplane would be fratricide—killing your brother the bass," says bassist Julius Levine.

So Mr. Levine and many other musicians buy seats on their flights for their instruments, so that the things can sit safely beside them. Smuggling them aboard as an economy measure has become increasingly difficult now that passengers are watched so closely to spot hijackers. Airlines charge half fare for an instrument.

The airlines require a name on an instrument's ticket, and that has led to some funny public-address announcements at airport terminals. Dick Kniss, bass man for the Peter, Paul & Mary folk group, says he has heard airline employes more than once page folks like "Mr. B. Fiddle" and "Mr. Harry Violin" to inform them of flight changes.

That has led to other funny things. One musician—or so his story goes— bought a half-fare seat for his instrument and then flew alone from Baltimore to New York, traveling as "Mr. Cello." Eastern Airlines, which brags that it will dispatch a shuttle flight to accommodate only one passenger, once had to do that—for a half-fare bass.

One cellist who insisted that his cello travel at half fare was never able to take his wife on trips because of the additional expense. His wife put up with the neglect for a while, but she finally delivered an ultimatum: Either Mr. Cello rode as baggage and she rode in Mr. Cello's seat, or the marriage was over. This cellist was a dedicated pro, and the marriage was over.

Elaine Jones is a New York tympanist (or percussionist)—she beats the drums—and she says that has had an adverse affect on her love life. "Anybody I go out with has to be strong," she says, "because sooner or later he has to carry those drums." A male friend recently was drafted to help her carry the drums to an engagement, she says, "and he never called back."

Packing instruments within New York City can be just as frustrating as taking them outside the city. Bass players claim buses will pass them by, and taxis no longer are much help. Now that most cabs are equipped with Plexiglas dividers separating the front seats from the back, they cannot hold a bass.

For the past 20 years, New York tuba player Don Butterfield has carried his tuba around New York in a custom-modified shopping cart. But soon he is supposed to begin a series of engagements across the country, and the shopping cart won't help him get to Dubuque. He's thinking of having the bell cut off to make a two-piece tuba that he can carry in special steel cases.

Challenging the subways with big instruments can lead to real hangups. One French horn player was stuck on a train for three stops beyond his destination because the bell of his horn kept getting stuck between passengers in the jammed car. "I could have gotten out okay, but I couldn't have taken my horn with me," says the musician, Lester Solomon. And a New York bass player once got trapped in a subway entrance turnstile. He wriggled there for two hours before he could be extricated.

LENGTH: 860 WORDS

13   Flying with Your Tuba

SCORING: Reading time: _____ Rate from chart: _____ W.P.M.

RETENTION	number right _____ × 4 equals _____ points
INFERENCES	number right _____ × 3 equals _____ points
COMPLETION	number right _____ × 4 equals _____ points
DEFINITIONS	number right _____ × 3 equals _____ points

(Total points: 100) **total** _____ points

RETENTION   Based on the passage, which of the following statements are True (T), False (F), or Not answerable (N)?

1. _____ Apparently, tubas are made in one piece.

2. _____ Unfortunately, airlines charge full fare for instruments.

3. _____ Musicians depend on airplanes for long-distance trips.

4. _____ Jacqueline du Pre's cello is worth as much as $5000.

5. _____ One Eastern Airlines flight had only a cello aboard.

6. _____ One bass player got stuck in a subway turnstile for two hours.

7. _____ Bass players find it easier to travel in taxis than in airplanes.

8. _____ Elaine Jones switched to the flute because of travel problems.

9. _____ Baggage compartments are not safe enough for cellos and basses.

10. _____ Don Butterfield played his tuba in Dubuque.

INFERENCES

1. _____ Which of the following statements is probably most accurate?
   (a) An airline with heated baggage compartments would attract musicians.

(b) Musicians never want to be far from their instruments.

(c) Cellists give everybody a headache when they travel.

2. _____ Which of the following statements is probably inaccurate?

(a) Traveling with instruments in New York City is as bad as going out of town.

(b) Traveling in New York City is easier for cellists than traveling by air.

(c) Bass players do not travel much easier than tuba players.

COMPLETION Choose the best answer for each question.

1. _____ On an instrument's ticket, the airline requires a: (a) receipt. (b) name. (c) small deposit. (d) confirmation of flight plans or cancellations.

2. _____ Julius Levine said that letting your bass go in the hold is like: (a) giving up music. (b) robbery. (c) hijacking. (d) fratricide.

3. _____ One French horn player got his horn caught in a: (a) train. (b) turnstile. (c) friend's purse. (d) shuttle dispatch.

4. _____ One marriage broke up over a dispute about a: (a) folk group. (b) Plexiglas divider. (c) cello. (d) tympanist.

5. _____ Tympanists play: (a) the field. (b) second fiddle. (c) the drums. (d) on buses and subways.

6. _____ Most large instruments are: (a) dentable. (b) woodwinds. (c) on the move. (d) in New York.

DEFINITIONS Choose the definition from Column B that best matches each italicized word in Column A.

Column A	Column B
1. airlines *page* folks	_____ a. annoying
2. Mr. Adam's *maneuverings*	_____ b. unwilling
	_____ c. final stop
3. overcoat bulging *ominously*	_____ d. more and more
4. *reluctant* to ship a cello	_____ e. not so burdened
5. as *frustrating* as flying	_____ f. shiftings
	_____ g. bad
6. beyond his *destination*	_____ h. call for
	_____ i. magnificently

7. before he could be *extricated*

8. most people are *unencumbered*

9. it is *increasingly* difficult

10. an *adverse* effect on her

_____ j. ineluctable

_____ k. suspiciously

_____ l. auspicious

_____ m. gotten out

_____ n. anniversary

14

ALANNA NASH

John Dillinger in Wax

John Dillinger, like many American outlaws, has become something of a legend. His memory is preserved most vividly in a small museum in the Midwest, the scene of some of his most daring exploits. The museum is a testament to America's fascination with crime and criminals.

"Dillinger captured the imagination," Joe Pinkston says. "I guess I wanted to be like him when I was a kid."

Joe Pinkston is an unlikely admirer of that Public Enemy Number One of the 1930's, John Dillinger. At 44, he's a part-time sheriff in Nashville, Ind., and a former Pinkerton detective and criminal investigator for the United States Air Force. But the fact is that Dillinger has long fascinated lawmen in general and this lawman in particular. Nashville, which is 40 miles south of Indianapolis, was Dillinger territory back then, part of the area where he was born and took refuge; now it is Dillinger territory again, courtesy of Joe Pinkston, who has established the John Dillinger Historical Museum in downtown Nashville.

Old radio themes blare from the RCA table radio in the converted Victorian house at Franklin and Van Buren Streets. Headlines shout from yellowed newspapers framed and hung on the walls. In the first room, photographs and documents tell of the first years of Dillinger, who at the age of 12 was stealing coal from railroad cars and selling it to neighbors. There's a letter he wrote in 1924 from the Indiana Reformatory, where he'd been sent, at age 21, for robbing and beating a grocer. In a corner is the original tombstone—chipped by vandals and souvenir hunters—from Dillinger's grave in Indianapolis's Crown Hill Cemetery (an identical replacement now stands in Crown Hill). It is the first hint amid the museum's lively atmosphere of the grim artifacts to come.

JOHN DILLINGER IN WAX   From "Maybe I'll Learn Someday, Dad, You Can't Win in this Game" by Alanna Nash. *New York Times*, March 7, 1976. © 1976/77 by The New York Times Company. Reprinted by permission.

The second room holds such items as the rabbit's foot Dillinger gave a reporter when he was arrested in Tucson, Ariz., early in 1934 . . . a detailed plan for a robbery in Dillinger's writing . . . a bullet removed from the leg of a Dillinger Gang victim. Tacked on a wall are the trousers—the bloodstains preserved—worn by the 31-year-old gangster the night of July 22, 1934, when he was shot down outside Chicago's Biograph Theater. Also on display are replicas of the dead man's effects: a .380 Colt automatic pistol, a straw boater, wire-rim spectacles worn for disguise, a La Corona cigar and a pocket watch.

Two special exhibits distinguish the museum from the average small-town repository: Lifelike, detailed wax figures of Dillinger at critical moments of his career. The first, on the main floor, re-creates the frequently published photograph of the bandit cradling a submachine gun and fingering the "wooden" gun used in his daring escape from the Crown Point, Ind., jail. The second is on the next floor. As the visitor reaches the top of the stairs, he hears the soft strains of a dirge. Then he sees an all-too-realistic reproduction of the funeral parlor in nearby Mooresville on July 26, 1934, the day—as the newspapers of the time declared—that John Dillinger "came home for the last time." Behind a glass partition lies the wax "body" of Dillinger in a custom-made, full-couch casket. There may be grins and wisecracks from visitors in the rest of the museum, but nobody leaves this room laughing.

Joe Pinkston, who established the museum in partnership with Barton N. Hahn, a former F.B.I. agent, is the co-author (with Robert Cromie) of the biography, "Dillinger: A Short and Violent Life." He grew up in Martinsville, hearing the Dillinger saga from residents of Mooresville, just 16 miles away, and from his uncle, who played pool with Dillinger as a teen-ager. Pinkston has spent 25 of his 44 years collecting Dillinger material. He has interviewed virtually everyone connected with the gangster, including his notorious girlfriend Evelyn "Billie" Frechette and the man generally credited with master-minding Dillinger's demise, F.B.I. Agent Melvin Purvis. Many of the museum's exhibits he acquired from the Dillinger family, some of whom still live in the area.

Some visitors to the museum have theorized that Pinkston laid out the museum as a memorial to Dillinger; Pinkston hedges when asked about it. "Dillinger was the type of man who captured the imagination of the public," he says. "The museum is dedicated to the genuine loss and sorrow on *both* sides of the law during his 14 months in the headlines."

Pinkston insists that he "offers the museum without social or moral comment." Yet his selection of Dillinger quotations, hanging on the museum walls, suggests his own involvement. One vivid example: "Maybe I'll learn someday, Dad, that you can't win in this game."

LENGTH: 800 WORDS

14   John Dillinger in Wax

```
┌─────────────────────────────────────────────────────────────────┐
│ SCORING:    Reading time: _____ Rate from chart: _____ W.P.M. │
├─────────────────────────────────────────────────────────────────┤
│                                                                   │
│      RETENTION      number right _____ × 4 equals _____ points  │
│                                                                   │
│      INFERENCES     number right _____ × 3 equals _____ points  │
│                                                                   │
│      COMPLETION     number right _____ × 4 equals _____ points  │
│                                                                   │
│      DEFINITIONS    number right _____ × 3 equals _____ points  │
│                                                                   │
├─────────────────────────────────────────────────────────────────┤
│              (Total points: 100) total _____ points              │
└─────────────────────────────────────────────────────────────────┘
```

RETENTION   Based on the passage, which of the following statements are True (T), False (F), or Not answerable (N)?

1. _____ Joe Pinkston became a Pinkerton agent because of Dillinger's threat.

2. _____ Dillinger was already an accomplished thief at the age of twelve.

3. _____ Dillinger died when he was forty-eight years old.

4. _____ Both people who established the John Dillinger Historical Museum are lawmen.

5. _____ Actually, Dillinger was in the headlines for less than two years.

6. _____ Melvin Purvis arranged for Dillinger's death in 1934.

7. _____ Pinkston actually has the original gravestone from Dillinger's grave.

8. _____ The Dillinger family would give nothing to the museum.

9. _____ When he was a kid, Pinkston never wanted to be like Dillinger.

10. _____ The casket contains Dillinger's genuine mummy.

INFERENCES

1. _____ Which of the following statements is probably most accurate?
    (a) People in downtown Nashville have forgotten Dillinger.
    (b) Dillinger simply captured people's imaginations.
    (c) Pinkston still envies Dillinger his courage.

2. _____ Which of the following statements is probably inaccurate?
   (a) Dillinger's rabbit-foot charm did not do him much good.
   (b) The bloodstained trousers were definitely a bad-luck charm.
   (c) Dillinger seems to have been superstitious.

COMPLETION Choose the best answer for each question.

1. _____ Dillinger is buried in: (a) the reformatory. (b) a vault on his farm. (c) Nashville. (d) Indianapolis.

2. _____ Dillinger's girlfriend was nicknamed: (a) "Pinky." (b) "Moll." (c) "Billie." (d) "Vivid."

3. _____ Some people think that Pinkston founded the museum as a: (a) quick-money scheme. (b) lark. (c) memorial to Dillinger. (d) warning to criminals.

4. _____ Some of Dillinger's family: (a) are still outlaws. (b) live in the area of the museum. (c) snub Pinkston. (d) have joined the FBI.

5. _____ Dillinger was shot down outside: (a) his car. (b) the immediate area. (c) the museum. (d) the Biograph Theater.

6. _____ Dillinger has long fascinated: (a) lawmen in particular. (b) tourists. (c) grave robbers especially. (d) the Colt plant in Hartford.

DEFINITIONS Choose the definition from Column B that best matches each italicized word in Column A.

Column A	Column B
1. *critical* moment in his career	_____ a. unfavorable
2. *replicas* of his things	_____ b. belongings
3. small-town *repository*	_____ c. intense
4. where he *took refuge*	_____ d. death
5. interview *virtually* everyone	_____ e. stole junk
6. the *grim* artifacts	_____ f. funeral hymn
7. the dead man's *effects*	_____ g. the good ones, moral people
8. credited with his *demise*	_____ h. reproductions
9. soft strains of a *dirge*	_____ i. causes
10. one *vivid* example	_____ j. morbid
	_____ k. important, crucial
	_____ l. museum
	_____ m. hid out
	_____ n. essentially, just about

15

MILTON RICHMAN

The One-Armed Bettenhausen

Race-car drivers are noted for their comebacks from serious accidents. But very few drivers have ever tried to race again after suffering an accident as serious as Merle Bettenhausen's. Very few drivers could imagine handling a high-speed car using only one arm. Bettenhausen could imagine it, and he could do it.

Merle Bettenhausen still keeps both hands on the wheel.

It's a little tougher in his case.

Particularly since he lost his right arm in a crack-up trying to win the Michigan International 13 months ago. He's back racing midgets now though and handling the wheel fine.

"Physically, I'm 100 per cent normal except I've got an arm missing and as far as I know, no one ever has run with one arm," says the friendly, outgoing 30-year-old son of the late Tony Bettenhausen, who was killed at Indianapolis 12 years ago practicing for the 500.

"I crashed at Cambridge Junction, Michigan, on July 16, 1972 and didn't race again until this past June 16. Eleven months to the day. At first, when I came back, it felt a little funny. I really didn't know what it would be like driving one-handed. It turned out much more comfortable than I anticipated. I found out I was doing 90 per cent of my driving left-handed."

Merle Bettenhausen, whose two brothers, Gary, 31, and Tony, Jr., 21, also race cars, is a remarkable young man on any number of counts.

First because he'd even care to get back in a race car of any kind again, and second because of his magnificent attitude since his accident. He's pleasant, cheerful and helpful.

THE ONE-ARMED BETTENHAUSEN "One Armed Bettenhausen Making Comeback" by Milton Richman. *Willimantic Chronicle*, August 30, 1973. Reprinted by permission of United Press International.

Those close to him say he has never grumbled or complained once about what happened to him. Nor does he go into a shell if the subject is brought up.

"I'm not sensitive about it," he says. "If you ask me what I think caused the accident I'd say it was a combination of my inexperience, my first Indy type car race and too fast a track. My car was not set up properly either but that's something I'd rather not go into.

"Anyway, I was just coming around the second corner and completing the third lap when I apparently lost control and hit the guard rail. My car caught fire and hit the wall. I was in the car one minute and 15 seconds and tried getting out while it was still in motion, but it hit the wall again. That's when my arm was severed. I don't remember losing it. What I was concerned about was the fire.

"The car finally stopped and the fire team got me out. My arm was gone. I was conscious through it all, and I remember going to the infield hospital and them working on me. Even though I knew I had lost my arm and was burned badly, it felt good to be out of the car.

"I remember them cutting off my fireproof long underwear. I was lying there only in my jockey shorts, and I thought to myself, okay, that's neat. Then they began cutting off my jockey shorts. That upset me. It seemed like there were hundreds of people running around. Nurses, doctors, everyone. Why were they cutting off my shorts? They weren't on fire."

Merle's older brother, Gary, came by to see him at University of Michigan Hospital shortly afterward.

"Well, kid, you still wanna drive race cars?" he inquired.

"Uh-huh," said Merle, nodding affirmatively.

This really isn't anything new with him.

Merle Bettenhausen has wanted to race cars, the same way his daddy did, since he was a kid.

"I remember the day he died, May 12, 1961," says Merle. "I was 17 years old. When they told me what happened, I was very upset. But I remember listening to the race that year and saying to myself I still want to drive in the Indy 500 some day."

Merle and Gary are very close. They frequently talk about their father and about young Tony, Jr., now driving in stock car races.

"Gary and I had more of a chance to learn from our father than Tony did," says Merle. "He was only 10 at the time. Hardly a day goes by that Dad's memory doesn't linger on our minds. I remember him saying 'if you do something, do it right or don't do it at all'."

That's the way Merle Bettenhausen is trying to do it now—the right way.

When he said he'd like to race again after losing his arm, the only others who believed in him besides Gary and his wife, Leslie, were Steed Industries, makers of automotive additives, and the Marathon Oil Company. Both sponsor him now, but basically he still has to do it on his own.

"I have no other income except what I make racing," he says.

His big dream is to qualify for the Indianapolis 500 and he'd like to see Gary and Tony, Jr., in the race with him some day.

"It would be something if we were the first three brothers to compete together at Indy," he says, his eyes lighting up. "My Dad tried to win in Indianapolis for many years and died there. Now it's up to one of us three brothers more or less to win the race for him."

To compete at Indianapolis, Merle Bettenhausen will have to get his license back again there and that may not be so easy.

"It all depends on me," he says, candidly. "In other words if I show them I can drive any other race car, and drive it as well as I did with two arms, then how can they really say no to me?"

LENGTH: 880 WORDS

15   The One-Armed Bettenhausen

SCORING: Reading time: _____ Rate from chart: _____ W.P.M.

RETENTION	number right _____ × 4 equals _____ points
INFERENCES	number right _____ × 3 equals _____ points
COMPLETION	number right _____ × 4 equals _____ points
DEFINITIONS	number right _____ × 3 equals _____ points

(Total points: 100) **total** _____ points

RETENTION   Based on the passage, which of the following statements are True (T), False (F), or Not answerable (N)?

1. _____ Tony Bettenhausen, Sr., won the Indianapolis 500 a few years ago.

2. _____ Merle Bettenhausen lost his right arm while racing.

3. _____ Oddly enough, Merle never lost consciousness during and after the accident.

4. _____ The accident occurred in a renovated Dodge Charger.

5. _____ Merle had been racing in Michigan.

6. _____ After recovering, Merle went back to midget racing.

7. _____ Because of Tony Bettenhausen's death, Merle is the only Bettenhausen who races.

8. _____ Since the accident, Merle has been subject to depression.

9. _____ At first, after the accident, Merle wanted to give up driving.

10. _____ Merle was seriously burned as a result of the accident.

INFERENCES

1. _____ Which of the following statements is probably most accurate?
   (a) Driving race cars seems to get out of control.
   (b) Driving race cars is not a profession; it's a hobby.
   (c) Driving race cars seems to "run in the family."

2. _____ Which of the following statements is probably inaccurate?
    (a) The shock of an accident apparently dulls even severe pain.
    (b) Merle Bettenhausen was mostly a left-handed driver anyway.
    (c) Getting back in shape for the Indy 500 will not be very tough.

COMPLETION   Choose the best answer for each question.

1. _____ When he cracked up, Merle Bettenhausen was trying to: (a) win the Indy 500.   (b) avoid a wreck.   (c) skim a wall.   (d) win the Michigan International.

2. _____ To compete in the Indy 500, Merle will have to: (a) learn to drive.   (b) get his license back.   (c) drive faster.   (d) compete more diligently.

3. _____ Merle remembered their cutting off his: (a) arm.   (b) approach.   (c) jockey shorts.   (d) battered door.

4. _____ The cause of the accident was: (a) an oil slick.   (b) loss of control.   (c) another accident.   (d) simple stupidity.

5. _____ The writer is most impressed by Merle's: (a) stamina.   (b) courage.   (c) attitude.   (d) speed.

6. _____ Merle said that one thing that contributed to his accident was his: (a) inexperience.   (b) overconfidence.   (c) drinking set ups.   (d) pit crew.

DEFINITIONS   Choose the definition from Column B that best matches each italicized word in Column A.

Column A	Column B
1. his *magnificent* ability	_____ a. finishing
2. better than I *anticipated*	_____ b. remain
	_____ c. remarked
3. a *remarkable* young man	_____ d. openly
4. *completing* the third lap	_____ e. awake and aware
5. I was *conscious* then	_____ f. alarmed, baffled
	_____ g. great, terrific
6. it doesn't *linger* in our minds	_____ h. cut off
7. to *compete* at Indianapolis	_____ i. expected
8. he spoke *candidly*	_____ j. surprising, interesting

9. when my arm was *severed*   _____ k. conceding

10. I was *concerned* about the car   _____ l.   worried

                                                            _____ m. race, vie

                                                            _____ n.   austerely

16 *ANTHONY RIPLEY*

Do Plants Like Rock or Bach?

We have known for a long time that plants respond to subtle changes in their environments. But do plants respond to music? And if they do, do they respond differently to different kinds of music?

It's certainly not pure science and Mrs. Dorothy Retallack is the first to concede it as she roars enthusiastically forward playing recorded music for her plants at Temple Buell College.

It seems that the plants cringe and die when she plays them a regular diet of acid rock by the Led Zepplin, the late Jimi Hendrix or the now-disbanded Vanilla Fudge. The plants lean sharply away from the sound and die in a few weeks. Even their roots grow aslant, rejecting the music.

When she plays them Bach, or "La Paloma," or, especially, Ravi Shankar's classical Indian music, they flourish, with petunias turning their trumpet-like flowers toward the source of the music and even reaching their leaves out to hug the loudspeakers.

Also cringing and dying are some of the professors at Temple Buell, the former Colorado Women's College that was renamed to honor one of its benefactors. They find the whole thing an excruciating embarrassment.

"We have been ridiculed professionally," said one biologist in an emotional telephone call. Each time a national television network or newspaper or magazine writes of Mrs. Retallack's plants, the whole thing boils up again.

The plants, which include beans, squash, grape ivy, primrose, aluminum plant, corn and annual flowers, sit inside controlled environmental chambers at the liberal arts college in northeast Denver. This week they were listening to

DO PLANTS LIKE ROCK OR BACH? "Rock or Bach an Issue to Plants, Singer Says" by Anthony Ripley. *New York Times*, February 21, 1977. © 1976/77 by The New York Times Company. Reprinted by permission.

country and Western music in one chamber, which they seemed to like a little bit, and "jazz" in another.

Mrs. Retallack's unscientific definition of "jazz" ranges from early Dixieland to "Strangers in the Night" played with strings. The plants also seem to like the "jazz." In a third, silent controlled environment chamber the plants apparently grow normally.

Mrs. Retallack, whose husband, Louis L. Retallack, is a Denver physician, has 16 grandchildren and is a professional singer, a mezzo-soprano performing at synagogues, churches and funeral homes. She entered college in 1964 after rearing three children and five stepchildren and found she had to take a year of science to graduate. She began putting music and plants together in 1968 in a biology course and has been at it ever since.

She is full of laughter and enthusiasm: "I love life. I love people. I love music. I find life terribly exciting.

"I'm a musician, wife, mother, a grandmother," she said and laughed. "A scientist? I'm trying to do things the way they should be done in this kind of an experiment."

She concedes that scientists can poke holes in some of her methods, but she has been through almost 20 experiments. She said the plants all seemed to agree with her personal music tastes, preferring classical, light classical and swing.

Thinking that perhaps her personal likes and dislikes may be perceived by the plants, she had someone else visit them to rewind the tapes and tend them. The results were the same, she said.

A similar story was told by the Rev. Franklin Loehr, of Princeton, N. J., who identifies himself as "a Congregational minister with a Presbyterian ordination—rather eclectic." Mr. Loehr was the author of a 1959 book called "The Power of Prayer on Plants."

"Very definitely a person can reach out invisibly, immaterially, and can affect the growth of plants for good or ill," he said in a telephone interview.

Prayed over seeds seem to sprout better and grow more quickly, Mr. Loehr said. He added that a few persons have the power to inhibit plant growth by prayer.

He agrees with Cleve Backster, of New York City, who hooked lie detectors to plants and said that readings indicate that plants had a wide range of emotions and could sense human attitudes.

Dr. Cleon Ross, a plant physiologist at Colorado State University, will discuss the subject reluctantly until it gets into plant responses to human thought. Then he bales out.

"Pure garbage," he said.

At Utah State University, Dr. Frank B. Salisbury of the Plant Science Department, is a bit kinder.

"I don't know what to make of it all," he said. "It's been going on since 1950. There was a report at the 1954 International Botanical Congress by a man from India who played violins to plants.

"I hate to just out-and-out say it's all baloney but there's been an awful lot of pseudo-science in this field for years. Most of this stuff just doesn't have the right kind of experimentation."

He said that as a graduate student at California Institute of Technology he and other students got some of Rev. Loehr's prayed over seeds of both kinds and planted them. Both types—those that were supposed to grow fast and those that were not—grew at the same rate, he said.

What is needed most in the field, he said, is solid scientific experimentation. Until that comes along, "I don't believe any of it," he said.

Thinking about the acid rock music and about the young who listen to it, Mrs. Retallack wondered if the music that destroys plants might not destroy people, too.

"Some of those plants look like the people who attend rock festivals," she said.

LENGTH: 885 WORDS

16   Do Plants Like Rock or Bach?

SCORING: Reading time: _____ Rate from chart: _____ W.P.M.

RETENTION   number right _____ × 4 equals _____ points

INFERENCES   number right _____ × 3 equals _____ points

COMPLETION   number right _____ × 4 equals _____ points

DEFINITIONS   number right _____ × 3 equals _____ points

(Total points: 100) **total** _____ points

RETENTION   Based on the passage, which of the following statements are True (T), False (F), or Not answerable (N)?

1. _____ Dorothy Retallack's research is conceded to be pure science.

2. _____ The plants actually seem to turn away from music they dislike.

3. _____ Mrs. Retallack has only worked with flowers so far.

4. _____ Oddly enough, Mrs. Retallack's plants agree with her own musical tastes.

5. _____ Everyone at Temple Buell is proud of this plant research.

6. _____ One minister is sure that plants respond favorably or unfavorably to prayer.

7. _____ Hard-rock groups never travel with live plants.

8. _____ Lie detector tests were used to show that plants have emotions.

9. _____ The music and plant research goes back to 1968.

10. _____ Mrs. Retallack is herself a musician.

INFERENCES

1. _____ Which of the following statements is probably most accurate?
   (a) The plants seem to respond to the desires of the researchers.
   (b) The whole thing is nonsense.
   (c) Most of the researchers do not even like plants.

2. _____ Which of the following statements is probably inaccurate?
   (a) More careful research is necessary to prove that plants like music.
   (b) Pseudo-science has many amusing aspects.
   (c) Mrs. Retallack is making vast claims for her research.

COMPLETION   Choose the best answer for each question.

1. _____ One kind of music the plants seemed to like a little bit was: (a) country and Western. (b) waltz music. (c) polka tunes. (d) lieder.

2. _____ The first report on plants and music was written by: (a) Mrs. Retallack. (b) a famous rock star. (c) a violinist from India. (d) a prayer group.

3. _____ Mrs. Retallack wonders if the music that destroys plants might: (a) be silly. (b) destroy people. (c) energize the soil. (d) be violin music.

4. _____ One tune the plants liked was: (a) "Wooden Ships." (b) "Fifty Ways to Leave Your Lover." (c) "C-Jam Blues." (d) "La Paloma."

5. _____ Mrs. Retallack is married to a: (a) physician. (b) violinist. (c) minister. (d) plant physiologist.

6. _____ One biologist at Temple Buell claimed that the biologists had been: (a) robbed. (b) underrated. (c) stunned by the research. (d) ridiculed professionally.

DEFINITIONS   Choose the definition from Column B that best matches each italicized word in Column A.

Column A	Column B
1. *excruciating* embarrassment	_____ a. thrive
2. excruciating *embarrassment*	_____ b. vivid
	_____ c. unwillingly
3. renamed to honor a *benefactor*	_____ d. see, observe
4. she roars *enthusiastically*	_____ e. donor, helper
5. plants *flourish* with Ravi Shankar	_____ f. detect
	_____ g. stop
6. she *concedes* the point	_____ h. excitedly

7. the plants might *perceive* her

8. plants *sense* human attitudes

9. *reluctantly* discuss the subject

10. power to *inhibit* plant growth

_____ i. accepts

_____ j. intensely painful

_____ k. austerely

_____ l. shame

_____ m. clandestinely

_____ n. admits

17 CARYL RIVERS

Cloning: A Generation Made to Order

Science has created many frightening prospects for humanity. One of the oddest is cloning–the reproduction from a single cell of a being that is the parent's genetic twin. The potential is so awesome that we hardly know what to make of it.

Human reproduction begins with the merger of the sex cells, sperm and egg. Since each contains only half a set of chromosomes, the joining of sperm with the egg is the first step in the creation of a new and unique individual, with traits inherited from both parents. But this is not the only possible way for life to begin.

The other type of cells in the human body already has a full set of chromosomes. All the genetic information necessary for an organism to reproduce itself is contained in the nucleus of every cell in that organism. If body cells could be made to divide, the result would be asexual reproduction—the production of offspring with only one parent. Such a process is already being used with other species—it is called cloning. It has been tried successfully with plants, fruit flies—and more significantly, with frogs.

In 1968, J. B. Gurdon at Oxford University produced a clonal frog. He took an unfertilized egg cell from an African clawed frog and destroyed its nucleus by ultraviolet radiation. He replaced it with the nucleus of an intestinal cell of another frog of the same species. The egg, suddenly finding itself with a full set of chromosomes, began to reproduce. It was "tricked" into starting the reproductive process. The result was a tadpole that was a genetic twin of the frog that

CLONING: A GENERATION MADE TO ORDER *Ms.,* June 1976. © *Ms.* Magazine Corp., 1976. Reprinted by permission.

donated the cell. The "mother" frog contributed nothing to the genetic identity of the tadpole, since her potential to pass on her traits was destroyed when the nucleus of her egg was obliterated.

How would it work with human beings? Roughly the same way. A healthy egg could be removed from a woman's body. But instead of fertilizing the egg with sperm, scientists could destroy the nucleus of the human egg and replace it with a cell taken from the arm or anywhere of a donor we'll call John X. The egg would be reimplanted in the uterus of a woman. Although its identity would be wiped out with the destruction of its nucleus, it could nonetheless start to divide, because it had received the proper signal—the presence of a full set of chromosomes. The baby that would be the result of that process would have only one parent—John X. It would, in fact, be a carbon copy of John X—his twin, a generation removed. (Or her twin, if the cell donor were female.)

In March of this year scientists announced major progress on the hunt for the substance that "switches on" the reproductive mechanisms of the cell. Gurdon's first experiments with the frog proved that such a mechanism exists and that all cells—not just sex cells—could be made to reproduce. Now, work done by Gurdon at Cambridge and by Ann Janice Brothers at the University of Indiana is moving science closer to discovering the identity of the "master switch."

Gurdon inserted the nuclei of human cancer cells into immature frogs eggs, and the human cell nuclei responded in dramatic fashion, swelling in size to as much as a hundredfold.

The consequences of human cloning are almost impossible to imagine. Widespread human cloning would alter human society beyond recognition. The family would no longer exist, sexuality would have no connection with reproduction. The idea of parenthood would be completely changed. The diversity of human beings provided by sexual reproduction would vanish. One could imagine entire communities of people who looked exactly the same, whose range of potential was identical. Some scientists have suggested that "clones and clonishness" could replace our present patterns of nation and race.

The misuses of cloning are not hard to predict. Would an aging dictator try to insure the continuance of his regime by an heir apparent who was his genetic double? Would women and men project their egos into the future by producing their own "carbon copies"? Would society choose to clone our most valued citizens? Artists? Generals? Members of elite groups? The capacity of our species to change and adapt may be rooted in the diversity of the gene pool. By tampering with that process we could be limiting our own ability to survive.

There are some who believe that current work in test-tube fertilization to extract eggs is a first step in the direction of cloning. There have been some estimates that human cloning will be a reality within the decade. Who will say where we draw the line?

LENGTH: 815 WORDS

17 Cloning: A Generation Made to Order

| SCORING: | Reading time: _____ Rate from chart: _____ W.P.M. |

RETENTION	number right _____ × 4 equals _____ points
INFERENCES	number right _____ × 3 equals _____ points
COMPLETION	number right _____ × 4 equals _____ points
DEFINITIONS	number right _____ × 3 equals _____ points

(Total points: 100) **total** _____ points

RETENTION Based on the passage, which of the following statements are True (T), False (F), or Not answerable (N)?

1. _____ Cloning is an asexual process.

2. _____ A full set of chromosomes signals an egg to begin dividing.

3. _____ A cloned egg produces a genetic copy of the donor of the chromosomes.

4. _____ Science demonstrates that only sex cells can be triggered to reproduce.

5. _____ The consequences of human cloning are not mentioned in the passage.

6. _____ Human cloning would have no effect on our ability to survive.

7. _____ Russian clones speak Russian; English clones speak Chinese.

8. _____ Clonishness could replace racial and national distinctions.

9. _____ A frog has been successfully cloned.

10. _____ Research in cloning is limited to the United States.

INFERENCES

1. _____ Which of the following statements is probably most accurate?
   (a) Widespread human cloning would change humanity entirely.
   (b) Cloning is not the kind of process that would alter society much.
   (c) Cloning will be limited to frogs and similar forms of life.

2. _____ Which of the following statements is probably inaccurate?
    (a) New laws will probably be needed to govern cloning.
    (b) Fortunately, cloning does not lend itself to misuse, nor will it.
    (c) Human cloning may be a reality in ten years or so.

COMPLETION Choose the best answer for each question.

1. _____ Human cloning could have a tremendous impact on: (a) women's liberation. (b) frog's legs meals. (c) the family. (d) inheritance taxes.

2. _____ J. B. Gurdon, in 1968, produced the first: (a) fertilized ovum. (b) clonal frog. (c) ultraviolet cell. (d) reproductive mechanism.

3. _____ The capacity of our species to change and adapt may lie in our: (a) ruggedness. (b) clonishness. (c) projected egos. (d) diverse gene pool.

4. _____ The most successful cloning has been with: (a) plants. (b) mammals. (c) arthropods. (d) the nucleus of the human egg.

5. _____ Destroying the nucleus of a human egg also destroys its: (a) ability to survive. (b) sensitivity. (c) capacity to adapt. (d) identity.

6. _____ In normal sexual reproduction, traits are: (a) clear and predictable. (b) not so important. (c) inherited from both parents. (d) freely admitted.

DEFINITIONS Choose the definition from Column B that best matches each italicized word in Column A.

Column A	Column B
1. *current* work in science	_____ a. place of worship
2. sexual reproduction would *vanish*	_____ b. change
	_____ c. undeveloped
3. to *alter* our behavior	_____ d. ability
4. the *diversity* of human beings	_____ e. qualities, characteristics
	_____ f. disappear
5. the *donor* of the cell	_____ g. destroyed
6. the *capacity* of our species	_____ h. differences
7. *immature* frogs eggs	_____ i. shiny
	_____ j. size
8. a new and *unique* individual	

9. their inherited *traits*

10. the nucleus was *obliterated*

_____ k. recent

_____ l. one who gives

_____ m. singular

_____ n. reiterated

18 *FELICIA AMES*

How Intelligent Is Your Dog?

Sometimes we need to be reminded that our best friend is also one of our smartest friends. Dogs think, and sometimes they think very clearly. Next to humans, they might well be among the smartest animals on earth. Felicia Ames raises a few questions about our intelligence in comparison.

Mr. and Mrs. Isenberg will never forget that day in Scarsdale, New York, and the intelligence of their three-year-old beagle, Snooper. They had gone shopping and had locked the dog in the car. Returning from the store, all heaven broke loose on them and they found themselves at the mercy of a torrential rain. It was then that they discovered they had locked more than Snooper in the car; they had no keys. The dog went to work and, with very little coaxing from the drenched pair, lifted the door lock with his teeth.

"How intelligent are dogs?" is a frequent question. Many owners believe absolutely that Rover or Fido or Schroeder has to be the smartest animal this side of a primate and there are some who won't stop there. On the other hand, quite a number of authorities feel that what passes for intelligence in canines is nothing more than cleverness, an ability to learn by rote or imitation.

We have to agree that cleverness is a better word for dogs who can stand on one leg or bow-wow to ninety. We are oversaturated with pictures of dogs swimming, diving, climbing trees and catching anything from fly balls to frisbees. Clever are those pets, too, who pose with cigar in mouth, nautical hat atop head and spectacles over eyes. And, of course, all those dogs who can roll over, play dead or jump through a flaming hoop.

Something other than cleverness, though, must account for dogs who have been known to find their way across strange and rugged miles, back to a house

HOW INTELLIGENT IS YOUR DOG? "How Intelligent Is Rover?" by Felicia Ames. *Around New York*, October 1972. Reprinted with permission of Felicia Ames.

whence they roamed or were removed, often long before. This trait—not all dogs reveal it—is mostly labeled the homing instinct or built-in radar, but no one has ever been able to explain it.

There is also the dog who, finding himself lost, determines to stay by a bit of his owner's clothing, often for days, apparently knowing that there is a chance of the owner's return.

Judgment reflects intelligence and many dogs are capable of making decisions. For example, consider any seeing-eye dog. If he stopped when the light turned red and moved on green, it might be possible to assume, first that he was trained to react to light changes and, secondly, that he wasn't color blind. But we have yet to observe any of these dogs who allow the light to be their only cue for action. Invariably, the dog will watch the traffic, in all directions, as well as any pedestrians nearby, before determining whether to wait or lead his master across the intersection.

A story involving an English seeing-eye dog and his master really does much to prove that dogs possess keen intelligence. The dog, named Kim, was taken suddenly ill while walking with his master in the city. Deliberately disobeying his master's pressures on the lead—the man was en route to an appointment—the dog went, instead, to a veterinarian whom he knew to have an office nearby. After the doctor had treated him for a severe stomach distress, he went on to help his master keep the appointment.

Another story we like involved another English guide dog. Simba was her name and she was a three-year-old Alsatian. Every day, in her house in Kent, she led Minky downstairs and then opened the door to let her outside. Minky was a seven-year-old spaniel. The owner of the two dogs, Esme Bidlake, said: "As soon as Minky went blind, Simba seemed to sense it and, with no training from me, started guiding the little spaniel about the house. She even leads Minky to her feeding bowl and sits beside her while she has her meal." When the dogs went out for a walk, Simba held onto Minky's ear, waited for traffic to pass, then gently escorted her across the road, still holding her ear.

Dogs have long been respected for their ability to hear and smell. But it also required some intelligence for a dog named Schmutz to rescue a man buried under an avalanche in the Swiss Alps. The man reported later that he could hear his would-be rescuers digging with their shovels. He screamed to them to keep digging, but they didn't hear him. The dog did hear him and went on digging after the men had abandoned the search. Fourteen others were eventually rescued from the same avalanche, thanks to the hearing of a dog and his intelligence to sense danger.

Another dog with a sense of danger and the intelligence to act was Spooky, a two-year-old pit bull terrier. The dog observed an injured sea gull struggling about a hundred yards offshore of Hutchinson Island, Florida. The dog's owner watched as the dog climbed down a bridge construction site, swam the distance, grabbed the gull in his mouth and brought it to shore without ruffling a feather.

The owner freed a fishing lure that had been hooked from the beak of the bird to its wing, and the gull was able to fly away.

For clinching arguments, though, there are Prince, a four-year-old Cock-apoo in Los Angeles and a moonshine dog in McNairy County, West Tennes-see. The owner of the latter used to operate a still and was in the habit of hiding his product. Since he was either drunk when he hid the stuff or drunk when he went to find it, the poor man never knew quite where to go. But the dog did. Confronted with a sale, the moonshiner would indicate with his fingers how many pint bottles the transaction required and the dog would do the rest. There was one problem. The man would become very ugly and offensive with too much to drink. When this happened, the dog would leave home and stay away until his boss was sober. This never lasted too long, of course, because the boss could never remember where he stashed the hootch. We never did find out if the dog took a drink, but we presume he was too smart for that.

As for Prince, the Los Angeles cocker and poodle cross, his thing is cigarettes. He hates them with such abandon that his owner wonders whether he might be of some use to the American Cancer Society. We're not sure how many people have given up smoking because of Prince, but we know that there isn't one smoker who dares practice his habit in the dog's presence. Ever since he was a pup, says his owner, Margaret Eiden, he's been curling his lip whenever he sees a cigarette being lit. If the lighter of the weed persists and takes a drag, Prince emits a low, horrifying snarl. If the dragger drags on, the dog goes into a crouch that can only spell kill. No one, needless to say, pushes at that point for another puff.

A dog with a cause, and more intelligent than many of us, it seems.

LENGTH: 1120 WORDS

18 How Intelligent Is Your Dog?

SCORING: Reading time: _____ Rate from chart: _____ W.P.M.

RETENTION	number right _____ × 4 equals _____ points
INFERENCES	number right _____ × 3 equals _____ points
COMPLETION	number right _____ × 4 equals _____ points
DEFINITIONS	number right _____ × 3 equals _____ points

(Total points: 100) **total**_____ points

RETENTION   Based on the passage, which of the following statements are True (T), False (F), or Not answerable (N)?

1. _____ Good judgment tends to reflect high intelligence.

2. _____ Schmutz's keen sense of smell helped him rescue some mountaineers.

3. _____ One English seeing eye dog took his master to the veterinarian.

4. _____ Primates react much the same way as dogs do to dangerous situations.

5. _____ Seeing eye dogs rely solely on the traffic lights at intersections.

6. _____ Minky was a blind spaniel.

7. _____ Dogs have been respected for their good sense of smell, but not for their good sense of hearing.

8. _____ Prince, the Los Angeles Cockapoo, had a good tolerance for cigarettes.

9. _____ Cleverness seems to be common in dogs.

10. _____ One dog in Florida actually rescued a sea gull.

INFERENCES

1. _____ Which of the following statements is probably most accurate?
   (a) Felicia Ames has done extensive scientific research on this subject.

(b) Cleverness is revealed in tricks; intelligence is revealed in decision making.

(c) Not many more examples could be found of this kind of behavior in dogs.

2. _____ Which of the following statements is probably inaccurate?

(a) All dogs have the homing instinct, or built-in radar.

(b) Dogs adapt to a wide variety of life styles of their masters.

(c) Dogs can sense a need in other creatures, not just in people.

COMPLETION   Choose the best answer for each question.

1. _____ The three-year-old beagle, Snooper, was able to: (a) foil a detective.   (b) chase a gull.   (c) unlock a car.   (d) catch a suspected robber.

2. _____ The product of a still is: (a) peace and quiet.   (b) liquor.   (c) seeing eye dogs.   (d) clothing.

3. _____ Occasionally a seeing eye dog will: (a) wander off.   (b) have built-in radar.   (c) disobey the master.   (d) collect blind friends.

4. _____ His owners thought Prince might have been a: (a) small lion.   (b) swimming or climbing dog.   (c) help to the American Cancer Society.   (d) primate in disguise.

5. _____ The dog owners trying to get into their car were: (a) unrelated.   (b) from a foreign country.   (c) laughing like mad.   (d) drenched.

6. _____ Dogs may be: (a) drafted.   (b) colorblind.   (c) amused by television.   (d) unknown in the Swiss Alps.

DEFINITIONS   Choose the definition from Column B that best matches each italicized word in Column A.

Column A	*Column B*
1. to learn by *rote*	_____ a. sale
2. pose with a *nautical* hat	_____ b. treatment
3. a *torrential* downpour	_____ c. convincing
4. the homing *trait*	_____ d. characteristic, quality
5. for *clinching* arguments	_____ e. signal
6. what the *transaction* required	_____ f. sailor's
	_____ g. respond
	_____ h. memorization

7. when the smoker *persists*

8. to *react* to light changes

9. a *cue* for action

10. *severe* stomach distress

_____ i. opposing

_____ j. soaking; intense

_____ k. to reach

_____ l. continues, keeps on

_____ m. big, colossal

_____ n. difficult to endure

19 *LYDEL SIMS*

Mark Twain's Speechmaking Strategy

Most Americans recognize Mark Twain as the author of such classics as Huckleberry Finn *and* A Connecticut Yankee in King Arthur's Court. *But Twain, in his own time, was probably almost as well known for his great ability as a speaker. One of his secrets suggests why this is so.*

The schoolboy in the old story explained the technique nicely. "Strategy," he wrote, "means that when you run out of bullets you keep on firing." It hasn't caught on in military circles, but speechmakers have been practicing that kind of strategy for generations.

Consider the problem:

You're going to a sales conference, a convention, a testimonial dinner, a meeting of department heads. You're scheduled to speak, or you know you'll be called on. So you organize your thoughts, scribble notes on a piece of paper . . . and worry.

You worry, because like all good speakers, you want people to believe the words just flow out—all the humor, the motivation, the drive, the matchless grasp of detail, the fresh and sparkling anecdotes.

But speakers who hold audiences in the palm of their hand don't speak from notes. Are you going to pause and consult those plaguey notes, thus admitting mere mortality? Or are you going to wing it and risk forgetting your best story, omitting your most important point? And if you run out of ammunition, are you going to try to keep on firing?

MARK TWAIN'S SPEECHMAKING STRATEGY "How Mark Twain Solved the Speechmaker's Dilemma." From *TWA Ambassador* Magazine. Copyright Trans World Airlines 1976. Used by permission.

Mark Twain faced that very same dilemma and solved it, becoming one of the most successful speakers in America's history.

In his early days on the lecture circuit, Mark Twain worked out a solution to the speechmaker's dilemma by trial and error, but he didn't explain it until years later in a little-known essay that was published after his death. The system was so good, he testified, that a quarter-century after he had given a lecture he could remember the whole thing by a single act of recall.

You have Twain's posthumous guarantee that it'll work for you.

When he first began his speaking career, Twain recalled, he used a full page of notes to keep from getting mixed up. He would write down the beginnings of key sentences, to take him from one point to another and to protect him from skipping. For a typical evening's lecture, he would write and memorize 11 key beginnings.

The plan failed. Twain would remember the sentences, all right, but forget their order. He would have to stop, consult his notes, and thereby spoil the spontaneous effect of the whole speech.

Twain then decided to memorize not only his key sentences, but also the first letter of each sentence. This initial-letter method didn't work either. Not even when, as he solemnly alleged, he cut the number of letters to 10 and inked them on his fingernails.

"I kept track of the fingers for a while," he wrote in his essay, "then I lost it, and after that I was never quite sure which finger I had used last."

He considered licking off the inked letters as he went along. People noticed he seemed more interested in his fingernails than his subject; one or two listeners would come up afterwards and ask what was wrong with his hands.

Then Mark Twain's great idea came—that it's hard to visualize letters, words and sentences, but *pictures* are easy to recall. They take hold. They can make things stick . . .

Especially if you draw them yourself.

Twain was no artist, mind you, but that didn't stop him. "In two minutes I made six pictures with a pen," he reported, "and they did the work of the 11 catch-sentences, and did it perfectly."

Having once drawn the pictures, he found he could throw them away. He discovered [and you can test it for yourself] that, having once made a crude series of drawings, he could recall their image at will.

He left us samples of three of those first six pictures, and they are pathetic things, indeed, by artistic standards. But they got the job done.

The first was a haystack with a wiggly line under it to represent a rattlesnake—that was to tell him to begin talking about ranch life in the West. Alongside it, he drew a few slanting lines with what could just possibly be an umbrella and the Roman numeral II—that referred to a tale about a great wind that would strike Carson City at 2 o'clock every afternoon. Next, he drew a couple of jagged lines—lightning, of course—telling him it was time to move on to the subject of weather in San Francisco, where the point was that there *wasn't* any lightning. Nor thunder either, he noted.

From that day, Twain was able to speak without notes, and the system never failed him. Each portion of his speech would be represented by a picture. He would draw them, all strung out in a row, then look at them and destroy them. When the time came to speak, there was the row of images sharply in his mind.

Twain observed you can even make last-minute notes based on the remarks of an earlier speaker. Just insert another figure in your set of images.

The magic of the Twain technique should be immediately obvious to the speaker who organizes remarks around anecdotes. Are you introducing your first point with a story about a nervous doctor in Dubuque? Draw the doctor. Are you following that with the principle that's best illustrated with the tale of the fellow who treed a wildcat? Draw a tree alongside the doctor. And so on.

The remarkable thing is that Twain's method can work just as well for concepts as it does for anecdotes. Sales must be increased? Draw a vertical arrow with a dollar sign. Something about productivity? A lopsided circle representing a wheel is sufficient. Research and development? Even you can draw what will be recognized—by you—as a mad scientist. And if you need figures, put them in the pictures, too, coming out of people's mouths, piled in pyramids, outlined in exclamation marks, lurking under bridges.

The wilder the image, the easier it'll be to remember. And once you have your scrawls in sequence and take a good look, you're fixed. Instant memory.

Mark Twain didn't mention it, but there's one more thing you might do. When you reach the end of your drawings, hence the end of your speech, you could add one more— a drawing of an octagonal sign: STOP!

That would be smart strategy, for then you really *are* out of bullets. No need to keep on firing.

LENGTH: 1170 WORDS

19   Mark Twain's Speechmaking Strategy

SCORING: Reading time: _____ Rate from chart: _____ W.P.M.

RETENTION	number right _____ ✗ 4 equals _____ points
INFERENCES	number right _____ × 3 equals _____ points
COMPLETION	number right _____ × 4 equals _____ points
DEFINITIONS	number right _____ × 3 equals _____ points

(Total points: 100) **total** _____ points

RETENTION   Based on the passage, which of the following statements are True (T), False (F), or Not answerable (N)?

1. _____ Even after scribbling notes, speechmakers can worry.

2. _____ Inking key letters on his fingernails did not work for Twain.

3. _____ Actually, Twain never tried making notes.

4. _____ Drawings are easier to memorize than sentences or even words.

5. _____ Twain was an artist.

6. _____ Speakers who use images for notes make no last-minute changes.

7. _____ The image system works for anecdotes, but not for concepts.

8. _____ Twain could not recall when he first began his speaking career.

9. _____ Unfortunately, we have no samples of Twain's pictures.

10. _____ The secret to Twain's technique was published after his death.

INFERENCES

1. _____ Which of the following statements is probably most accurate?
    (a) Other speechmakers caught on to Twain's system pretty fast.
    (b) Twain kept the system pretty much to himself.
    (c) Most people do not mind if a speech is read from notes.

2. _____ Which of the following statements is probably inaccurate?
    (a) Speechmakers try to affect effortlessness.

(b) Most of the hard work is really done before the speech is given.
(c) Other successful speechmakers had no system at all.

COMPLETION   Choose the best answer for each question.

1. _____ Twain left us a posthumous: (a) guarantee.   (b) legend.   (c) ghost story.   (d) jibe.

2. _____ Twain could recall a speech he had made: (a) while drunk.   (b) in England.   (c) in a foreign language.   (d) years before.

3. _____ To use notes is to admit: (a) nothing.   (b) mere mortality.   (c) cocky complacency.   (d) lack of courage.

4. _____ The wilder the image, the: (a) worse the speech.   (b) easier it is to remember.   (c) quicker the speech.   (d) more impressive the speech.

5. _____ Twain liked to make his speeches seem: (a) fanciful.   (b) spiteful.   (c) significant.   (d) spontaneous.

6. _____ One reason for using a system such as Twain's is to: (a) move up the ladder.   (b) make friends fast.   (c) not leave out anything.   (d) end quickly.

DEFINITIONS   Choose the definition from Column B that best matches each italicized word in Column A.

Column A	Column B
1. a *typical* lecture	_____ a. important
2. beginnings of *key* sentences	_____ b. medicines
	_____ c. imagine
3. to consult *plaguey* notes	_____ d. stories
4. *organize* your thoughts	_____ e. order
5. as he solemnly *alleged*	_____ f. usual
6. to *visualize* letters	_____ g. interlocking
7. each *portion* of his speech	_____ h. part
	_____ i. assign
8. just *insert* another figure	_____ j. asserted
9. it works for *anecdotes*	_____ k. annoying
10. put your images in *sequence*	_____ l. plan
	_____ m. pledged
	_____ n. fit in

SECTION III

Vocabulary Preview

The following words come from the seven reading selections in Section III. Study the list carefully, pronouncing the words aloud if possible. Conceal the definitions with a card or your hand and test your command of the meanings of the words.

abolish, *verb*   to end; to get rid of

adage, *noun*   saying

aeons, *noun*   great ages of time

allegations, *noun*   accusations; charges

ambulatory, *adj.*   able to get around; capable of walking

apocalyptic, *adj.*   having to do with the end of the world

belligerently, *adv.*   in a warlike manner; violently

benighted, *adj.*   in the "dark"; ignorant

bigoted, *adj.*   prejudiced

bilking, *verb*   cheating; defrauding

breach, *verb*   to break through

cache, *noun*   supply; something stored away

caper, *noun (slang)*   crime

cessation, *noun*   ending of something

coercion, *noun*   force; being forced against one's will

coincides, *verb*   comes at the same time

compensatory, *adj.*   making up for something

conjured, *verb*   did magically

consternation, *noun*   confusion; dismay

contended, *verb*   held, believed; fought (as in, contended with)

cryptic, *adj.*   mysterious; not intelligible

debunk, *verb*   to expose; to put down

demagogue, *noun*   leader who stirs up the worst feelings of the people

demented, *adj.*   crazy, insane

demurred, *verb*   turned down; did not accept the offer

deposition, *noun*   testimony or evidence taken in writing

dire, *adj.*   serious; awful

disclosures, *noun*   revealed information

disdain, *noun*   contempt

disenchant, *verb*   to lose one's illusions

dismemberment, *noun*   loss of legs or arms or both

disperse, *verb*   to send off; to scatter

disruptive, *adj.*   causing trouble

divulge, *verb*   to reveal; to tell

euthanasia, *noun*   painless killing of sick people

exorbitant, *adj.*   excessive; too costly

expertise, *noun*   skill

exploitation, *noun*   taking advantage of someone or something

fallacy, *noun*   untruth

fetish, *noun*   compulsive attraction to something

flux; fluctuations, *noun*   flow; changes and flow of things

formidable, *adj.*   strong; significant

fraud, *noun*   deceit; dishonest cheating

genealogical, *adj.*   relating to family descent

gullibility, *noun*   too-willing readiness to believe

heresy, *noun*   belief or idea that is not accepted as true

impending, *adj.*   about to happen; approaching

stop⟶**implausible,** *adj.*   unlikely

impose, *verb*   to weigh on others; to set up or establish something

incipient, *adj.*   beginning; just starting

inexorably, *adv.*   inevitably; fated

juncture, *noun*   meeting place; arrival point

ludicrously, *adv.*   ridiculously

malicious, *adj.*   specifically evil

mannerism, *noun*   odd behavior; exaggerated or strange habit

memorabilia, *noun*   mementos; souvenirs

modus operandi, *noun*   way of operating

mogul, *noun*   important person

monitor, *verb*   to watch carefully

moribund, *adj.*   dying

myriad, *adj.*   diverse; various

non-plused, *adj.*   surprised

obtain, *verb*   to get; to acquire
periodic, *adj.*   happening from time to time
perspective, *noun*   point of view; seeing relationships
precariously, *adv.*   uncertainly
premises, *noun*   bases for decisions or arguments
purport, *noun*   apparent meaning
quadriplegic, *noun*   without the use of any limb
rebuffs, *noun*   refusals; setbacks
repressed, *adj.*   held back; held in
resounds, *verb*   rings; reverberates; sounds loudly
seclusion, *noun*   in hiding
sepulchral, *adj.*   referring to a burial vault
sham, *noun*   something false
shrewd, *adj.*   cunning; artfully wise
staunch, *adj.*   strong
subsidize, *verb*   to give special support to
suppressed, *adj.*   stifled; put down
surveillance, *noun*   being watched or observed
tactic, *noun*   scheme; bit of strategy
tampering, *verb*   interfering or meddling with
termination, *noun*   ending
tribulations, *noun*   sufferings; trials
tycoons, *noun*   powerful businessmen
undermined, *verb*   weakened
unique, *adj.*   one of a kind; singular
unprecedented, *adj.*   new; without a former instance
verge, *verb*   to come close to; to move toward a beginning

Complete the following sentences, using the correct words from the list.

1. He wanted to buy that watch, but the price was _____.

2. Jefferson resented the British economic _____ of the American colonies.

3. The _____ legislation frightened the former governor.

4. He was completely _____ by her unexpected response.

5. Ramona's _____ in public speaking helped her to succeed.

6. Giraldo undermined the _____ of the argument.

7. The speaker used an unprecedented _____ in arguing her point.

8. Marcia _____ the notion that euthanasia was desirable in this country.

9. The committee was abolished because of its highly _____

_____ tactics.

10. Leon _____ the secret about his foot fetish.

11. Patrice's gullibility led to his being a victim of _____.

12. The teacher _____ the examination carefully to avoid any breach of ethics.

13. Although he spoke clearly, his speeches were _____

_____ and vague.

14. The _____ of his message was that surveillance would not be used.

15. It was a fallacy to think that Peter would act in anything but a

_____ emergency.

16. The demagogue did not want the public to know it, so the news was

_____.

17. My uncle had an odd mannerism: saving matchbook covers as

_____.

18. Madeline was on the verge of giving a totally _____ answer.

19. Stu made periodic attempts to see things from a new _____

    _____.

20. The woman became belligerent when her enemy came out of

    _____.

21. Phyllis almost did not _____ a license for her dog.

22. My friend was perched _____ on the ledge.

23. Miguel's favorite _____ was to begin with a malicious joke.

24. The preacher's stories always dealt with _____ warnings.

25. Senator Onslew announced the _____ of hearings with this, the final meeting.

20 *JACKIE ROBINSON*

I Never Had It Made

In this somewhat bitter memoir, Jackie Robinson recalls what it was like to be the first black major-league baseball player. He was aware of the problems, the risks that his manager took. But he was also aware that he was being used as a box-office attraction. He recalls his own pain throughout the experience and realizes things were never easier for him than for other players.

I guess if I could choose one of the most important moments in my life, I would go back to 1947, in the Yankee Stadium in New York City. It was the opening day of the world series and I was for the first time playing in the series as a member of the Brooklyn Dodgers team. It was a history-making day. It would be the first time that a black man would be allowed to participate in a world series. I had become the first black player in the major leagues.

I was proud of that and yet I was uneasy. I was proud to be in the hurricane eye of a significant breakthrough and to be used to prove that a sport can't be called national if blacks are barred from it. Branch Rickey, the president of the Brooklyn Dodgers, had rudely awakened America. He was a man with high ideals, and he was also a shrewd businessman. Mr. Rickey had shocked some of his fellow baseball tycoons and angered others by deciding to smash the unwritten law that kept blacks out of the big leagues. He had chosen me as the person to lead the way.

It hadn't been easy. Some of my own teammates refused to accept me because I was black. I had been forced to live with snubs and rebuffs and rejections. Within the club, Mr. Rickey had put down rebellion by letting my teammates know that anyone who didn't want to accept me could leave. But the

---

problems within the Dodgers club had been minor compared to the opposition outside. It hadn't been that easy to fight the resentment expressed by players on other teams, by the team owners, or by bigoted fans screaming "nigger." The hate mail piled up. There were threats against me and my family and even out-and-out attempts at physical harm to me.

Some things counterbalanced this ugliness. Black people supported me with total loyalty. They supported me morally; they came to sit in a hostile audience in unprecedented numbers to make the turnstiles hum as they never had before at ball parks all over the nation. Money is America's God, and business people can dig black power if it coincides with green power, so these fans were important to the success of Mr. Rickey's "Noble Experiment."

Some of the Dodgers who swore they would never play with a black man had a change of mind, when they realized I was a good ballplayer who could be helpful in their earning a few thousand more dollars in world series money. After the initial resistance to me had been crushed, my teammates started to give me tips on how to improve my game. They hadn't changed because they liked me any better; they had changed because I could help fill their wallets.

My fellow Dodgers were not decent out of self-interest alone. There were heartwarming experiences with some teammates; there was Southern-born Pee Wee Reese who turned into a staunch friend. And there were others.

Mr. Rickey stands out as the man who inspired me the most. He will always have my admiration and respect. Critics had said, "Don't you know that your precious Mr. Rickey didn't bring you up out of the black leagues because he loved you? Are you stupid enough not to understand that the Brooklyn club profited hugely because of what your Mr. Rickey did?"

Yes, I know that. But I also know what a big gamble he took. A bond developed between us that lasted long after I had left the game. In a way I feel I was the son he had lost and he was the father I had lost.

There was more than just making money at stake in Mr. Rickey's decision. I learned that his family was afraid that his health was being undermined by the resulting pressures and that they pleaded with him to abandon the plan. His peers and fellow baseball moguls exerted all kinds of influence to get him to change his mind. Some of the press condemned him as a fool and a demagogue. But he didn't give in.

In a very real sense, black people helped make the experiment succeed. Many who came to the ball park had not been baseball fans before I began to play in the big leagues. Suppressed and repressed for so many years, they needed a victorious black man as a symbol. It would help them believe in themselves. But black support of the first black man in the majors was a complicated matter. The breakthrough created as much danger as it did hope. It was one thing for me out there on the playing field to be able to keep my cool in the face of insults. But it was another for all those black people sitting in the stands to keep from overreacting when they sensed a racial slur or an unjust decision. They could have blown the whole bit to hell by acting belligerently and touching off a race riot. That would have been all the bigots needed to set back the cause of progress of black men in sports another hundred years. I knew this. Mr. Rickey knew this. But this never happened. I learned from Rachel who had spent hours in the stands that clergymen and laymen had held meetings in the black community to spread the word. We all knew about the help of the black press. Mr. Rickey and I owed them a great deal.

Children from all races came to the stands. The very young seemed to have no hangup at all about my being black. They just wanted me to be good, to deliver, to win. The inspiration of their innocence is amazing. I don't think I'll ever forget the small, shrill voice of a tiny white kid who, in the midst of a racially tense atmosphere during an early game in a Dixie town, cried out, "Attaboy, Jackie." It broke the tension and it made me feel I had to succeed.

The black and the young were my cheering squads. But also there were people—neither black nor young—people of all races and faiths and in all parts of this country, people who couldn't care less about my race.

Rachel was even more important to my success. I know that every successful man is supposed to say that without his wife he could never have accomplished success. It is gospel in my case. Rachel shared those difficult years that led to this moment and helped me through all the days thereafter. She has been strong, loving, gentle, and brave, never afraid to either criticize or comfort me.

There I was the black grandson of a slave, the son of a black sharecropper, part of a historic occasion, a symbolic hero to my people. The air was sparkling. The sunlight was warm. The band struck up the national anthem. The flag billowed in the wind. It should have been a glorious moment for me as the stirring words of the national anthem poured from the stands. Perhaps it was, but then again perhaps the anthem could be called the theme song for a drama called *The Noble Experiment*. Today as I look back on that opening game of my first world series, I must tell you that it was Mr. Rickey's drama and that I was only a principal actor. As I write this twenty years later, I cannot stand and sing the anthem. I cannot salute the flag; I know that I am a black man in a white world. In 1972, in 1947, at my birth in 1919, I know that I never had it made.

LENGTH: 1240 WORDS

20   I Never Had It Made

RETENTION   Based on the passage, which of the following statements are True (T), False (F), or Not answerable (N)?

1. _____ Blacks had been kept out of the major leagues by a written law.

2. _____ Black fans did little to help the "Noble Experiment" succeed.

3. _____ Children of all races watched Jackie Robinson play.

4. _____ Robinson was unaware that he was a symbolic hero to blacks.

5. _____ Robinson felt his wife, Rachel, was very important to his success.

6. _____ Branch Rickey's wife took special care of Rachel.

7. _____ Jackie Robinson's father was a sharecropper.

8. _____ People in baseball tried to change Branch Rickey's mind about Jackie.

9. _____ Branch Rickey was not officially connected with the Dodgers.

10. _____ In 1947, the Dodgers were a Brooklyn team.

11. _____ Jackie played his first World Series game in Yankee Stadium.

12. _____ Eventually, Jackie thought of his experience as a kind of drama.

13. _____ The old and the weak were Jackie's cheering squads.

14. _____ Jackie's fellow players rallied around him from the start.

15. _____ Pee Wee Reese was particularly friendly toward Jackie.

16. _____ Fortunately, those were times before hate mail.

17. _____ Jackie felt that Branch Rickey was really an inspiring man.

18. _____ Playing in the World Series can mean a few thousand dollars more per man.

19. _____ Sad to say, the Yankees won that World Series.

20. _____ Money was not the only thing at stake for Branch Rickey.

INFERENCES Which three of the following statements, based on the passage, are probably justifiable? _____, _____, and _____.

1. At first, Jackie was a starry-eyed idealist about playing baseball.

2. Branch Rickey and Jackie maintained almost a family tie with each other.

3. Black people were really unaware of the significance of Jackie's action.

4. Rickey's book, *The Noble Experiment,* was long awaited.

5. Even many years after breaking into the majors, Jackie still felt like a stranger in America.

6. Jackie knew that there was nothing but money involved in Rickey's experiment.

7. There were many times when Jackie wanted to give it all up and go home.

8. It took the combination of idealist and businessman to get Jackie into the majors.

COMPLETION Choose the best answer for each question.

1. _____ On opening day of the World Series they played: (a) like crazy. (b) the national anthem. (c) an exhibition game. (d) a waiting game.

2. _____ Many of the Dodgers accepted Jackie because he could: (a) sing and dance. (b) keep quiet. (c) see what was happening. (d) help them earn more money.

3. _____ The possibility of racial rioting was lessened by: (a) the black press. (b) the police. (c) Branch Rickey's genius. (d) Jackie's soft voice.

4. _____ During the actual games, Jackie got most of his inspiration from: (a) blacks. (b) whites. (c) opponents. (d) children.

5. _____ A racial riot might have: (a) been in order. (b) harmed black progress in sports. (c) stopped everything. (d) changed Rickey's mind entirely.

6. _____ Jackie felt that Rickey took: (a) special pains. (b) a terrific gamble. (c) his time. (d) a strange interest in his new ballplayer.

DEFINITIONS   Choose the best definition for each italicized word.

1. _____ baseball *moguls:*   (a) players   (b) fans   (c) owners   (d) critics

2. _____ a *shrewd* businessman: (a) calculating   (b) big   (c) bad   (d) paltry

3. _____ by acting *belligerently:*   (a) passively   (b) subtly   (c) quickly   (d) aggressively

4. _____ a *staunch* friend: (a) solid   (b) favorite   (c) mere   (d) white

5. _____ to live with *rebuffs:*   (a) failures   (b) rejections   (c) frights   (d) fears

6. _____ a racial *slur:*   (a) insult   (b) law   (c) crime   (d) fact

7. _____ his health was *undermined:*   (a) very bad   (b) being examined   (c) a very real question   (d) weakened

8. _____ *participate* in a World Series: (a) win   (b) go   (c) take part   (d) have a friend

9. _____ problems had been *minor:*   (a) widespread   (b) off-key   (c) great   (d) slight

10. _____ the flag *billowed:*   (a) wafted   (b) slunk   (c) sagged   (d) snapped

11. _____ a *principal* actor: (a) smart   (b) cool   (c) major   (d) scholarly

12. _____ the *bigoted* fans: (a) alarmed   (b) prejudiced   (c) fighting   (d) shrewd

13. _____ a *hostile* audience: (a) hustling   (b) unfriendly   (c) Indian   (d) savage

14. _____ a fool and a *demagogue:*   (a) businessman   (b) crook   (c) agitator   (d) saint

15. _____ *suppressed* for many years: (a) not cheerful   (b) hurt   (c) held back   (d) admirable in its way

21 *ROBERT S. COWEN*

Wandering Continents

The continents—the great land masses—have traditionally been thought of as solid, very solid. To imagine them as moving in any sense is almost beyond belief. Yet, current research shows that the continents may, indeed, drift, although very slowly. New studies in geology have made some remarkable contributions to our knowledge of the earth's crust.

If you take the long-term view of real-estate investment, don't put your money into Los Angeles. It's moving inexorably toward the Aleutian sea-bottom trench.

Sixty million years hence, it may slip down that trench to be forever lost in the hot, plastic matter that underlies earth's crust.

This apocalyptic vision springs from geophysicists' fast-evolving new concepts of processes that shape the earth's surface. Where once they thought they saw vast stability, they now see restless change.

Discoveries supporting this view flood in from many parts of the world, especially from deep-sea explorations. They have revolutionized the science that studies our planet's face.

Fifteen years ago, geophysicists had little to do with such concepts. They knew that mountain ranges grew and eroded on vast scales. They recognized that land and sea underwent alteration over aeons of time.

Yet they thought of such change against a background of general stability. Ocean basins were fixed features, and land masses stayed put.

WANDERING CONTINENTS *The Christian Science Monitor,* December 4, 1970. Reprinted by permission from *The Christian Science Monitor* © 1970 The Christian Science Publishing Society. All rights reserved.

Earth scientists scarcely imagined ocean basins being born, growing, or disappearing within 200 million years or less of geological time. To suggest continents might split apart, come together, or otherwise drift about, they generally considered heresy. They gave little thought to such processes as are going on and being observable today.

Ten years ago, the geophysicists began to loosen up. As one of them put it, you no longer had to go to the washroom to talk about continental drift. By five years ago, the growth of oceans and drift of land masses had become the centerpiece of earth-surface research.

But over the past few years, the scientists concerned have realized that merely to think of changing seas and continents is to take a superficial view of a more fundamental process. For both sea floor and land now appear to be just the upper part of large plates of earth's crust whose growth, destruction, and maneuvering keep our planet's face in constant flux.

To recognize this has at last put these geophysicists on a par with experts in many other fields.

When an astronomer looks outward at the stars, he fits his discoveries into a general scheme of our galaxy and of the universe. When a biologist probes processes of organic life, he has a general concept of that life to guide him. So too does a physicist have an overall frame for his studies of the atom.

But up to now, geophysicists had no such overview to which they could relate their scattering of facts about earth's surface. They had no theory of crustal processes to make sense of their findings.

Now, for the first time, they can see those processes as a unified whole. They can predict the future world map, as Robert S. Dietz and John C. Holden of the (American) National Oceanic and Atmospheric Administration did recently when they forecast Los Angeles' demise.

They can also hope to measure the mapmaking processes directly as Dr. P. L. Bender of the Joint Institute for Laboratory Astrophysics, Boulder Colo., is trying to do by bouncing laser beams off the moon.

The laser beams are reflected by an array of mirrors left behind by Apollo 11 astronauts. Measuring the laser beam round-trip travel time to within billionths of a second, Dr. Bender can compute the distance between reflector and his earth-based instrument to within 30 centimeters. He hopes to cut this to within 15 centimeters over the next couple of years.

Then he should be able to measure the change in a laser station's relative position due to continental drift, a matter of a few centimeters a year. A pair of stations being set up in Hawaii and Japan should be able to detect the 8 to 10 centimeters a year by which these islands are thought to be moving apart.

As geophysicists have built up their theory over the past two to three years, they envision earth's 100-kilometer thick outer shell, or lithosphere, as cracked into about 10 plates, each thousands of kilometers across. There are a number of smaller plates, too.

You can imagine it as being like a cracked eggshell. Only with earth, the shell fragments are moving and bumping together. Sometimes one overrides the other.

Where two plates move apart, lava wells up from the hot, plastic upper-mantle material below. It solidifies to become part of the drifting plates which thus grow as they move apart.

Where plates crush together, their edges may crumple into mountain ranges. Where one plate underrides another, the inferior plate plunges down into the mantle material. There it dissolves into the general mantle substance. The underriding plate thrusts up mountains and creates earthquakes on the upper plate as it goes.

Here is an all-embracing theory that unifies seemingly unconnected features of today's globe, as well as allowing scientists to judge how earth's surface has evolved in the past and may change in the future.

For example, it makes sense of the Pacific "ring of fire" and the 40,000-mile-long system of oceanic ridges that long puzzled geophysicists. They knew that many of the world's earthquakes and volcanic actions occurred around the Pacific Ocean rim and along the ocean ridges. The Pacific rim also has many deep-seabottom trenches. Relatively high flows of heat mark the ocean ridges.

Geophysicists now take the ridges to be regions between the edges of crustal plates that are moving apart. They are regions of upwelling lava that adheres to the drifting plates, forming new plate material. The encircling Pacific trenches are considered regions where one plate plunges below another.

The great earthquake that rocked Peru was probably due to the motion of the east Pacific plate that underthrusts South America. It moves eastward about 5 centimeters a year. Diving beneath the plate that carries the continent at a 45-degree angle, it thrusts up the Andes and creates strains that build up until earthquakes relieve them.

The boundaries of the great crustal plates are marked by rifts and faults as well as ridges of lava upwelling and down-thrusting trenches. Many fracture zones on the seabed now are thought to mark such regions. California's San Andreas fault probably is the juncture between a Pacific Ocean plate and the plate that carries the bulk of the North American continent.

Where this juncture enters the Gulf of California, Dr. H. W. Menard of the Scripps Institution of Oceanography and others think the relative motion of the plates may be opening up a new sea.

This new science of plate tectonics, as geophysicists call it, also makes sense of the once-despised concept of continental drift. Geophysicists used to find it hard to imagine how continents moved.

They rejected the notion of land masses plowing through the seabed like a ship through water. Now it's "natural" to think of the continents as being passively carried along by moving underlying crustal plates like passengers on a raft.

Imagine the "cinema film" of plate motions run backward, and you can see the continents fitting together again into two or even one compact mass. Laurasia, the mass from which North America and Eurasia came, and Gondwanaland, ancestor of the other continents, may once have been a single mass called Pangaea.

Prof. Edward Bullard of Cambridge University and some others have found a very good fit in putting together masses like Africa, South America, India, Australia, and Antarctica. They use the shape of the offshore 500-fathom line as being more representative than the changeable water's edge.

Such reconstructions usually put Gondwanaland and Eurasia together about 200 million years ago, although the age is debatable.

More recently, Drs. Dietz and Holden made a reconstruction based on the 1,000-fathom contour. They figure all present continents were one 225 million years ago. This primitive land, Pangaea, broke into Laurasia and Gondwanaland, as crustal plates moved about.

Last summer, the two scientists published maps showing how subsequent plate movements opened up the Atlantic, formed the Mediterranean Sea, and positioned the present continents. India moved from being part of lower Africa to bump against Asia. The crunch between the plate carrying India and the opposing plate carrying part of Asia has thrown up the Himalayas.

More recently, the two scientists carried their calculations into the future to show the world map 50 million years hence. With continents still looking somewhat familiar, the Mediterranean has been crushed to a narrow sea.

A new incipient sea has opened in East Africa. And California has broken away from North America as the plate on which it rides slowly plunges into the Aleutian trench.

All of this, of course, may turn out to be a scientist's daydream if new discoveries are made that don't fit the scheme. Indeed, even the most enthusiastic exponents of plate tectonics admit that no one has yet satisfactorily explained what moves the plates about.

Many theorists suggest slow-moving convection currents within the underlying mantle. A few object to this as implausible. Britain's famed earth scientist, Sir Harold Jeffreys, maintains that the mantle can't support such convection.

In November, C. McCann of Reading analyzed Sir Harold's theoretical arguments and concluded that the mantle could probably support the needed convection.

Some experts, such as R. Meservey of the Massachusetts Institute of Technology, suggest that earth may be expanding and cracking its crust into plates in the process.

Indeed, no geophysicist, if pressed on the point, would argue that plate tectonics was more than a rough theory or that no surprises lie in store for geophysical explorers. But at the same time, it has given a unity and perspective to their science they have never known before.

Whether the theory stands up over time or not, Dr. Menard observes, the subject will never be the same again. For the new view of earth's future has taken the stuffiness out of what seemed a moribund subject a couple of decades ago and put it on a course of creative knowledge building.

LENGTH: 1370 WORDS

21   Wandering Continents

SCORING: Reading time: _____ Rate from chart: _____ W.P.M.	

RETENTION	number right _____ × 2 equals _____ points
INFERENCES	number right _____ × 2 equals _____ points
COMPLETION	number right _____ × 4 equals _____ points
DEFINITIONS	number right _____ × 2 equals _____ points

(Total points: 100) **total** _____ points

RETENTION   Based on the passage, which of the following statements are True (T), False (F), or Not answerable (N)?

1. _____ Geophysicists once discounted the idea of continental drift.

2. _____ Plate tectonics must be thought of as a fully reliable theory.

3. _____ The current continents may once have been fused together.

4. _____ Pangaea is the name that geophysicists give to the first continent, which existed 225 million years ago.

5. _____ Fifty million years from now, California may be separate from the rest of North America.

6. _____ The moon's surface is extraordinarily like the earth's.

7. _____ Japan and Hawaii, at least, are not moving apart.

8. _____ Those areas that are moving apart travel at almost one-half mile a year.

9. _____ According to this theory, the continents are like passengers on a raft.

10. _____ Theory suggests the first two continents were Laurasia and Gondwanaland.

11. _____ The Pacific "ring of fire" had long been understood by geophysicists.

12. _____ Twenty years ago theories suggesting splitting continents were heresy.

13. _____ None of the quoted experts suggests that the earth is shrinking.

14. _____ Before astronauts reached the moon, measuring continental drift was totally impossible.

15. _____ Now scientists use laser beams from moon-based reflectors to measure continental drift.

16. _____ The earth's outer shell is called the lithosphere.

17. _____ No one knows how thick the earth's outer shell really is.

18. _____ One theorist suggests that plate shifts are caused by the earth's expansion.

19. _____ Far into the future, the Mediterranean may be crushed to a narrow sea.

20. _____ The experts quoted in this article cite a military value to their research.

INFERENCES Which three of the following statements, based on the passage, are probably justifiable? _____, _____, and _____.

1. Theories of plate tectonics have radically devalued California properties.

2. The fact that the moon is in motion invalidates most theories of continental drift.

3. The earth is basically like a soft-boiled egg.

4. Plate tectonics offers a unified theory for geologists.

5. Evidence for the plate-tectonics theory has arrived from many parts of the world.

6. Peru is critical for any thoroughgoing theory of noncrustal movement.

7. The crustal movement is best described as "cinematic."

8. In a sense, plate tectonics has given geology a lively "new look."

COMPLETION Choose the best answer for each question.

1. _____ Los Angeles is said to be moving toward: (a) New Jersey. (b) Australia. (c) Gondwanaland. (d) the Aleutian trench.

2. _____ A great mountain range is described as a: (a) catastrophe. (b) crunch between plates. (c) strayed land mass. (d) general scheme.

3. _____ Some scientists believe the great continents were: (a) better off before. (b) fixed. (c) once joined. (d) part of the earth's biosphere

4. _____ The earth's interior is described as being: (a) rough. (b) plastic. (c) enormously stable. (d) like a trench.

5. _____ The laster beam helps scientists measure: (a) height. (b) time and space. (c) speed. (d) significance.

6. _____ Fifteen years ago, geologists knew: (a) mountains eroded. (b) seas spilled over. (c) plates cracked. (d) the apocalypse was coming.

DEFINITIONS   Choose the best definition for each italicized word.

1. _____ a general *concept* of life: (a) theory (b) love (c) contempt (d) sense

2. _____ *Revolutionize* the science: (a) ruin (b) boost (c) slur (d) change

3. _____ how the earth has *evolved:* (a) developed (b) decayed (c) been (d) spun

4. _____ an *incipient* sea: (a) sluggish (b) beginning (c) rough (d) saline

5. _____ they rejected the *notion:* (a) delivery (b) scientist (c) trinket (d) idea

6. _____ an *array* of mirrors: (a) assembly (b) dealer (c) instrument (d) technology

7. _____ scientists *scarcely* imagined: (a) often (b) alone (c) hardly (d) blithely

8. _____ a *once-despised* theory: (a) beloved (b) imagined (c) hated (d) coherent

9. _____ *exponents* of the theory: (a) opponents (b) engineers (c) supporters (d) roots

10. _____ the shell *fragments:* (a) parts (b) surfaces (c) colors (d) crusts

11. _____ one *compact* mass: (a) portable (b) teensie (c) big (d) dense

12. _____ the age is *debatable:* (a) significant (b) important (c) uncertain (d) great

13. _____ it *solidifies* soon after: (a) gets heavy (b) hardens (c) dies (d) moves

14. _____ the ridges are *regions:* (a) uplifts (b) seams (c) hills (d) areas

15. _____ the earth's *mantle:* (a) crust (b) region beneath the crust (c) entire structure (d) general shape

JAMES EMMETT

The Magic
of Remembering Names

Remembering names seems like a simple enough process, but frequently it is quite difficult. How often have we met someone, talked a few minutes, and then realized we have already forgotten his or her name? How often have we been amazed at someone else's memory for names? James Emmett outlines a few tricks for remembering names.

"The new vice-president called me by name," reports a twenty-five year old Los Angeles junior executive. "Makes me feel like a member of the team!"

"I go out of my way to shop at that market," says a Houston housewife. "The manager always remembers my name."

"Glad to see Ken got promoted," comments a Kansas City stock clerk. "He's the kind of fellow that knows who you are."

Such instances confirm the adage that to any person the sweetest sound in the world is the sound of his own name. Psychologists tell us why. Within each of us is a built-in need to belong, to be part of the action, to be recognized as a person of importance.

Business consultants and leadership trainers go further and point out that by helping to fulfill this need in others we're also helping ourselves. As one authority puts it, "Our recognition of the importance of others is reflected in their friendship and goodwill. This increases our own self-confidence, greatly improving our chances for success."

Former US President Harry Truman, Dale Carnegie, and Conrad Hilton credit much of their success to their ability to remember names. Master of the art

---

THE MAGIC OF REMEMBERING NAMES *The Kiwanis Magazine,* February 1975. Reprinted by permission of *The Kiwanis Magazine* and James McMahon.

Jim Farley memorized the names and faces of thousands of acquaintances. President Franklin D. Roosevelt said of his valuable campaign manager, "Jim Farley wins campaigns with his wonderful memory for people."

Recently I complimented a successful office equipment salesman on his ability to recall the names of everyone in our office. I knew he visited many offices similar to ours. "The people here," I told him, "know you as the man who never forgets a name. What's your secret?"

He smiled. "They have no idea," he said, "of the time I spend maintaining a file of the names of people I meet. I always carry a few three-inch by five-inch cards. As soon as I have an opportunity after meeting someone I record his name, where he works, what he does, and some brief notes of description. I file the cards according to the offices that I visit. So I wouldn't want to disenchant your people by telling them that less than two hours ago I was busy reviewing each of their names. Yes, I have a secret—hard work."

We can all develop the ability to remember names and faces. Like other career skills—public speaking, letter writing, management techniques—it can be learned. By continual practice it can be developed to a degree surprising to ourselves as well as to our acquaintances.

A few time-tested techniques (based largely on the principle of association of ideas) will help you master the three basic steps of getting the name correctly, really seeing the person to whom you are introduced, and fixing this information permanently in your memory.

A business acquaintance had this to say about the problem of getting the name: "The most common problem is that we're much more concerned about the impression we're making on the new acquaintance than we are about hearing his name."

Your new friend won't mind being asked to repeat his name. However, with practice we can train ourselves to approach each introduction with the thought, "Get the name."

The time immediately following introductions is critical. It's then that we need some mental hook if we are to avoid losing the name in the next few seconds. Some make it a habit of inventing a little rhyme as a quick memory aid—anything to snare that name before it gets away.

John McGuire joined the choir
Frank Harris flew in from Paris

Later the name can be converted to a more permanent word picture. Another helpful device at this initial stage is to use the name in conversation with the new acquaintance to better fix in your memory. It might be worked in at the end of a sentence or when leaving the new acquaintance.

Just as important as getting the name is getting a clear mental picture of the person. Said one master of the art, "I make use of two devices. First I imagine myself an accomplished artist and in my mind's eye quickly do a colored sketch of the person's face. What color hair? Straight? Wavy? Bald? Is face round or oval? Shape of features? Color of eyes?

"A second device I've found effective is to ask myself, 'Who among all my acquaintances, does this person most nearly resemble?' The resemblance may be in a mannerism, in some particular feature, or in general appearance. Coming up with an answer to this question forces a mental process of comparison that brings the picture into sharper focus. It also provides an additional clue to recalling the person's appearance."

Bodily characteristics should not be overlooked. Tall or short? Heavy or slight? This information will be helpful for future recognition. With practice all of these mental processes can be accomplished in a few seconds.

The next step is to tie the name and face together in ways that will fix this information permanently in our memory. Again, psychologists come to our aid. Pictures, they tell us, are remembered more easily than words. The trick, then, is to convert the name into a mental picture, a kind of mental cartoon. The name Barton might be converted into a steel bar that weighs a ton. The name Caldwell into a caldron in the bottom of a well.

To permanently tie the name and face together, the important point is to devise a combined mental picture that includes both the name and the face. Barton tugging at the bar that weighs a ton. Caldwell stirring a potion in the caldron in the bottom of the well. So much the better if the action fits the build, facial appearance, or mannerisms of the individual.

The more mental hooks one has, the more certain the ability becomes to recall the name. Repeating the name aloud works well for some. In this way facial muscles as well as the sound of the name are brought into play to aid the memory. Writing the name is another way of involving physical movement, as well as the appearance of the name, in the memory process.

Repetition fixes information in our minds. Periodic review of a card file of names and brief notes of description helps to recall the mental pictures and etch them deeper in our memory. One supervisor has developed a file that he periodically reviews. The file includes a snapshot of each employee with the name typed on a tab fixed to the picture. He never forgets a name.

Says one successful businessman, "Sure, I have to work at it, but taking a genuine interest in others in a way that contributes so much to my personal success is well worth the time and effort."

Think of it as a game that's fun to play. Results come quickly, and you'll marvel at the magic of remembering names.

LENGTH: 1150 WORDS

22   The Magic of Remembering Names

SCORING: Reading time: _____ Rate from chart: _____ W.P.M.

RETENTION   number right _____ × 2 equals _____ points

INFERENCES   number right _____ × 2 equals _____ points

COMPLETION   number right _____ × 4 equals _____ points

DEFINITIONS   number right _____ × 2 equals _____ points

(Total points: 100) **total** _____ points

RETENTION   Based on the passage, which of the following statements are True (T), False (F), or Not answerable (N)?

1. _____ The ability to remember names is a knack only a few people have.

2. _____ People can train themselves to "get the name."

3. _____ Sometimes a rhyme can help fix a person's name in our memory.

4. _____ Psychologists have little to say on remembering names.

5. _____ Repeating a person's name aloud almost never works to help us remember it.

6. _____ However, using facial muscles can help fix a name in our memory.

7. _____ People seem to have a basic need to be remembered and to feel important.

8. _____ Artists are noted for their ability to recall names.

9. _____ Jim Farley was Franklin Roosevelt's office-equipment salesman.

10. _____ Dale Carnegie was described as a former president of the United States.

11. _____ The salesman who remembered names used a card-file system.

12. _____ The passage mentions a Kansas City stock clerk.

13. _____ Pictures are easier to remember than words.

14. _____ Remembering appearances does not help in remembering names.

15. _____ Public speaking and letter writing are career skills.

16. _____ The time right after introductions is critical for remembering names.

17. _____ Tying the name and the face together is not very important.

18. _____ Apparently, Ken got promoted.

19. _____ A cartoon can be a kind of memory aid.

20. _____ There is no mention of writing names down as an aid to memory.

INFERENCES   Which three of the following statements, based on the passage, are probably justifiable? _____, _____, and _____.

1. Conrad Hilton was an enormously successful hotel man.

2. After the embarrassment of forgetting Franklin Roosevelt's name, Jim Farley became a wizard at memorizing names.

3. Remembering names can play a direct part in one's own success.

4. Remembering names is really most important for salesmen and politicians.

5. Working up an association with a name is the clue to remembering it.

6. Recalling names is nothing but pure magic.

7. A good memory depends on hard work, careful planning, and concern.

8. Psychologists are not likely to have a good memory for names.

COMPLETION   Choose the best answer for each question.

1. _____ The techniques for remembering are called: (a) Carnegie's method. (b) the real thing. (c) time tested. (d) the Farley Maneuver.

2. _____ Remembering names depends on: (a) magic. (b) file-cards. (c) love for other people. (d) mental hooks.

3. _____ One man with a good memory for names uses a: (a) shoebox. (b) mental sketch. (c) portable tape recorder. (d) team photo.

4. _____ Success can depend on: (a) a genuine interest in others. (b) being on the spot at the right time. (c) teamwork. (d) gladly sharing the load.

5. _____ Developing the skill for remembering names demands: (a) participation. (b) continual practice. (c) leadership training. (d) art training.

6. _____ The sweetest sound in the world is the sound of: (a) music. (b) nature's call. (c) one's own name. (d) success.

DEFINITIONS   Choose the best definition for each italicized word.

1. _____ remember the old *adage:*   (a) saying   (b) name   (c) hook   (d) aged man

2. _____ this *increases* self-confidence: (a) intensifies   (b) makes   (c) adds to   (d) manifestly voids

3. _____ a new *acquaintance:*   (a) relative   (b) associate   (c) good pal   (d) office mate

4. _____ another *device:*   (a) failure   (b) method   (c) compliment   (d) problem

5. _____ do not *disenchant* your people: (a) disturb   (b) amuse   (c) unfix   (d) disappoint

6. _____ time *maintaining* a file: (a) having   (b) seeing   (c) keeping up   (d) making do

7. _____ an *accomplished* artist: (a) skilled   (b) failed   (c) associate to   (d) mediocre

8. _____ a *particular* feature: (a) serious   (b) weak   (c) lovely   (d) specific

9. _____ his *periodic* review: (a) unofficial   (b) occasional   (c) careful   (d) permanent

10. _____ *convert* the name to a song title: (a) change   (b) make   (c) compare   (d) relate

11. _____ a person's *mannerism:*   (a) expertise   (b) worldliness   (c) looks   (d) behavior

12. _____ an *effective* device: (a) mental hook   (b) useful   (c) weak   (d) harmful

13. _____ good at the *initial* stage: (a) beginning   (b) crucial   (c) worst   (d) final

14. _____ *confirm* the saying: (a) deny   (b) undo   (c) recall   (d) verify

15. _____ I *record* his name: (a) resay   (b) write down   (c) sing   (d) repeat and repeat

23 *KENNETH HARVEY*

How to Lose a Job
—the Hard Way

We all know how uncertain a career in show business can be. Ken Harvey recalls the time he found out that he was written out of the script. His soap-opera script called for his dying slowly in a hospital bed. The other actors began to treat him as if he were already dead.

"There isn't any easy way to tell you this, Ken." It was the voice of *Search for Tomorrow*'s producer on the telephone. "You are being written out of the show."

"Why? What happened?" I asked.

"You know the kind of trouble we've been having with ratings. Everybody's job is on the line."

Everybody's job, I thought, except I'm the one being written out.

"The decision," he went on, "was to get a major character into trouble. Keep the audience wondering what is going to happen."

"I see."

"There will be an automobile accident. You will be severely injured—your spine. You will have to have a brain operation. It will be unsuccessful."

"You mean I die on the operating table?"

"No, no, of course not. That would be too quick."

Indeed it would. Time on a soap opera moves more slowly than ordinary time, and only villains die quickly. Heroes linger. No doubt, the storyline would require that I hang on for some time while the audience rooted for me to pull through, tuning in each day, week after week, to monitor my progress. It is the stuff of which ratings are made.

HOW TO LOSE A JOB—THE HARD WAY *TV Guide*, June 21, 1975. Reprinted with permission from *TV Guide*® Magazine. Copyright © 1975 by Triangle Publications, Inc. Radnor, Pennsylvania.

"When," I asked, "do I leave?"

"A month," he replied, "six weeks at the most." He proceeded to outline the manner of my demise: "We will play the euthanasia thing. You ask various people to kill you—put you out of your misery. You don't want to be a burden to anybody, a vegetable—you know."

"What finally happens?" I asked.

"Somebody pulls the plug on the respirator."

"Murder?"

"Right."

"Who does it?"

"Well, I am not at liberty to divulge," he said, "but Scott [my son] will be arrested and brought to trial. That could mean a good four, five months of suspense."

"Sure," I said. "Sure."

"Ken, I'm sorry. I really am sorry. Why did it have to be you?"

Why indeed, I thought, some five weeks later as I lay flat on my back on a bed in Studio 41 at the CBS Broadcast Center in New York. We were preparing to tape my death on *Search for Tomorrow,* and it was no fun at all.

For seven years I had been a happy actor on *Search for Tomorrow.* For seven years I was Doug Martin, husband, father, attorney at law, adviser to the young and pillar of the community of Henderson, U.S.A. For all that time I had endured the myriad ills a soap-opera hero's flesh is heir to. I had overcome a severe mental breakdown just in time to conduct a successful courtroom defense of my best friend Sam, falsely accused of attempted murder. I met, loved, courted and married Sam's sister-in-law, Eunice, who, in something more than due course, gave birth to our little girl, Susan. I discovered Scott, a grown son I never knew I had. For a time, I became a male chauvinist pig, accusing my poor, innocent wife of infidelity, neglect of husband and child and, worst of all, of taking a job as a magazine writer. Later, I recovered my senses sufficiently to attempt to rescue her from a demented editor who was trying to shoot her.

In short, I was an actor gainfully employed in the practice of my craft on television. The *Search for Tomorrow* company to which I belonged is a group of talented professionals. We worked in close, if not always harmonious, proximity, and prior to that fateful telephone call, we had been a loose, exuberant bunch, serious about our craft, yet able to laugh at ourselves and at some of the bizarre twists of plot we were expected to make believable on the television screen.

I cannot say precisely when the mourning began. I know that the news of my impending termination sent a collective shudder through the cast, since actors know just how expendable they are.

The storyline that launched me toward extinction was concerned, in the first week, with my automobile accident, my subsequent brain operation, and with the emotional impact these had on the members of the "family." As the week wore on, I noticed a slight tapering off of the early-morning high jinks.

The following week, I lay unconscious, hovering between life and death. Eunice, now my ex-wife and married to John, the idiot who had given her that job on the magazine, simply fell apart with guilt and possessiveness and insisted on spending all her time in the intensive-care unit, staring at my unconscious form through a glass panel. This made John's life miserable. My son Scott, who was also my law partner, neglected his wife, our practice and his mistress, in that order, while he agonized over me.

By the third week, the emotional wear and tear on the actors had become considerable, and the change of mood in the studio during rehearsals was beginning to make itself felt. In the middle of that week, I was called upon to show signs of coming to. But in the Friday episode, Dr. Tony Vincente, Henderson's best-looking brain surgeon, made the awful discovery that I was totally paralyzed below the neck, with no hope of recovery short of a miracle.

The following Monday morning, we did the read-through without any energy. A couple of attempts at banter fell flat and, for the most part, people just sat around, studying scripts, sipping coffee, waiting their turn to rehearse.

That week, there was a surprise development. I received a visit from the drunken driver who was the cause of my accident. By a coincidence peculiar to this art form, he turned out to be a distant relative by a previous marriage—Dr. Len Whiting, a somewhat disreputable internist at the hospital who, driven by guilt and remorse, had come to me to confess his crime. I threatened to denounce him to the police unless he agreed to do me in. He demurred without enthusiasm, and slunk out.

It was about this time that I began to notice that cast members had taken to removing themselves from the studio during many of my scenes, and that people actually began to avoid the area of the studio where I lay. My own depression was deepening daily. There was almost no casual conversation in the studio any more.

I observed that people had begun to perform odd little rituals, more proper to sickrooms and funeral chapels than to a television studio. Stagehands would tiptoe their way carefully around me, turning their eyes away from where I was lying. I would find myself, at odd times, the recipient of gentle pats on the back, sudden silent embraces, impulsive kisses on the cheek, and wide, sympathetic stares from across the room. Some of my less stable colleagues, coming upon me unexpectedly, simply burst into tears and fled.

By the fifth week, we were in the homestretch and the pace of the writing began to quicken. Eunice arrived at my bedside to inform me that she had left John and was going to devote the rest of her life (or mine) to caring for me. John burst past a protecting nurse to offer the less than complimentary sentiment that I was a greater threat to his marriage as a quadriplegic than I had ever been as an ambulatory divorcé.

I developed respiratory difficulties. This required an emergency tracheotomy, and my attachment, quite literally, to a device known as a Bennett respirator. This is a machine, no bigger than a breadbox, having some dials on its front panel and an ordinary electric plug going to a wall socket. I was connected to it by something resembling a vacuum-cleaner hose, that was firmly taped to the "hole" in my throat. The stage was set for murder.

And so now, at last, I lie speechless in a sepulchral studio, waiting for the end. Sidney, our stage manager, shouts "Quiet! Tape is rolling!" Out of the corner of my eye, I catch his final hand cue and it looks like a gesture of absolution.

There is a pause, and then the sound of a door opening softly off-camera, a shuffle of footsteps. Camera 1 catches the shadow of a person moving across the floor toward the bed. Camera 2 cuts to the respirator and pans the electric cord to the wall socket and holds there. Another pause. Suddenly, the cord goes taut, as if grasped by an unseen hand. A sharp pull, and the plug comes out of the wall. Quickly, the camera moves to my face. I am struggling to breathe. My mouth moves in a vain effort to call out. Bewildered, I turn my head to look for the nurse and I see—my murderer. My eyes widen in recognition and, even as I gasp for breath, a faint smile edges my lips. Mercifully, the camera swings from my face to a tight close-up of the plug, dangling uselessly in midair. The sounds of my tortured breathing grow fainter, fading gradually into silence. The screen goes to black. It is over. Doug Martin is dead.

I have left that benighted bed forever, and have not returned to the studio since, but it is certain that no one mourns there now, and I am sure the place resounds again with laughter. Still, I wonder at the sorrow that assailed us in the weeks of my "dying," and I marvel at the mystery of the actor's art. For there is no doubt in my mind that we were moved ourselves by the anguish we had conjured up for other hearts to feel.

LENGTH: 1385 WORDS

23   How to Lose a Job—the Hard Way

SCORING: Reading time: _____ Rate from chart: _____ W.P.M.

RETENTION	number right _____ × 2 equals _____ points	
INFERENCES	number right _____ × 2 equals _____ points	
COMPLETION	number right _____ × 4 equals _____ points	
DEFINITIONS	number right _____ × 2 equals _____ points	

(Total points: 100) **total** _____ points

RETENTION   Based on the passage, which of the following statements are True (T), False (F), or Not answerable (N)?

1. _____ Ken Harvey played the part of a lawyer.
2. _____ Ken Harvey—as Doug Martin—had both a son and a daughter.
3. _____ Scott Martin was a surgeon.
4. _____ Doug Martin died in order to boost the audience ratings.
5. _____ Before taping a show, the actors read through their lines.
6. _____ Doug Martin was a quadriplegic before he died.
7. _____ The Bennett respirator is the size of a large vacuum cleaner.
8. _____ Doug's wife, Eunice, was now married to John, from the magazine.
9. _____ Doug Martin had always been a fair-minded character.
10. _____ In a soap opera, time moves as it does in real life.
11. _____ The sponsor tried to stop Doug's death.
12. _____ Doug had once been an ambulatory divorcé.
13. _____ Scott Martin was arrested and brought to trial after Doug's death.
14. _____ Even the stagehands began to treat Ken Harvey as if he were dying.
15. _____ On soap operas, only the heroes die quickly.
16. _____ *Search for Tomorrow* is set in Bellows Falls, U.S.A.
17. _____ Ken Harvey had acted in the show for seven years.
18. _____ This incident caused soap operas to change significantly.
19. _____ Doug Martin had been in an automobile accident.
20. _____ The death scene was taped in a real hospital.

INFERENCES Which three of the following statements, based on the passage, are probably justifiable? ____, ____, and ____.

1. Soap-opera actors are a hard-boiled group.

2. Actors on such a series become rather close.

3. Ken Harvey was really grateful for the chance to move on to something else.

4. The producers never can tell how their audience is going to react to episodes in a soap-opera series.

5. The whole crew began to become involved in Ken Harvey's own "misfortune."

6. Actually, Harvey could have refused to die by acting his part improperly.

7. People did not talk to Harvey when he returned to the set months later.

8. "Soaps" thrive on a wide variety of unlikely misfortunes and miseries.

COMPLETION Choose the best answer for each question.

1. ____ Doug Martin's death could have been: (a) accidental. (b) improbable. (c) euthanasia. (d) self-inflicted.

2. ____ All the action of the drama took place in: (a) a real chapel. (b) the county hospital. (c) Manhattan. (d) Studio 41.

3. ____ Doug's law partner was: (a) John. (b) his own son. (c) Eunice's brother. (d) his own mother-in-law.

4. ____ Tony Vincente was the town's best-looking: (a) brain surgeon. (b) dentist. (c) policeman. (d) auto mechanic.

5. ____ The man who had caused the accident was: (a) from out of town. (b) a distant relative of Doug's. (c) unspeakable. (d) anxious to silence Doug forever.

6. ____ While Doug was "dying," people tuned in: (a) and out again. (b) as always. (c) to monitor his progress. (d) out of an abnormal morbid curiosity.

DEFINITIONS Choose the best definition for each italicized word.

1. ____ I cannot *divulge:* (a) recall (b) tell you (c) figure it (d) separate them

2. _____ he cried and *fled:* (a) left   (b) lost blood   (c) flopped   (d) fell apart

3. _____ *respiratory* difficulties: (a) breathing   (b) legal   (c) bad   (d) emotional

4. _____ my *demise:* (a) severance pay   (b) lines   (c) part in the script   (d) death

5. _____ *bizarre* twist of plot: (a) complex   (b) bad   (c) neat   (d) weird

6. _____ I *endured* the ills: (a) contracted   (b) put up with   (c) caught   (d) sought out

7. _____ the *myriad* problems: (a) silly   (b) worst   (c) many   (d) most painful

8. _____ worked *in proximity:* (a) harmoniously   (b) slowly   (c) happily   (d) closely

9. _____ *prior to* that call: (a) before   (b) after   (c) since   (d) as a result of

10. _____ *conjure up* anguish: (a) create   (b) put down   (c) cure   (d) depend on

11. _____ all *banter* fell flat: (a) hopes   (b) efforts   (c) small talk   (d) good humor

12. _____ an *exuberant* bunch: (a) canny   (b) vivid   (c) happy   (d) suspicious

13. _____ a *gesture* of absolution: (a) pointer   (b) signal   (c) maneuver   (d) power

14. _____ he *demurred:* (a) refused   (b) sang   (c) produced   (d) spoke quietly

15. _____ a *demented* editor: (a) power-hungry   (b) insane   (c) silly   (d) shrewd

24 *GRANT HENDRICKS*

When Television Is a School for Criminals

The author of this article did his research the hard way: while serving time in jail! His findings were so startling that the editors double-checked them to be sure they were authentic. Hendricks suggests that television is a kind of school for criminals who can learn new tricks by watching crime shows.

For years, psychologists and sociologists have tried to find some connection between crime and violence on television and crime and violence in American society. To date, no one has been able to prove—or disprove—that link. But perhaps the scientists, with their academic approaches, have been unable to mine the mother lode of information on violence, crime and television available in our prison systems.

I'm not about to dismiss the scientists' findings, but as a prisoner serving a life sentence in Michigan's Marquette maximum-security prison, I believe I can add a new dimension to the subject. Cons speak much more openly to one of their own than to outsiders. And because of this, I spent three weeks last summer conducting an informal survey of 208 of the 688 inmates here at Marquette, asking them what they felt about the correlation between the crime and violence they see on television and the crime and violence they have practiced as a way of life.

Making this survey, I talked to my fellow prisoners in the mess hall, in the prison yard, in the factory and in my cell block. I asked them, on a confidential basis, whether or not their criminal activities have ever been influenced by what they see on TV. A surprising 9 out of 10 told me that they have actually learned new tricks and improved their criminal expertise by watching crime programs. Four out of 10 said that they have attempted specific crimes they saw on television crime dramas, although they also admit that only about one-third of these attempts were successful.

Perhaps even more surprising is the fact that here at Marquette, where 459 of us have television sets in our individual cells, hooked up to a cable system, many cons sit and take notes while watching *Baretta, Kojak, Police Woman, Switch* and other TV crime shows. As one of my buddies said recently: "It's like you have a lot of intelligent, creative minds—all those Hollywood writers—working for *you*. They keep coming up with new ideas. They'll lay it all out for you, too: show you the type of evidence the cops look for—how they track you, and so on."

What kinds of lessons have been learned by TV-watching criminals? Here are some examples.

One of my prison-yard mates told me he "successfully" pulled off several burglaries, all patterned on a caper from *Police Woman*.

Another robbed a sporting-goods store by following the *modus operandi* he saw on an *Adam-12* episode.

By copying a *Paper Moon* scheme, one con man boasts he pulled off a successful bunco fraud—for which he has never been caught (he's currently serving time for another crime).

Of course, television doesn't guarantee that the crime you pull off will be successful. One inmate told me he attempted to rip off a dope house, modeling his plan on a *Baretta* script. But the heroin dealers he tried to rob called the cops and he was caught. Another prison-yard acquaintance mentioned that, using a *Starsky & Hutch* plot, he tried to rob a nightclub. But to his horror, the place was owned by underworld people. "I'm lucky to still be alive," he said.

On the question of violence, however, a much smaller number of Marquette inmates feel they were influenced by watching anything on television. Of the 59 men I interviewed who have committed rape, only 1 out of 20 said that he felt inspired or motivated to commit rape as a result of something he saw on television. Forty-seven of the 208 men I spoke to said that at one time or another they had killed another person. Of those, 31 are now serving life sentences for either first- or second-degree murder. Of these 31, only 2 said their crimes had been television-influenced. But of the 148 men who admitted to committing assault, about 1 out of 6 indicated that his crime had been inspired or motivated by something he saw on TV.

Still, one prisoner after another will tell you how he has been inspired, motivated and helped by television. And crime shows and TV-movies are not the only sources of information. CBS's *60 Minutes* provides choice viewing for Marquette's criminal population. One con told me: "They recently did a segment on *60 Minutes* on how easy it was to get phony IDs. Just like the hit man in

'Day of the Jackal,' but on *60 Minutes* it wasn't fiction—it was for real. After watching that show, you knew how to go out and score a whole new personality on paper—credit cards, driver's license, everything. It was fantastic."

Sometimes, watching television helps you learn to think on your feet. Like an old friend of mine named Shakey, who once escaped from the North Dakota State Penitentiary. While he hid in the basement of a private residence, they were putting up roadblocks all around the city of Bismarck. But Shakey was smart. He knew that there had to be some way for him to extricate himself from this mess. Then, all of a sudden it occurred to him: Shakey remembered a caper film he'd seen on television once, in which a fugitive had managed to breach several roadblocks by using an emergency vehicle.

With this basic plan in mind, he proceeded to the Bismarck City Hospital and, pretending to be hysterical, he stammered to the first white-coated attendant he met that his brother was lying trapped beneath an overturned farm tractor about 12 miles or so from town. He then climbed into the back of the ambulance, and with red lights blazing and siren screaming, the vehicle drove right through two roadblocks—and safely out of Bismarck.

Two days or so later, Shakey arrived back on the same ranch in Montana where he'd worked before his jail sentence. The foreman even gave him his job again. But Shakey was so proud of what he'd done that he made one big mistake: he boasted about his escape from the North Dakota state prison, and in the end he was turned over to the authorities, who sent him back to North Dakota—and prison.

A burglar associate of mine—a member of the so-called Pike Street Gang— had his eye on the large safe in a certain store in Seattle. There was only one problem that kept him from going ahead with the crime: the safe was built into the front interior wall of the store in plain view of traffic and pedestrians, to say nothing of the police station directly across the street. The entire front of the store was plate glass, and the interior was well illuminated at night. He calculated that it would take him 20 minutes to peel [open] the safe door, and there was no way he could do it without being spotted.

One night, as he was watching *Mission: Impossible,* the IMF heroes were faced with a similar situation, and they showed my friend exactly how to pull his job off. The next day, he purchased a large piece of canvas, some paint, brushes and a few bamboo fishing poles. He then built a large folding frame, which worked on the same basic principle as an Army cot. He stretched the canvas over the frame and, using a color photo of the store wall, he painted the canvas to look identical to the area of wall where the safe was located. Placing his professional tools on the center of the dried canvas, he folded the frame and rolled the entire thing into a small bundle, which he carried under his arm. He broke into the back room of the store through the roof. Then he opened the frame, stretched out the canvas, and within minutes a fake wall was in place a few feet in front of the real wall. He went to work on the safe, completely hidden from view of all who passed by, including several patrol cars. An hour later, he was back in his apartment, counting over $9000 in cash, thanks to *Mission: Impossible*. What's more, he was never caught for that caper!

An 18-year-old inmate told me that while watching an old *Adam-12* show, he had learned exactly how to break open pay-phone coin boxes. He thought it seemed like a pretty good idea for picking up a couple of hundred dollars a day, so he gave it a try. To his surprise and consternation, the writers of *Adam-12* had failed to explain that Ma Bell has a silent alarm system built into her pay phones. If you start tampering with one, the operator can notify the police within seconds—even giving them the location of the phone being ripped off. He was arrested on his first attempt and received a one-year sentence.

Another prisoner told me that he had learned to hot-wire cars at the age of 14 by watching one of his favorite TV shows. A week later he stole his first car—his mother's. Five years later he was in Federal prison for transporting stolen vehicles across state lines.

This man, at the age of 34, has spent 15 years behind bars. According to him, "TV has taught me how to steal cars, how to break into establishments, how to go about robbing people, even how to roll a drunk. Once, after watching a *Hawaii Five-O,* I robbed a gas station. The show showed me how to do it. Nowadays [he's serving a term for attempted rape] I watch TV in my house [cell] from 4 P.M. until midnight. I just sit back and take notes. I see 'em doing it this way or that way, you know, and I tell myself that I'll do it the same way when I get out. You could probably pick any 10 guys in here and ask 'em and they'd tell you the same thing. Everybody's picking up on what's on the TV."

Some of the plans are downright bloodcurdling. One man, after watching a recent movie on TV called "The Doberman Gang," plans, after his release, to train a couple of German shepherds to pick up ransom money. Then he'll kidnap and kill a child, and use the dogs to pick up the ransom and bring it to him over an obstacle course. He says that way, even if the police capture the dogs, he'll still be scot-free.

Of the 59 men I interviewed who have committed rape at least once, only 3 of them suggested a connection with television. And in all those cases, they say it wasn't a matter of television giving them the idea or passion, but that it only nudged them in that direction.

One of them had already served time for rape, and he wanted to do it again, but was gun-shy from his first experience. One evening, while drinking heavily, he saw a television police show—he thinks it was *The Streets of San Francisco*—about a successful rapist. This inmate said that he was already on the verge of rape, and this TV show didn't really inspire or motivate him, but simply showed him *how* to get away with it. Thus, he followed the *modus operandi* of the TV rapist and broke into the apartment of a girl he'd been wanting to rape for several weeks. Unfortunately, he made one mistake. He pounced on her bed in the dark, and a moment later her six-foot boy friend was beating him to a pulp!

One of my friends here in Marquette says that TV is just a reflection of what's happening "out there." According to him, "The only difference is that the people out there haven't been caught—and we have. But our reaction to things is basically the same. Like when they showed the movie 'Death Wish' here, the people reacted the same way they did on the outside—they applauded Charles Bronson when he wasted all the criminals. The crooks applauded Bronson!"

Still, my research—informal though it is—shows that criminals look at television differently than straight people. Outside, TV is entertainment. Here, it helps the time go by. But it is also educational. As one con told me, television has been beneficial to his career in crime by teaching him all the things *not* to do. Another mentioned that he's learned a lot about how cops think and work by watching crime-drama shows. In the prison factory, one guy said that he's seen how various alarm systems operate by watching TV; and here in my cell block somebody said that because of television shows, he's been kept up-to-date on modern police procedures and equipment.

Another con told me: "In the last five to seven years we've learned that the criminal's worst enemy is the snitch. TV has built that up. On *Starsky & Hutch* they've even made a sympathetic character out of a snitch. So we react to that in here. Now the general feeling is that if you use a partner to commit a crime, you kill him afterwards so there's nobody to snitch on you."

For most of us cons in Marquette, it would be hard to do time without TV. It's a window on the world for us. We see the news shows, we watch sports and some of us take great pains to keep tuned into the crime shows. When I asked one con if he felt that watching TV crime shows in prison would be beneficial to his career, he just smiled and said, "Hey, I sit and take notes—do my homework, you know? No way would I sit in my cell and waste my time watching comedies for five hours—no way!"

LENGTH: 2180 WORDS

24   When Television Is a School for Criminals

SCORING:	Reading time: _____ Rate from chart: _____ W.P.M.

RETENTION	number right ____ × 2 equals ____ points
INFERENCES	number right ____ × 2 equals ____ points
COMPLETION	number right ____ × 4 equals ____ points
DEFINITIONS	number right ____ × 2 equals ____ points

(Total points: 100) **total** ____ points

RETENTION   Based on the passage, which of the following statements are True (T), False (F), or Not answerable (N)?

1. _____ Prison is a prime source of information on the relationship of television, crime, and violence.

2. _____ Convicts do not speak very openly to outsiders.

3. _____ The author is writing from an Illinois jail.

4. _____ There are over one thousand prisoners at Marquette.

5. _____ Most of the prisoners have television sets in their own cells.

6. _____ The convicts pay attention to, but do not take notes on, the shows they watch.

7. _____ The warden used to be a regular on *Baretta*.

8. _____ In a sense, the television writers are educating the convicts.

9. _____ Murder is a crime that is specifically incited by television.

10. _____ One showing of *60 Minutes* explained how to set up a false identification.

11. _____ Some of the crimes described in the article were never solved.

12. _____ Crime shows are the only ones criminals watch.

13. _____ Television shows teach criminals how to "think on their feet."

14. _____ One criminal actually has planned a kidnap-murder involving dogs.

15. _____ Television helps out-of-circulation convicts learn new police tactics.

16. _____ The convicts actually applauded the "good guy" in a recent crime drama.

17. _____ A rapist was actually inspired by a *Streets of San Francisco* episode.

18. _____ Baretta did time once, but swears he's straight now.

19. _____ On television crime shows, the criminal's worst enemy is the snitch.

20. _____ Television crime shows seem to inspire more robbery than anything else.

INFERENCES   Which three of the following statements, based on the passage, are probably justifiable? _____, _____, and _____.

1. The maximum-security prisons are not doing an outstanding job in reforming criminals.

2. Criminals should not have any forms of entertainment in prison.

3. Hendricks interviewed mainly professional criminals.

4. The criminals at Marquette can watch what they choose on television.

5. Hendricks has established that television definitely causes crime.

6. The connection between television and violence is particularly strong.

7. Many criminals watch violent shows because of peer pressure.

8. The producers of violent shows do not care if the shows have an audience.

COMPLETION   Choose the best answer for each question.

1. _____ From television shows, criminals seem to learn: (a) everything.   (b) new techniques.   (c) what people think of them.   (d) their *ABC*'s.

2. _____ The man who took $9000 from an exposed safe must have been a good: (a) climber.   (b) counter.   (c) experienced fellow.   (d) painter.

3. _____ Pay telephones have a: (a) built-in alarm.   (b) weak money box.   (c) way of enticing youngsters.   (d) subtle fascination.

4. _____ Hendricks did not interview all the prisoners in Marquette, only about: (a) one-tenth.   (b) 80 percent.   (c) 4 percent.   (d) one-third.

5. _____ The author's friend, Shakey, escaped in: (a) the nick of time.   (b) a police car.   (c) an ambulance.   (d) a pie-delivery truck.

6. _____ The author interviewed fifty-nine men who: (a) were innocent.   (b) would not talk.   (c) committed rape.   (d) thought television was a menace to society.

DEFINITIONS   Choose the best definition for each italicized word.

1. _____ television has been *beneficial:*   (a) harmful   (b) useful   (c) alarming   (d) abused

2. _____ one man was *gun-shy:*   (a) deaf   (b) slow-handed   (c) frightened   (d) dangerous

3. _____ *on the verge of* rape: (a) close to   (b) opposed to   (c) beginning   (d) used to

4. _____ television *motivates* him: (a) teaches   (b) bores   (c) excites   (d) directs

5. _____ a *sympathetic* character: (a) harmful   (b) likeable   (c) silly   (d) rude

6. _____ he *extricated* himself: (a) removed   (b) alarmed   (c) confused   (d) incriminated

7. _____ *patterned* on a caper: (a) fixed   (b) postured   (c) based   (d) printed

8. _____ provides *choice* viewing: (a) limited   (b) excellent   (c) bad   (d) rank

9. _____ the *mother lode* of information: (a) feel   (b) height   (c) tip   (d) source

10. _____ on a *confidential* basis: (a) secret   (b) public   (c) moral   (d) criminal

11. _____ criminal *expertise:*   (a) scholars   (b) skill   (c) types   (d) schools

12. _____ *correlation* between crime and television: (a) relationship   (b) feedback   (c) scenes   (d) dependency

13. _____ *influenced* by television: (a) simulated   (b) refused   (c) harmed   (d) inspired

14. _____ *informal* research: (a) strict   (b) structural   (c) unscientific   (d) meaningful

15. _____ practiced as a *way of life:*   (a) style   (b) feeling   (c) career   (d) rule

25 ROBERT WALTERS

J. Edgar Hoover's Fortune

The once-powerful director of the FBI was in office longer than most public servants can hope for. During that time, Hoover devoted himself so completely to his job that he spent very little of his salary. He died "at his desk" with a sizeable fortune. The question now is, what has become of it?

In death as in life, J. Edgar Hoover, Director of the FBI for 52 years, remains a subject of controversy.

For more than four years—he died on May 2, 1972—a bizarre struggle has been going on over Hoover's estate.

Almost all of the estate was willed to FBI Associate Director Clyde A. Tolson, Hoover's longtime confidant and close companion. When they were working together at the FBI, Hoover's bullet-proof Cadillac limousine would pick up Tolson every morning at his apartment at precisely the same time. And they invariably lunched at the same restaurant in Washington's Mayflower Hotel.

Every summer, the pair would travel to the Del Mar Racetrack outside San Diego. On the first day of every year, they went to New York to celebrate Hoover's birthday. And every winter, they fled to Miami Beach.

Hoover and Tolson also made numerous trips around the country, always shepherded by FBI agents who temporarily abandoned their crime-fighting tasks to act as tour guides.

Former agent Joseph L. Schott, in a book called *No Left Turns*, describes the often hilarious aspects of preparing for a Hoover and Tolson visit to a Texas hotel. Four down pillows had to be placed on each man's bed, typed operating

---

J. EDGAR HOOVER'S FORTUNE "What's Happened to J. Edgar Hoover's Fortune?" by Robert Walters. *Parade* Magazine, January 16, 1977. Reprinted by permission.

instructions had to be put next to all appliances, and a doctor had to be on call in case of medical emergencies.

On the night of Hoover's death, Tolson moved into the Hoover home on 30th Place, a quiet residential street in Northwest Washington, where he went into seclusion for several days.

Following Tolson into the Hoover home was an assessor assigned to inventory the household possessions. He found a grab bag of statues, figurines, rugs, mementos, photographs, cartoons and artifacts from every corner of the world.

Among the items that occupied almost every nook and cranny of the Hoover house were a celluloid figure of Buddha, a gold-plated Colt .22 revolver with a mother-of-pearl handle, a mounted golden railroad spike, an airplane propeller, a marble fragment of Hitler's bookcase, a pottery dish with the Justice Department seal and a pair of Chinese opium pipes.

Also in the home were twenty-six miniature elephants made of ivory, crystal, teak and bronze, twenty-three Indian rugs, a dozen miniature ivory horses, eight miniature wooden horses, numerous female nude figures made of a variety of materials, and countless trinkets from Haiti, Japan, Mexico, Germany, China, Switzerland, Hungary, India and Morocco.

Shortly after Hoover's death, The Washington Star interviewed his neighbors and reported on his fetish about orderliness in the house:

"Hoover rarely switched a picture or art object after he had assigned it a place in his house. In fact, when everything had to come down one year so that the wallpaper could be cleaned, he had photographs of the walls taken first, to make certain that everything would be put back in the same place."

The complete list of Hoover's household possessions took forty-nine legal-size pages, included more than 1200 items and carried an estimated value of just under $70,000. Additional assets—in the form of cash, insurance policies, stocks and bonds—brought the total value of the Hoover estate to slightly more than $425,000.

Bachelor Hoover's will called for small bequests totaling about $11,500 to a handful of distant relatives and personal aides. His funeral cost slightly more than $5000, and the federal estate tax took $135,000.

Everything remaining, valued at approximately $280,000, was willed to Tolson, although Hoover specified that if Tolson should die before or at the same time he did, the money should be divided equally between two charities.

One early, ominous sign of what was to befall Hoover's estate involved a pair of cairn terriers which were his pets when he died. A dog fancier, Hoover had at least seven dogs as pets during his time in Washington, and he thought enough of the animals to purchase grave sites and perpetual care for them at a suburban Washington pet cemetery.

His will, although relatively short, contained a clause which specifically said: "I would like Clyde Tolson to keep or arrange for a good home for my two dogs." But according to one source familiar with the estate, the two dogs were killed shortly after Hoover's death because "they were pretty old."

Hoover's will was processed in the District of Columbia courts with few complications, although there were some unexpected claims. Among those shrugged off by court officials were:

A Richmond, Va., man who claimed to be a "a first cousin nine times removed" and offered a genealogical chart to identify others in the family.

Three Michigan men who claimed the FBI had violated their civil rights through illegal electronic surveillance, thus entitling them to a compensatory payment from the estate.

A Gainesville, Ga., woman who wrote: "I am his wife. We were married in Hall County, Georgia, in 1945. We have a son . . ."

The bulk of the Hoover estate was transferred to Tolson, apparently without a hitch—until Tolson died on April 14, 1975, almost three years after Hoover. Touching off the controversy was a clause in Tolson's will which specified that "I leave nothing . . . to my brother," Hillory A. Tolson, or to any of his brother's children or grandchildren.

The brother promptly filed a lawsuit charging that at the time of Hoover's death Tolson "suffered from many ailments which resulted in his permanent disability" and made Tolson "an easy prey for undue influence and coercion, which was exhibited upon him" by John P. Mohr, the FBI's third highest ranking executive under Hoover's administration.

Hillory Tolson contended that his brother was improperly influenced not only by Mohr, who received $26,000 under Clyde Tolson's will, but also by Dorothy S. Skillman, Clyde Tolson's secretary at the FBI and the intended recipient of a $27,000 bequest.

Before that lawsuit was settled in an out-of-court agreement, it produced a series of startling admissions by present and former FBI employees, all required to testify under oath, in their depositions.

The most significant of those disclosures involved a series of events which began on May 22, 1972—less than three weeks after Hoover's death.

Mrs. Skillman's sworn testimony was that on that date Mohr brought her a "power of attorney" document authorizing him to handle Tolson's financial affairs. Mohr asked Mrs. Skillman to sign the name of her boss—and she never bothered to check with Tolson to see if he approved.

"I knew Mr. Mohr was taking care of matters for Mr. Tolson," said Mrs. Skillman, "and I didn't question any order he gave me or any instructions he gave me from Mr. Tolson."

Three days later, on May 25, Mrs. Skillman again signed Tolson's name to a crucial legal document, a letter to a Washington bank containing detailed instructions for the handling of Hoover's estate. Again, she acted only on Mohr's instructions and never consulted Tolson.

The next day, the process was repeated again with another "power of attorney" document. As in the first case, Tolson's signature was supposedly witnessed by two high-ranking FBI officials, James B. Adams and Nicholas P. Callahan.

During the legal struggle over the Tolson will, Adams admitted that "Mr. Tolson did not sign it [the power of attorney] in my presence," and Callahan said he did not believe the signature was Tolson's, although it was "similar to signatures of his in the past."

Although Hoover named Tolson executor of his estate, the series of legal documents signed, witnessed and notarized by FBI employees using Tolson's name but without his knowledge had the effect of transferring control of the Hoover legacy to Mohr—and it is he who now also serves as executor of the Tolson estate.

Tolson's estate—including Hoover's house, knickknacks and cash—totaled more than $725,000. His will called for distribution of almost $200,000 among more than a dozen friends and colleagues. Another $100,000 was accepted by his brother Hillory under terms of the agreement that settled the lawsuit.

The remainder of the estate is to go to the same two charities designated by Hoover, the Boys Clubs of America and the Damon Runyon-Walter Winchell Memorial Fund for Cancer Research. But neither group has yet received any money and by the time it is delivered the amount may be very small. "I'm not sure there will be much left after the lawyers get through," says one man who has followed the tribulations of the Hoover-Tolson estate.

All of the bills for the legal fight within the Tolson family have not yet been submitted but will probably cost the Tolson estate close to $100,000. And soon after that court case was settled there emerged another serious threat to the disposition of the Hoover-Tolson assets.

It is a civil suit filed in mid-1976 in federal court in Washington. A group of former officers and members of the Southern Christian Leadership Conference, the civil rights group headed by the late Dr. Martin Luther King Jr., charge that they were the subject of illegal FBI wiretapping and eavesdropping during the 1960's.

The SCLC members who initiated the lawsuit are asking that the defendants—including Tolson—be required to pay $6 million. The lawsuit may well entangle the estate in a new, costly and lengthy legal battle.

The story of Hoover's legacy is one of dismemberment. Even his collection of awards, honors and mementos now faces an uncertain future. Tolson's will instructs his executor "to install these memorabilia and personal property . . . in the J. Edgar Hoover Room in the new FBI Building."

The current FBI Director, Clarence M. Kelley, late last year discovered still another cache of Hoover treasures—packed in boxes at FBI headquarters—but he's not notably anxious to display them.

In a letter to court officials, Kelley cited eighteen separate boxes of scrolls, certificates, plaques, photos and trays from police chiefs' organizations, Boy Scout groups, American Legion posts and a host of other organizations.

In addition, said Kelley, another sixty-eight "boxes, crates and packets" of newspaper articles, photographs, certificates, diplomas and honorary degrees have not even been inventoried by the FBI.

The FBI is retaining custody of the materials while the Justice Department considers whether their rightful owner is the federal government or the Hoover and Tolson estates. And the FBI has no current plans to establish a room for display of the memorabilia—a far cry from the days when whatever Hoover wanted, Hoover got.

LENGTH: 1780 WORDS

25   J. Edgar Hoover's Fortune

SCORING: Reading time: _____ Rate from chart: _____ W.P.M.

RETENTION	number right _____ × 2 equals _____ points
INFERENCES	number right _____ × 2 equals _____ points
COMPLETION	number right _____ × 4 equals _____ points
DEFINITIONS	number right _____ × 2 equals _____ points

(Total points: 100) **total** _____ points

RETENTION   Based on the passage, which of the following statements are True (T), False (F), or Not answerable (N)?

1. _____ Clyde Tolson's estate was actually larger than J. Edgar Hoover's.

2. _____ The FBI has no immediate plans to set up a "J. Edgar Hoover Room."

3. _____ Tolson was just a friend of Hoover's, not a member of the FBI.

4. _____ Hoover and Tolson drove to work in a Mayflower sedan.

5. _____ Hoover kept much of his memorabilia at the FBI headquarters.

6. _____ Hoover came up through the Boys Clubs.

7. _____ FBI agents acted as tour guides for Hoover and Tolson.

8. _____ Hoover was FBI chief for almost thirty years.

9. _____ Hoover's estate totaled well over $1 million.

10. _____ Legal battles have tied up the Hoover-Tolson estate.

11. _____ Clyde Tolson left most of his belongings to his brother, Hillory.

12. _____ Before his death, Tolson had his signature affixed to documents he never saw.

13. _____ Apparently, Tolson suffered from many ailments late in his life.

14. _____ Despite court battles, legal fees will not amount to much of Tolson's estate.

15. _____ Most of Hoover's estate went to charity, not to Tolson.

16. _____ Hoover and Tolson were exceptionally close friends.

17. ____ Hoover's house was jammed full of pictures, sculptures, and knickknacks.

18. ____ A simple listing of Hoover's belongings took almost fifty legal-size pages.

19. ____ Hoover usually stayed in Washington and did not travel around the country.

20. ____ Hoover owned no stocks or bonds.

INFERENCES   Which three of the following statements, based on the passage, are probably justifiable? ____, ____, and ____.

1. Hoover's belongings were primarily American mementos.

2. Tolson liked travel, too, but not as much as Hoover did.

3. The estate of a prominent person is vulnerable to legal threats.

4. Apparently, such struggles over estates are quite common in Washington.

5. Tolson's power of attorney documents may have been illegal.

6. Hoover and Tolson kept close ties with their families.

7. Hoover was once a great deal more popular than he is now.

8. Hoover's charities stand to gain enormous sums from the estate.

COMPLETION   Choose the best answer for each question.

1. ____ Among Hoover's effects were twenty-six: (a) bags of garbage.   (b) miniature elephants.   (c) Colt revolvers.   (d) railroad memorabilia.

2. ____ The SCLC, Martin Luther King's organization, is suing because of: (a) an unsolved crime.   (b) the assassination.   (c) forgery.   (d) wiretapping.

3. ____ Tolson was sure the FBI would set up a: (a) charity.   (b) legal defense.   (c) Hoover room.   (d) team to research Hoover's death.

4. ____ The eighteen boxes of Hoover belongings found at FBI headquarters contained: (a) questionable materials.   (b) nothing.   (c) honors and plaques.   (d) dog mementos.

5. ____ One woman actually claimed that she was Hoover's: (a) daughter.   (b) wife.   (c) mistress.   (d) mother-in-law.

6. _____ After his death, Hoover's two Cairn terriers were: (a) put to death. (b) lost in a storm. (c) Tolson's source of strength. (d) put on a diet.

DEFINITIONS   Choose the best definition for each italicized word.

1. _____ a marble *fragment:* (a) statue (b) piece (c) bomb (d) game

2. _____ the *tribulations* of the estate: (a) valuations (b) troubles (c) sizes (d) ages

3. _____ his *fetish* for orderliness: (a) concern (b) fear (c) sense (d) hatred

4. _____ she never *consulted* Tolson: (a) asked (b) hurt (c) alarmed (d) offended

5. _____ *improperly* influenced: (a) soon (b) rudely (c) wildly (d) wrongly

6. _____ *shepherded* by FBI agents: (a) moved (b) dogged (c) guided (d) fleeced

7. _____ an *estimated* value: (a) approximated (b) declined (c) real (d) flexible

8. _____ electronic *surveillance:* (a) measurement (b) scan (c) cloud (d) observation

9. _____ they *initiated* the lawsuit: (a) terminated (b) held (c) started (d) feared

10. _____ *entangle* the estate: (a) tie up (b) sew up (c) irritate (d) unsolve

11. _____ charities *designated* by Hoover: (a) befriended (b) seen (c) helped (d) chosen

12. _____ he went into *seclusion:* (a) a depression (b) illness (c) hiding (d) remission

13. _____ often *hilarious* aspects: (a) funny (b) serious (c) meaningful (d) various

14. _____ female *nude* figures: (a) rude (b) wood (c) unclothed (d) standing

15. _____ an *ominous* sign of trouble: (a) immediate (b) threatening (c) full (d) big

26 *TAKASHI OKA*

The Hungry World

Food may become the world's most important political weapon in the next few decades. We already have seen the effects of famine in Bangladesh and other developing nations. The question now is; How much can the United States do to keep food supplies stable and thus avoid famine?

Remember Bangladesh?

How long is it since all those pictures of starving infants stared out accusingly from television screens and newspaper front pages? How long since those equally accusatory reminders that while people in the rich nations were gobbling up more and more meat, many citizens of poor countries were fortunate if they got two meals a day?

The nasty shock of 1972–74—when world grain production fell by 33 million tons, the Soviet Union cornered U.S. grain exports, and wheat prices quadrupled—is fading from memory. The United States, the Soviet Union, even the Indian subcontinent, have had bumper harvests. World food stocks are beginning to build up again. The anchovies have returned to the coasts of Peru, increasing supplies of fertilizer and feed.

And yet the fundamental problem of too many mouths chasing after too little food remains. Half a billion of the world's 4 billion inhabitants suffer from malnutrition, estimates Jean Mayer, former Harvard professor and now president of Tufts University. Another billion could do with a more varied diet. Population growth has slowed, but the developing nations are going to have to increase food production at least 4 percent a year if their food import bills are not to reach prohibitive levels by 1985.

THE HUNGRY WORLD "U.S. and the Hungry World" by Takashi Oka. *The Christian Science Monitor,* January 7, 1977. Reprinted by permission from *The Christian Science Monitor* © 1977 The Christian Science Publishing Society. All rights reserved.

Two years ago, here in Rome, the nations of the world assembled in the World Food Conference solemnly pledged to abolish hunger and malnutrition in a decade.

It was a noble promise, but implementation has lagged sadly behind. The United States, the world's largest exporter of grain, has been entangled in sterile argument over how much control should be exercised in the international grain market.

Other nations have dragged their feet also, for the promise, to be realized, requires a large allocation of resources and a restructuring of the world grain market.

The fundamental problem is that the developing nations of the world—in Africa, Latin America, and Asia—have not managed to increase food production to a point where it can keep up with the growth in their populations and with the increase in their demand for food.

From this failure arises the need:

1. For capital investment by the developing nations themselves to increase food production at least 4 percent a year (4.3 percent, says the World Food Council established by the 1974 Rome conference).

2. For the world grain trade to be structured in such a way that poor countries will not be victimized by sudden rises in grain prices, as occurred in 1974 when both oil and wheat prices quadrupled. This means setting up an international grain reserve that would keep price fluctuations within tolerable limits, say between $2 and $3 per bushel of wheat.

The first point, which holds out the only practical possibility that the world will overcome its food crisis, has become the focus of much controversy.

Many experts believe it is simply unattainable. The developing countries are not serious about population control. They are not interested in improving agriculture, but waste their money on prestige industrial projects. Their use of foreign aid is wasteful and corrupt, these experts say.

Therefore, the argument goes, it would be better to separate developing countries into those that are capable of helping themselves and those that are not. The first category will be helped. The others will be abandoned, just as those inside a lifeboat would try to keep too many others from clambering aboard lest the boat be swamped.

There are others who maintain that the present gap between the food needs of the developing nations and the enormous amounts consumed as livestock feed in the developed nations (400 million tons a year, more than human beings in China and India together consume) is the result of centuries of exploitation by the rich nations and that food, along with wealth, must be redistributed from the rich nations to the poor.

Finally, there is a third school—of natural scientists, aid administrators, and development experts—who point out that technically, there is no reason mankind, including the developing nations, should not be able to feed itself. Population growth is restrainable. Encouraging progress has already been made.

In a recent issue of Scientific American devoted to food and agriculture, W. David Hopper estimates that the southern Sudan alone, if drained of its swamps, could produce as much food as the entire world does today.

Similarly, the northern part of the Indian subcontinent, drained by three mighty rivers, the Indus, the Ganges, and the Brahmaputra, could be made vastly more productive than it now is—perhaps yielding up to 20 metric tons of grain per hectare (2.47 acres), or about 80 percent of the world's present grain output.

These are spectacular projects. Much more modest efforts, carried out on a global scale, could make hunger a thing of the past. As hunger is wiped out, population also can decline, even if living standards remain modest, as the experience of China has shown.

Effort on the part of the developing nations is certainly required. So is a reordering of priorities to give agriculture the first call on national resources. Equally required is capital. Many of the world's developing nations are small. In nearly 80 of them, the population is less than 5 million.

They may have the will but lack the capital to carry out the projects that would transform agriculture in their countries. For them, capital assistance from the rich countries is vital. This is the purpose of the International Fund for Agricultural Development (IFAD)—a billion-dollar fund, again promised by the World Food Conference, which is only coming into being this year because of the time required to obtain the needed money.

The development fund is unique because it will be controlled, in equal proportions, by the rich industrialized nations, by the newly rich oil-producing nations of the Organization of Petroleum Exporting Countries (OPEC), and by the non-oil-producing developing nations. Voting strength, in other words, will not be in proportion to the amount of money put into the kitty.

But the fund alone is only a drop in the bucket. At least $5 billion a year would need to be transferred every year from the rich countries to the poor if the goal of an annual 4 percent increase in food production were to be realized, according to officials of the World Food Council.

The second major task the world community faces to wipe out hunger in the next decade is to restructure the international grain market. This is not as formidable a task as the first one, but it has run into a great deal of controversy between American officials, who wish to keep the grain trade essentially uncontrolled, and third-world advocates, who see the need for at least some limits of price to be observed in the international marketplace.

The American argument, essentially, is that for 20 years after World War II, the United States and Canada held the world's only sizable reserve grain stock. Emergencies such as the periodic failures of the monsoon in India or of harvests in the Soviet steppes were met by drawing on this reserve stock.

But the storage was costly. The existence of the reserve acted to depress grain prices and thus kept farmers' incomes low. Periodic efforts were made to clear the stock by sales of grain at concessional prices to developing nations. Now that world grain prices finally are higher, so the argument goes, why should the United States bear the exclusive burden of keeping a grain reserve? Why should not other countries share the cost, if that is what they want to do?

The counterargument put forward by international development officials is that there never has been such a thing as a completely free market in grain. Domestically, food is too important a commodity to be left exclusively to the vagaries of the market, and many governments take measures from time to time to subsidize grain production when prices are unreasonably low, even if from the viewpoint of the market it would be cheaper to buy grain from abroad. Conversely, governments take action to protect consumers, or groups of consumers, when price rises impose too heavy a burden on them.

Should not these principles be applied internationally? By all means, protect farmers from grain prices that are too low to provide a reasonable margin of profit. At the same time, if the world is to become a genuine community, and not just to remain a market, should not the poorer nations of the world be protected in some way from exorbitant upward swings of the international market?

In the final analysis, both on agricultural aid to developing countries and on managing the international grain trade, the United States plays a pivotal role. The American role is no longer dominant, as it was during the 1950s and 1960s. But it remains essential, and it has to be played with increasing subtlety and sophistication.

Rich nations, poor nations, nations with oil and nations without, nations with food to spare and nations where hunger is endemic, all share responsibility for a world community in which the disruptive actions of a determined few could lead to the collapse of the entire edifice. No issue is more emotion-rousing than food, because no issue is as basic to individual and national survival. By the same token, no issue challenges the world community to act as a genuine community as does this one.

"If the human race cannot agree on food, on what can they agree?" asks a British economist, Dame Barbara Ward, in a recent book (foreword to "Hunger, Politics, and Markets"). "If those self-proclaimed Christian countries of the West who pray 'Give us this day our daily bread' are not prepared to give it to anyone else, they deserve the mockery and collapse that follow upon too wide a breach between principle and practice."

LENGTH: 1800 WORDS

26   The Hungry World

SCORING: Reading time: _____ Rate from chart: _____ W.P.M.

RETENTION	number right _____ × 2 equals _____ points
INFERENCES	number right _____ × 2 equals _____ points
COMPLETION	number right _____ × 4 equals _____ points
DEFINITIONS	number right _____ × 2 equals _____ points

(Total points: 100) **total** _____ points

RETENTION   Based on the passage, which of the following statements are True (T), False (F), or Not answerable (N)?

1. _____ At least food is not an emotional issue today.

2. _____ A 4 percent annual growth rate in grain production is essential.

3. _____ The United States prefers an open market for grain.

4. _____ The earth's surface is almost overexploited for food now.

5. _____ Population control is a key to avoiding malnutrition and famine.

6. _____ World population now stands at 2 billion.

7. _____ The World Food Conference met in Rome.

8. _____ Recently, developed nations have had terrible harvests.

9. _____ Russia actually grows more rice than wheat.

10. _____ Food production has not kept up with population growth in developing nations.

11. _____ Unhappily, population growth is unrestrainable.

12. _____ China has moved toward wiping out hunger.

13. _____ The Sudan could never produce large quantities of grain.

14. _____ Some officials say there has never been a free market in grain.

15. _____ The world's developing nations, like India, are all very large.

16. _____ During the 1950s, the United States had sizable grain holdings.

17. _____ Capital assistance from rich countries to poor countries is vital.

18. _____ Actually, there is little hope that nations can feed themselves.

19. _____ America's role in increasing world food supplies is not really pivotal.

20. _____ The United States is concerned with control over the international grain market.

INFERENCES   Which three of the following statements, based on the passage, are probably justifiable? _____, _____, and _____.

1. If the Indians can erase poverty, so can we.

2. The food supplies in the world depend mostly on grain.

3. Lately, there has not been much international concern about food.

4. People in developed nations eat more meat than those in developing nations.

5. Right now world food stocks are beginning to be depleted.

6. No one has any theories about developing nations' plans for increasing food production.

7. Christian countries depend on bread.

8. It is crucial that developing nations invest in their own agriculture.

COMPLETION   Choose the best answer for each question.

1. _____ If the Sudan drained its swamps, it: (a) would be powerful.   (b) could feed the world.   (c) would have no rice.   (d) would become a desert.

2. _____ More grain is fed to livestock than to all the people in: (a) Hungary.   (b) China.   (c) India.   (d) China and India.

3. _____ One of the countries that held sizable grain storage in the 1950s is: (a) Spain.   (b) France.   (c) Canada.   (d) Brazil.

4. _____ Grain storage is a problem because it is: (a) impossible.   (b) very messy.   (c) expensive.   (d) liable to corruption.

5. _____ Some governments take action to protect: (a) consumers.   (b) cattle.   (c) offshore deposits.   (d) individual interests.

6. _____ Many potential food-producing lands could be: (a) inundated.   (b) farmed-out by 1985.   (c) improved considerably.   (d) internationalized in the 1980s.

DEFINITIONS   Choose the best definition for each italicized word.

1. _____ to *obtain* the money: (a) spend   (b) get   (c) see   (d) feel

2. _____ the fund is *unique:*   (a) new   (b) old   (c) unusual   (d) singular

3. _____ to *abolish* hunger: (a) suffer   (b) see   (c) erase   (d) cope with

4. _____ *spectacular* projects: (a) doomed   (b) remarkable   (c) sad   (d) necessary

5. _____ population *decline:*   (a) rise   (b) scene   (c) plight   (d) reduction

6. _____ a *formidable* task: (a) difficult   (b) slight   (c) mean   (d) neat

7. _____ *subsidize* grain sales: (a) fake   (b) claim   (c) corrupt   (d) support

8. _____ *exorbitant* upswings: (a) extant   (b) excessive   (c) wild   (d) surprising

9. _____ *disruptive* actions: (a) persistent   (b) smooth   (c) damaging   (d) sudden

10. _____ *periodic* failures: (a) early   (b) occasional   (c) late   (d) grain

11. _____ *impose* a burden: (a) relieve   (b) set up   (c) have   (d) put on

12. _____ centuries of *exploitation:*   (a) tilling   (b) unfair use   (c) integration   (d) consolation awards

13. _____ *capital assistance:*   (a) help   (b) planning   (c) dollar aid   (d) food

14. _____ growth is *restrainable:*   (a) powerful   (b) useless   (c) helpful   (d) controllable

15. _____ price *fluctuations:*   (a) rises   (b) flights   (c) changes   (d) controls

SECTION IV

Vocabulary Preview

The following words come from the eight reading selections in
Section IV. Study the list carefully, pronouncing the words aloud if
possible. Conceal the definitions with a card or your hand and test
your command of the meanings of the words.

abated, *verb*   ended; gave way
abbreviated, *adj.*   shortened
abundant, *adj.*   plentiful
acquire, *verb*   to get; to obtain
advanced, *verb*   move ahead
advise, *verb*   to give advice; to help
alternatives, *noun*   possible choices; other choices
amid, *prep.*   in the middle of
amply, *adv.*   sufficiently; fully
analogy, *noun*   useful comparison
antiquated, *adj.*   old
apprentice, *noun*   assistant in training for a trade or profession
appropriateness, *noun*   rightness; suitability
arid, *adj.*   dry; barren
aspect, *noun*   view; part of something
bagged, *verb*   captured
basis, *noun*   foundation of something (like an idea or argument)
belie, *verb*   to make false; to give a false impression
bizarre, *adj.*   weird
cardiovascular, *adj.*   pertaining to the heart and blood vessels
cherishing, *verb*   loving; valuing highly

climatic, *adj.* having to do with the climate

coed, *adj.* mixing male and female, particularly in schools

conform, *verb* to shape up; to meet certain standards

convulsions, *noun* violent shakings or fits

criterion, *noun* standard of judgment

detectable, *adj.* noticeable; observable

deter, *verb* to prevent, stop

devise, *verb* to set up; to invent

disillusioned, *adj.* having lost illusions; disappointed

dismal, *adj.* bleak

domestic, *adj.* homey; relating to home and family

donning, *verb* putting on clothing or a disguise

elusive, *adj.* difficult to catch

emitting, *verb* letting off; releasing something

employ, *verb* to use

exhilarated, *adj.* excited; refreshed

extensive, *adj.* considerable; spread out; far-reaching

falter, *verb* to weaken; to slow down

fledgling, *noun* beginner; inexperienced person

forecast, *noun* prediction; outlook

forfeited, *verb* lost; gave up

format, *noun* plan; structure

full-fledged, *adj.* experienced; complete

fused, *adj.* joined

heightened, *adj.* increased

idiosyncratic, *adj.* peculiar

immune, *adj.* unable to be infected or hurt

intolerable, *adj.* unbearable

isolated, *adj.* separated

lethal, *adj.* deadly, fatal

lurked, *verb* lay concealed and waiting

magnitude, *noun* degree; size

mandatory, *adj.* required

meager, *adj.* sparse, lean, slight

menacing, *adj.* threatening

minute, *adj.* tiny, small

mirage, *noun* visual illusion, usually created by heat

moderate, *adj.* not extreme

novices, *noun* beginners

ominous, *adj.* threatening

optional, *adj.* not required; available by choice

panaceas, *noun* cure-alls; universal remedies

panic, *noun*   sudden loss of control; fear

perished, *verb*   died

plummeting, *verb*   dropping, falling

potential, *noun*   capability

precipitate, *verb*   to make something happen suddenly

precipitously, *adv.*   suddenly; without much thought

prevailing, *adj.*   current; ongoing

profusion, *noun*   abundance; plenty

prompted, *verb*   caused; urged

punitive, *adj.*   relating to punishment

ramifications, *noun*   branches; offshoots; further consequences

ravenously, *adv.*   greedily; hungrily

readily, *adv.*   easily

rebutting, *verb*   arguing successfully against something

recidivism, *noun*   rate of criminal return to prison

recreation, *noun*   refreshment; play

rehabilitate, *verb*   to fix up; to restore to good behavior (as with criminals)

reluctant, *adj.*   unwilling; hesitant

reveled, *verb*   delighted

seismic, *adj.*   relating to earthquakes

significant, *adj.*   meaningful; important

spate, *noun*   sudden outpouring; host of things

speculate, *verb*   to think over; to consider; to imagine

spurred, *adj.*   urged; stimulated

staple, *noun*   necessity; main item

stipulation, *noun*   requirement; necessary condition

tendency, *noun*   leaning toward

tenuous, *adj.*   flimsy, weak, unsubstantial

tragic, *adj.*   awful; terrible

transpires, *verb*   happens; takes place

tremors, *noun*   shock waves

turmoil, *noun*   upset; confusion

unearthed, *verb*   discovered; found

unstable, *adj.*   shaky; weak

vaguest, *adj.*   most unclear; most unprecise

vary, *verb*   to change, alter

version, *noun*   variation; one form of something

visage, *noun*   face; expression

witnessed, *adj.*   authorized or approved by others

wreaked, *verb*   took revenge; visited punishment on

Complete the following sentences, using the correct words from the list.

1. One would expect to see a mirage in an _____ climate.

2. Manfred was an expert at _____ other people's arguments.

3. Solitary confinement is a _____ measure used against troublemakers.

4. The Republicans _____ with the Socialists, but very reluctantly.

5. Doris was tough, but she was not _____ to criticism.

6. They had remarkable expertise for such _____.

7. We can achieve a great deal, but we have no _____ for our country's problems.

8. By what _____ did you reject her candidacy?

9. By comparison with last week's long meeting, this was an _____ _____ session.

10. The high rate of _____ meant that the prison's rehabilitation program was not successful.

11. An _____ can be made between a lion and a hero.

12. Luis already owned a shoe store; now he wanted to _____ _____ a hat business.

13. John looked bizarre when he laughed, but his _____ returned to normal when he grew solemn.

14. Paul was deeply _____ when he realized that all his expectations were in vain.

15. There was no _____ for making such a stipulation against talking.

16. Marilyn did a good job even though she was only an _____

   _____ carpenter.

17. Margo seemed to be in the center of the crowd, but she felt _____

   _____.

18. I think I got it right, although those instructions were the _____

   _____ I ever saw.

19. Whittier was paid _____ for his services.

20. I thought Jimmie would panic, but he kept right on and didn't even

   _____.

21. Even though Joan was advanced last year, her prospects for advancement

   this year are _____ indeed.

22. Frankie was really _____ at the prospect of living in a coed dorm.

23. The heat was intolerable in August, but I almost _____

   _____ with the cold in February.

24. I don't know what kind of scheme you could _____
   that would have no serious ramifications.

25. He had terrific potential, but he _____ a successful career by fooling around with drugs.

27 DONALD D. SCHROEDER

Earthquakes

During the last decade we have experienced an epidemic of earth-quakes. Even more will occur in the coming decade, and California will almost certainly be hit by a number of the worst. The ways in which quake stresses build up and the extent of the influence of quakes on the earth's surface are the subject of this article.

Killer quakes have hit the headlines with disturbing frequency in recent months.

"Guatemala's 39 Second Eternity of Terror," "Death Toll in Hundreds in Italy," "10,000 Left Homeless by Soviet Quake," and others in Mexico, Bali, and New Guinea hit in rapid succession. Then China was devastated by the most gigantic quake of the decade, killing tens of thousands.

Even before the China disaster, earthquakes in 1976 had killed over 24,000, making it the deadliest year for quakes since 1970, according to the U.S. Geological Survey.

Instinctively we don't like to think about earthquakes happening to us. Yet hundreds of millions of people live in major earthquake belts. And other areas—seemingly immune from quakes—may nonetheless be subject to damaging tremors caused by stresses building up over centuries of time.

Failure to face the possibility of experiencing an earthquake crisis can lead to uncontrolled panic, immobilizing fear, and dangerous rumors, as well as disregard for basic safety precautions when a quake hits. The tragic result is many unnecessary injuries, deaths, and property losses added to disaster columns.

One has but to map the geography of large earth tremors or major quakes in the last decade alone to realize that very few regions of the earth have been untouched by upsetting jolts if not some type of tragic destruction.

EARTHQUAKES *The Plain Truth,* September 1976. Reprinted by permission.

The truth is that terra firma, in an absolute sense, is a myth. Thousands of tremors occur daily. Most are detectable only with ultra-sensitive instruments. Still, about a dozen or so "major" quakes (7 to 7.9 on the Richter Scale) occur yearly. A "great" quake, such as occurred in San Francisco in 1906 and in Alaska in 1964, measures 8 or more on the same scale. Yet, even "moderate" quakes measuring little more than 6 can cause extensive damage in areas of poor construction.

In the last ten years major quakes have wiped out whole regions and villages in Sicily, Turkey, Pakistan, and Latin America and severely jarred many other areas around the Circum-Pacific "Ring of Fire."

In this same period, temblors have been felt in England, France, Austria, and other parts of Europe.

All but forgotten to most Americans is the tremor that jolted 23 Midwest States in 1968. Ceilings and walls cracked, windows broke, chimneys toppled, and tall buildings swayed over a wide area.

Earthquakes east of the Mississippi River are much less frequent and in most cases milder than those in Western States. Nevertheless, a three-hundred-mile strip of the central Mississippi Valley, Boston, Charleston (South Carolina), and other East Coast areas are vulnerable to major quakes, say experts.

The most widely accepted theory explaining many, but not all, earthquakes is plate tectonics. At least a dozen great crustal slabs 80 or so miles thick have been found covering the planet. These huge plates are floating on the earth's semimolten mantle and are kept in motion by powerful internal forces which are not as yet very well understood by geologists.

Imperceptible to human senses in most cases, these plates are constantly interacting at their edges—bumping, grinding, pulling apart or plunging beneath one another—producing tremendous strains from a few to several hundred miles below the surface.

The earthquake-plagued Japanese islands are the summits of a young and still evolving mountain chain which marks the boundaries of several of these plates.

Friction frequently locks sections of these huge plates in place, causing great strains that suddenly release themselves as earthquakes.

In California, two great plates are sliding past each other. A sliver of California coastal area is moving northwest a few inches a year. The famous San Andreas Fault marks the edges of these two plates.

Unfortunately, a section of this fault near Los Angeles (an area including the "Palmdale Bulge" that has risen a foot in the last fifteen or so years) and another near San Francisco appear locked while other sections of the plate have moved around twenty feet.

For years a major earthquake has been forecast for California on the order of the 1906 magnitude. "There will be a big earthquake in California sooner or later," said one official of the U.S. Geological Survey. "It could be decades away, but it could occur tomorrow."

While earthquakes most frequently occur along jostling plate edges, violent convulsions can and do occur far from the edges.

In fact, one of the greatest series of quakes in United States history devastated a huge area around New Madrid, Missouri, in 1811 and 1812. It was so strong that it reversed the Mississippi River in some places and created new lakes.

Recent quakes have killed thousands at a time, but for the most part, they have hit relatively unpopulated land or ocean areas, or in villages with poor building standards. (Often these villages have many stick-frame dwellings plastered over with mud that collapse in even a moderate quake.)

Modern construction and heavily populated areas in highly advanced nations have not yet been put to a "great" quake test. Yet earthquake experts fear hundreds of thousands could be injured or killed, because buildings, building codes, and human preparations have been greatly neglected in many areas.

The earthquake that ripped Nicaragua in late 1972 was a "moderate" quake (6.3 on Richter Scale), no bigger than the early morning Los Angeles quake (6.5) of 1971. Yet, downtown Managua resembled ground zero after an atom bomb blast. Thousands died in Managua while less than 100 died in the Los Angeles area.

Building construction, soil conditions, and time of day differences produced a wide disparity between these two disasters. Had the Los Angeles quake hit during hours of busy streets, occupied schools, and factories, casualties would have been much higher.

At the time of the devastating quake of 1906, San Francisco was relatively undeveloped compared to the present city. Today many officials are alarmed at the extensive housing projects built right on or along the San Andreas Fault that were not there in 1906.

In recent years, scientists have found that most big earthquakes do not come like a bolt out of the blue. Tell-tale seismic evidence will usually be present to signal the impending temblor.

Many seismologists now theorize that rocks in the vicinity of the future earthquake break apart slightly under increasing pressure. As a result, the speed of sound waves passing through these fracturing rocks slows down slightly as the rocks become filled with greater amounts of air. Many of these scientists feel that as water fills the minute cracks, a return to normal sound-wave measurement occurs. In several cases, this "normalizing" has been the tip-off that a quake is about to strike. Changes in tiltmeters, creepmeters, electrical conductivity, and magnetism in the earth also may be additional tip-offs.

Already, as a result of using detectable changes in the earth, several earthquakes around the world have been predicted accurately as to place, approximate time, and magnitude. (However, it is not known how many other predictions have failed.)

The most startling success in earthquake prediction occurred in the Manchurian province of Liaoning in China in late 1974 and early 1975. As a result of numerous instrument-recorded premonitory signs (as well as signs from alarmed animals: cattle behaving fitfully, frogs jumping through holes in ice on frozen ponds, rats surging from their dens) villages in several Chinese cities were evacuated several days before a devastating 7.3 quake tore the area. The town of Haicheng was leveled. Because of the advance orderly evacuation, casualties were largely among those who refused to heed the warning.

Late last year, Dr. James Whitcomb of Caltech's Seismology School successfully predicted a moderate quake east of Riverside, California. He predicts another for Southern California in the 5.5 to 6.5 magnitude range by May next year.

However, some public officials point out earthquake predictions could be a curse as well as a blessing. "A prediction itself could in some ways be worse than an actual earthquake," says Dr. Vincent E. McKelvey, director of the U.S. Geological Survey. "Visions of stalled economic growth, thousands of autos streaming over bridges in a mass evacuation are frightening indeed. Many would rather take their chances with no warning."

Still, most seismologists feel they have a moral obligation not to keep secrets and to at least give a warning to responsible government and public agencies.

The energy released in a major earthquake could actually be more than several hydrogen bombs. It would seem that governments that scarcely flick an eyebrow to spend additional millions or billions of dollars on military defense should expand their (so far usually meager) budgets for earthquake research and prediction.

Next, it is vital to upgrade building codes and improve their enforcement. Dr. Charles Richter, the famous seismologist who developed the scale bearing his name, says, "Ninety percent of the loss of life [from earthquakes] results from the collapse of structures that any engineer could have established as unsound." These deaths and half of the property losses are unnecessary and preventable, according to Richter.

Well-built, modern, steel-framed skyscrapers are, in most cases, safer from complete collapse than lower, multi-story buildings built before earthquake codes were enforced.

Yet equally as important as good earthquake structural engineering are the surface conditions upon which a building rests.

An area underlain by unstable ground (sand, clay, volcanic rubble, or other unconstituted materials) is likely to experience much more damage than an area equally distant or even nearer the earthquake epicenter but underlain by firm ground such as granite.

Apart from these considerations, the most the average individual can do is prepare himself or herself to act as calmly and sensibly as they can before, during, and after an earthquake.

LENGTH: 1880 WORDS

27   Earthquakes

SCORING: Reading time: _____ Rate from chart: _____ W.P.M.

MAIN SENTENCE	number right _____ × 4 equals _____ points	
GENERALITIES	number right _____ × 4 equals _____ points	
RETENTION	number right _____ × 2 equals _____ points	
COMPLETION	number right _____ × 3 equals _____ points	
DEFINITIONS	number right _____ × 2 equals _____ points	

(Total points: 100) **total** _____ points

MAIN SENTENCE   Each of these sentences appears in the text. Which one best describes or best summarizes the content of the passage? _____

1. For years a major earthquake has been forecast for California on the order of the 1906 magnitude.

2. Instinctively we don't like to think about earthquakes happening to us.

3. In recent years, scientists have found that most big earthquakes do not come like a bolt out of the blue.

GENERALITIES   Based on the passage, which of the following generalities seem justifiable? _____ and _____.

1. Fortunately, earthquakes are limited to predictable areas.

2. Rigidly enforced building codes can save lives in an earthquake.

3. People should avoid California until after the next quake hits it.

4. A good early-warning system ought to be an international priority.

RETENTION   Based on the passage, which of the following statements are True (T), False (F), or Not answerable (N)?

1. _____ The 1906 California quake was limited to Sacramento.

2. _____ During a quake, a new skyscraper is safer from collapse than an old four-story building.

3. _____ On the Richter Scale, 6 indicates a moderate quake.

4. _____ The "Palmdale Bulge" is in Boston.

5. _____ Large housing projects are actually built on the San Andreas Fault.

6. _____ Luckily, most recent quakes have hit unpopulated areas.

7. _____ Japan is earthquake plagued.

8. _____ As of yet, no quakes have been predicted accurately with instruments.

9. _____ There have been no recent quakes in the Soviet Union.

10. _____ Fortunately, rivers are rarely affected by quakes.

11. _____ One Chinese town was evacuated before a major quake.

12. _____ Frogs and rats can actually help signal major quakes.

13. _____ Almost one hundred major quakes can be expected yearly.

14. _____ The earth's crust is about eighty miles thick.

15. _____ Actually, there was a serious quake in the American Midwest recently.

16. _____ A relatively small number of people have seen quakes.

17. _____ A Caltech scientist expects a quake to hit Southern California very soon.

18. _____ Terra firma is a myth.

19. _____ Rocks in the vicinity of a future quake stay solid.

20. _____ Earthquakes killed a very small number of people in 1976.

COMPLETION   Choose the best answer for each question.

1. _____ The best theory explaining earthquakes is: (a) no theory.   (b) lack of planning and detection.   (c) plate tectonics.   (d) Chinese.

2. _____ The most startling success with quake detection was in: (a) Milwaukee.   (b) Bismark.   (c) Manchuria.   (d) Herzegovina.

3. _____ The slabs making up the earth's crust number at least: (a) a dozen.   (b) just under a hundred.   (c) hundreds.   (d) four thousand.

4. _____ Most earthquakes occur along: (a) natural borders.   (b) coastline shores.   (c) rivers.   (d) plate edges.

5. _____ The force of an earthquake could actually be more: (a) if planning is

bad.   (b) during the rush hour.   (c) in Asia.   (d) than that of a few hydrogen bombs.

6. _____ In 1906, San Francisco was: (a) less developed.   (b) like ground zero after a bomb.   (c) sunny and peaceful.   (d) thought to be immune.

DEFINITIONS   Choose the best definition for each italicized word.

1. _____ highly *advanced* nations: (a) developed   (b) safe   (c) immune   (d) forward

2. _____ *regions* of the earth: (a) countries   (b) areas   (c) deserts   (d) fields

3. _____ violent *convulsions:*   (a) wrecks   (b) faults   (c) haunts   (d) disturbances

4. _____ fill *minute* cracks: (a) small   (b) timely   (c) single   (d) empty

5. _____ large *tremors:*   (a) quakes   (b) sings   (c) premonitions   (d) faults

6. _____ *meager* budgets: (a) tremulous   (b) stingy   (c) insufficient   (d) generous

7. _____ chimneys *toppled:*   (a) rose   (b) smoked   (c) split   (d) fell

8. _____ *detectable* tremors: (a) new   (b) big   (c) noticeable   (d) unanswerable

9. _____ areas seem *immune:*   (a) safe   (b) sick   (c) sorry   (d) involved

10. _____ *tragic* destruction: (a) near-total   (b) serious   (c) disastrous   (d) mean

11. _____ *extensive* damage: (a) avoidable   (b) considerable   (c) some   (d) limited

12. _____ quakes *forecast* for California: (a) planned   (b) seen   (c) had   (d) predicted

13. _____ the 1906 *magnitude:*   (a) event   (b) temblor   (c) size   (d) experience

14. _____ total *seismic* evidence: (a) quake   (b) plate   (c) tectonic   (d) scientific

15. _____ codes have been *neglected:*   (a) maintained   (b) redone   (c) engineered   (d) ignored

28 *PATRICK A. LANE*

My Igloo Home

As Patrick A. Lane points out, when most people think of igloos, they think of dog sleds and the movies made of the far north. However, Patrick Lane actually built an igloo and made some interesting discoveries about this practical and remarkable dwelling.

Think of igloos. What springs to mind? Intense cold, driving snow, polar bears and seals, Eskimos, and—for those with a geographical "bent"—the forbidding wastes of Canada's central arctic region? These are the thoughts which the word *igloo* brings to *my* mind: visions of dog sleds, endless nights or days, seal hunting through holes in the ice, and a life that none of us would really want to exchange for our comfortable, "civilized" existence. In the Eskimo language, the word igloo means a house, of any kind. The Eskimos have the word *igloovigag* for the dome-shaped shelter made of snow. Despite its size and frozen material, this structure has done much to protect that people from the intolerable elements of the Arctic region.

But these intriguing dwellings have been used by others—men like Peary and Stefansson in their Arctic explorations and efforts to reach the North Pole. When Peary finally reached that fabled spot, he pitched camp only a few miles away—in an igloo. These remarkable structures have tremendous advantages over a typical tent shelter. They are roomier, quieter, drier, and they offer 100-percent protection during the blizzards that can so easily overcome a traveler in those northern wastes.

In 1912, Canadian Arctic explorer Vilhjalmur Stefansson pointed out that it could be 56 degrees centigrade (100° Fahrenheit) warmer inside an igloo than outside. When it was $-45.6°C$ ($-50°F$) outside, the temperature was $-6.7°C$ (20°F) at floor (bed) level, 4.44°C (40°F) and as high as 15.6°C (60°F) near the

MY IGLOO HOME *The Rotarian*, January 1977. Reprinted by permission.

ceiling. In fact, an igloo is comfortable enough to raise a family in—precisely what the Eskimos did.

So, I was delighted when Edward L. "Ted" Carpenter, 1977-78 president-elect of the Rotary Club of the University District of Seattle, Washington—and an inveterate mountaineer and outdoors enthusiast—invited me to join a party of Seattle Scoutmasters-in-training who were to travel to Mount Rainier National Park to build and live in igloos.

We reached our goal, at an altitude of 1,800 metres (6,000 feet), directly below the summit of Mount Rainier. There were 3.5 to 4.3 metres of snow on the ground (12 to 14 feet), but we were amply equipped: alpine boots, snowshoes, long woolen underwear, wind-resistant parkas, waterproof trousers and leggings, and our packs full of a variety of emergency kits. First we chose our site. Flat ground, of course; the risk of avalanches in this area is considerable, and we had no intention of unnecessarily calling out the mountain rangers. A dozen igloos were started that day by a group of enthusiastic novices in the art of building with snow. I worked with Mark Carpenter, Ted's 15-year-old son.

Under the guidance of the expedition's three leaders, we flattened the snow—first Mark with his snowshoes, then me with my size 8 boots. This compacted the snow in preparation for cutting it into blocks 50 by 75 by 10 centimetres (20 by 30 by 4 inches). After allowing 20 minutes for the snow to set and acquire the essential cohesiveness, we began what I was soon to discover was hard work. We followed the instructions of George Ushida, a Seattle Scoutmaster who earlier had instructed us on "igloo theory." George, who has even taught this skill to members of Himalayan expeditions, said that it took him two hours to complete an igloo. I felt that we were in for a much longer day.

Having dug a hole at least 100 centimetres (40 inches) deep, we then cut the blocks to a double depth with an aluminum saw. First make a transverse cut perpendicular to the ground—not as easy as it sounds—followed by two end cuts, careful not to sever the snow where the following block begins. Then a cut 50 centimetres (20 inches) below, and—"thump"—the block drops, and you know it is ready to lift. Ten, 20, 30, and more of them were thus extracted. I never realized that I could get so thirsty. Mark and I worked at it in turns, with occasional guidance and help from Ted. Some two hours later, we had all the snow blocks we needed. We felt exhilarated and extremely hungry, as we stopped for lunch and then prepared ourselves for the somewhat more technical aspect of the actual construction.

The basic principle of igloo building is that a block can be held in any position, including horizontal, by supporting it at two diagonally opposite corners. A third point of support will eliminate any tendency to rotate. With this in mind, we set to work. Our first layer of blocks leaned dramatically inward, a necessity if one wants an igloo and not a cone! We molded corners with our snow saw and filled cracks and crevices with abundant loose snow. In fact, we were delighted. The result looked good, and heightened our enthusiasm.

That emotion didn't last very long. The next step seemed to be a backward one, because it appeared to undo so much of our hard work. In the first layer, Mark made the long, bias cut essential to create the contact points between blocks. We carried on, fascinated by our work, and the second level was soon in place. A third level quickly followed, and we were soon left with only the last block to be dropped in from above. It held.

We filled the holes and stood back. After more than four hours' work, we had cut our own real igloo. It was hard to believe that this was the type of structure in which thousands of Eskimos had lived. Many more people, I hope, will have the experience. But we were not yet finished. We needed a large lintel for the entrance, two "A" frames (snow-block gabled "wings") for added sleeping space in the igloo, and an entranceway with enough room for our packs and equipment. The igloo had been built with the entrance at a right angle to the prevailing wind. This prevented snow drifts forming around the door. But we wanted to make our igloo even more comfortable. So our final step was to build a windbreak to reduce the effect of the severe winds which often blow over these Cascade slopes.

In our enthusiasm we had almost forgotten how our colleagues were getting on. We looked around to see that our bare white slope was now adorned with small roundish shapes and many excited and delighted figures. We swapped experiences, dared to offer advice, and behaved like schoolboys with new toys. Mark and I naturally thought ours was best, and on reflection it did look remarkably symmetrical. We planted our flags on the roofs, stood our skis and snowshoes by the side of the igloo, and carried our supplies inside.

I crept through a winding tunnel, so low that I went on all fours. I ducked underneath the lintel and rose inside. How pretty it looked. Whereas outside the structure appeared rounded, low, and smooth, inside one could see all the shapes of the blocks quite clearly. It was almost like having put lots of clear mints together. We twisted round, examined the "A" frames, and explored every last inch of our new home. It was surprisingly warm and light inside, and when we spread our ground sheets, packs, and sleeping bags, it took on an almost comfortable air.

By now we were ravenously hungry, so Ted quickly got to work on the small stove. After punching a small hole in the roof for ventilation, Ted, Mark, Mike (our fourth companion), and I squatted cheerfully over our delicious dinner: spaghetti, meatballs, biscuits, apples, and plain ice water. This may not sound very mouth-watering, but to us it tasted like ambrosia and nectar. Our stumpy candles illuminated the igloo dramatically, and we reveled in the simplicity of our existence and the satisfaction of a job we thought well done.

We discussed our programme for the remainder of the weekend—skiing, snowshoeing, hiking, and a visit to the ranger station for an outline of the dangers in these apparently benign mountains. There we learned that it never pays to treat these slopes with complacency, because they have caused many fatalities.

I wondered how my children would have viewed this whole adventure. I thought much more about these delightfully plain structures that provide so much protection, allow one to stand inside, and, when frozen solid the next day, permit several men to stand together on the roof. Unbelievable? It's true, I witnessed it.

My thoughts ran on in profusion, but one sad question kept coming back: where, in England, could I find enough snow to repeat this adventure?

LENGTH: 1400 WORDS

28   My Igloo Home

SCORING: Reading time: _____ Rate from chart: _____ W.P.M.

MAIN SENTENCE   number right _____ × 4 equals _____ points

GENERALITIES   number right _____ × 4 equals _____ points

RETENTION   number right _____ × 2 equals _____ points

COMPLETION   number right _____ × 3 equals _____ points

DEFINITIONS   number right _____ × 2 equals _____ points

(Total points: 100) **total** _____ points

MAIN SENTENCE   Each of these sentences appears in the text. Which one best describes or best summarizes the content of the passage? _____

1. In the Eskimo language, the word igloo means a house, of any kind.

2. In fact, an igloo is comfortable enough to raise a family in—precisely what the Eskimos did.

3. The basic principle of igloo building is that a block can be held in any position, including horizontal, by supporting it at two diagonally opposite corners.

GENERALITIES   Based on the passage, which of the following generalities seem justifiable? _____ and _____.

1. Patrick Lane built his first igloo on this journey.

2. The Eskimos have virtually all moved into wooden shelters.

3. Admiral Peary had his first igloo experience at the North Pole.

4. The igloo has much to teach us about survival in the wilderness.

RETENTION   Based on the passage, which of the following statements are True (T), False (F), or Not answerable (N)?

1. _____ The floor is the coldest spot in an igloo.

2. _____ Igloos get stronger after they are built.

3. _____ Patrick Lane expects to go to England.

4. _____ Peary never actually reached the North Pole.

5. _____ Stefansson refused to enter Peary's igloo.

6. _____ Unfortunately, one cannot cook in an igloo.

7. _____ *Igloovigag* is the Eskimo word for "skyscraper."

8. _____ There can be a 100° F difference between the temperatures outside and inside an igloo.

9. _____ The entry tunnel should be built at right angles to the wind.

10. _____ Loose snow makes the best igloo "brick."

11. _____ Patrick Lane was taught igloo theory by Vilhjalmur Stefansson.

12. _____ The igloo described here was built in Mount Rainier National Park.

13. _____ Lane associates igloos with central Canada.

14. _____ Himalayan explorers need know nothing about igloo building.

15. _____ Lane proved that only Eskimos can build satisfactory igloos.

16. _____ Lane worked with Peary's son to build his igloo.

17. _____ Igloo building is now a popular local sport in Seattle.

18. _____ The first layer of blocks must lean inward.

19. _____ Lane got very thirsty while cutting the snow blocks.

20. _____ The Mount Rainier area can be exceptionally dangerous.

COMPLETION   Choose the best answer for each question.

1. _____ Lane associated igloos with: (a) baked Alaskas. (b) dog sleds. (c) snow shoes. (d) snow blindness.

2. _____ The hole they punched in the roof was for: (a) visibility. (b) identification. (c) stress-testing. (d) ventilation.

3. _____ Before they cut the blocks, they: (a) dug a hole. (b) established contact. (c) drew up plans. (d) made time trials with George.

4. _____ The "A" frames were built for: (a) good looks. (b) the challenge. (c) sleeping space. (d) cooking facilities.

5. _____ Lane was surprised that the inside of the igloo was: (a) small. (b) roughened up. (c) light. (d) oppressive.

6. _____ The final step in building the igloo was to make a: (a) windbreak. (b) door. (c) welcome mat. (d) small address plate.

DEFINITIONS   Choose the best definition for each italicized word.

1. _____ my thoughts ran on in *profusion:*   (a) confusion   (b) stead   (c) deed   (d) abundance

2. _____ I *witnessed* it: (a) acknowledged   (b) was in   (c) saw   (d) legalized

3. _____ the *remainder* of the weekend: (a) worst   (b) rest   (c) best   (d) top

4. _____ we felt *exhilarated:*   (a) elated   (b) worn out   (c) edgy   (d) illuminated

5. _____ the *intolerable* elements: (a) terrific   (b) good   (c) unbearable   (d) best

6. _____ with *abundant* snow: (a) packed   (b) cut   (c) some   (d) plenty of

7. _____ enthusiastic *novices:*   (a) beginners   (b) snowmen   (c) Eskimos   (d) friends

8. _____ it *heightened* our mood: (a) lifted   (b) stretched   (c) intensified   (d) made

9. _____ we *reveled in* the simplicity: (a) fell in   (b) were delighted by   (c) partied in   (d) were confused by

10. _____ a *tendency* to rotate: (a) cause   (b) effort   (c) move   (d) inclination

11. _____ the *risk* of avalanches: (a) number   (b) size   (c) danger   (d) cause

12. _____ *ravenously* hungry: (a) intensely   (b) stupidly   (c) still   (d) birdlike

13. _____ to *acquire* cohesiveness: (a) get   (b) see   (c) be   (d) collect

14. _____ we were *amply* equipped: (a) soon   (b) over   (c) plentifully   (d) ill

15. _____ the *prevailing* wind: (a) worst   (b) best   (c) dominant   (d) cutting

29 *WILLIAM LEGGETT*

Cauthen: New Kind of Jockey

In the last twenty-five years, racing fans have seen some prodigies. The "Shoe," Willie Shoemaker, and Eddie Arcaro are two of the most remarkable jockies in racing history. But a third star is now destined to join that luminous group: Steve Cauthen. He's only a very young man now, but if he continues to ride as he has been doing, he will be the match of any rider who ever lived.

Steve Cauthen attended his first Kentucky Derby in 1963, the year Chateaugay defeated Candy Spots. He was taken to the Churchill Downs backstretch by his mother and father, and through the long afternoon he romped on the grass and dug away at the family picnic hamper. Steve Cauthen remembers little about that day because, like the horses running in the Derby, he, too, had only recently become a 3-year-old. The young man has been back for several Derbies since then, most recently last spring when Bold Forbes outgamed Honest Pleasure through the stretch. He remembers the date of that Derby—May 1, 1976—more readily than the race itself, because on that day he became 16 years old and could start his career as an apprentice jockey.

"Jockey" may not be quite the right word to use for Steve Cauthen. There are some 3,000 officially certified "jockeys" scuffling, whipping and emitting banshee screams as they break out of starting gates from Vancouver's Exhibition Park to El Comandante in San Juan. In a little more than seven months of riding professionally Cauthen has become accepted as a "race-rider," a term granted by racetrackers to only the very best: Shoemaker, Cordero, Hawley, Pincay, Velasquez, Baeza. Since being put up on a 136–1 shot named King of Swat last

---

CAUTHEN: NEW KIND OF JOCKEY "That Baby Face Will Fool You" by William Leggett from *Sports Illustrated,* January 3, 1977 © 1977 Time Inc. Reprinted by permission.

May 12, Cauthen has won 240 races and purse money in excess of $1.2 million. His own take during his abbreviated first season is more than $150,000.

Cauthen is now in the third "kiss" stage of his stunning apprenticeship. Kisses in racetrack terminology denote the asterisks placed alongside a fledgling rider's name in the entries. When he starts out, an apprentice is given three asterisks, allowing him to ride 10 pounds lighter than a full-fledged jockey. After five winners, the first kiss goes and the youngster competes with a seven-pound allowance until he has won 35 races. After that, the apprentice rides with a five-pound allowance until one year has elapsed since his first winner. Cauthen thus has nearly five more months to ride as an apprentice. Former Jockey Sammy Renick, who has studied riders for nearly 50 years, says, "Getting Steve Cauthen to ride your horse with a five-pound allowance is like having a license to steal, and trainers know it. Cauthen looks like the best young rider to come onto the racetrack since Willie Shoemaker in 1949."

Cauthen is 5′ 1″ and weighs 95 pounds. He began winning last spring at River Downs near Cincinnati and has moved onward and upward to Arlington Park and to Hawthorne near Chicago and, four weeks ago, to Aqueduct in New York, the track where jockeys are most critically judged.

Cauthen arrived in New York on the last day of November. After losing on his first four mounts, he took a 4-year-old named Illiterate out for the featured $25,000 eighth race. Illiterate was the lightweight at 110 pounds and had won but one claiming race since early April. Cauthen kept her close to the leaders and, with an eighth of a mile to go, rammed her through an opening to win by half a length. The tote board lit up at $61.20.

In his next 51 rides at Aqueduct, Cauthen had seven winners and was disqualified from another, a good but not extraordinary showing. There is an interesting thing about that disqualification, however. Cauthen's mount veered out in the stretch, but the rider was held blameless by the stewards. Being disqualified unsettles any rider and often causes inexperienced jockeys to become cautious. Not Cauthen. Two races after the disqualification, he drove a horse up along the rail to win.

In one 17-race stretch he bagged 12 winners. He was hot at all distances. He won the first stakes race of his career by taking the $55,050 Gallant Fox Handicap with a 19–1 shot named Frampton Delight. In just 21 days of riding at Aqueduct the 16-year-old apprentice won 29 races and $375,000 in purses. Projected over a full racing season, that would give Cauthen 425 winners and perhaps as much as $6 million in purses. No New York rider has won as many as 300 races in a year (though Velasquez just missed with 299 when Aqueduct closed last week), and no jockey has ever earned $5 million in purses.

Cauthen grew up in Walton, Ky., about 20 miles from Cincinnati and 60 miles from the bluegrass country of Lexington. His father, 44-year-old Ronald (Tex) Cauthen, is a blacksmith who works the Kentucky-Ohio circuit, and his mother Myra is a licensed owner/trainer. Two of his uncles are trainers.

At birth Cauthen weighed in at a normal enough 7 pounds, 12 ounces. But when he became five, his weight lingered at around 35 pounds. Young Steve was around horses on the family's 40-acre farm and his father would take him to work with him on the backstretches. "One summer he seemed to be with the starters in their stand at River Downs for almost every race," Tex Cauthen recalls. "He was beginning to learn things. At 12 he came to me and said, 'Dad, I think I want to be a jockey.' We sat down and I told him that if he was going to gain weight I didn't want him to even think about being a rider. I've seen too many jockeys practically commit suicide by starving themselves to death to make riding weight. That was the stipulation—no reducing.

"He wanted to ride everything that moved and even some things that didn't. When there wasn't a horse available he would sit on a bale of hay and use a stick as a whip. He chopped up many a $2.50 bale of hay that way. He kept getting better at using that stick, and the year before he went out to ride as an apprentice he could switch the whip so well that he could hit within an eighth of an inch of where he wanted to hit."

Tex Cauthen got some film of races at River Downs and Latonia, borrowed a projector, and he and his son would go up to Steve's room in the evening and watch the films, endlessly playing them backward and forward to see how moves were made, correctly or incorrectly. "There were maybe 80 or 90 races," says Tex, "and we just about wore the film out. We talked about things that people don't talk about too much anymore—wind resistance and balance. The rider we watched the most was Larry Snyder, because he has an excellent style. If you look at Steve now, you can see that he rides really low, which cuts down the wind resistance and makes him seem like one with his horse."

Cauthen rides so low and so close to his mounts that several opposing jocks have glanced over at his horses during races and thought he had fallen off. His back is always parallel to the ground and it looks as though a bowl of soup could be balanced there without ever losing a drop.

At River Downs' 56-day meeting last summer Cauthen had a record 94 winners. So one day he and his father flew to Saratoga to look things over for a possible invasion of the East. They checked out potential agents, then went back to River Downs to complete the meeting before moving on to Arlington Park. Cauthen won 40 races in 164 rides at Arlington to finish third in the standings. (The leading rider was Larry Snyder, the man Cauthen had looked at so many times on film, who won 54 races out of 271 mounts.) Moving south to Hawthorne, Cauthen finished second to Snyder, riding 27 winners to the veteran's 32.

When Hawthorne closed, Cauthen returned home and rode at Churchill Downs, where he had 24 winners in 120 mounts. One day Don Brumfield, perenially the top rider at Churchill, went to New York to win a stakes race, and when he came back he advised Cauthen to "take a shot" there.

On their visit to Saratoga, Cauthen and his father had talked to Lenny Goodman about the possibility of the agent's taking Cauthen's book. Goodman has handled the very best—Bobby Ussery, Johnny Rotz, Bill Hartack and, for the past dozen years, Hall of Famer Braulio Baeza—and had not taken on an apprentice in a quarter of a century. "I saw him ride in two races at Saratoga," Goodman says, "and he finished next to last in both on horses that didn't have a chance. But the talent was there. He wasn't afraid, he knew how to wait. He could switch the whip, he had balance. A feeling comes over you when you see one like him. So few have what he has." He took Cauthen on.

Last week Steve Cauthen was wearing a bathrobe in the jockeys' room at Aqueduct, nursing a severe cold he had caught while working horses early in the morning and then riding them in the afternoon in winds that gusted to 40 mph, dropping the wind-chill factor to minus 13°. "It's so cold riding in New York at this time of year that I have to wear gloves and earmuffs and sometimes wrap Saran Wrap around my feet to keep them warm," he was saying. "But I love to ride horses and I'm getting a chance. Sure, the days are long and I'm in bed by 9 o'clock. One of the things my father and I agreed on was that I had to finish high school, and I'm taking correspondence courses to finish up my senior year. I had mostly A's and B's back in school. I'm amazed by the attention I've gotten in New York. A lot of this is just being lucky. Television did a thing about me but I never saw it because I was asleep when the 11 o'clock news went on.

"I'm going to ride in New York all of next year if I'm good enough. But I'll be happy to get home for Christmas. I've been living in a hotel and I miss my family and my two brothers, who are 13 and seven. I'm looking forward to just being home."

On the first Saturday of this May, the chances are that Steve Cauthen, 17, will be at Churchill Downs once again. Riding in the feature.

LENGTH: 1720 WORDS

29   Cauthen: New Kind of Jockey

SCORING: Reading time: _____ Rate from chart: _____ W.P.M.

MAIN SENTENCE	number right _____ × 4 equals _____ points	
GENERALITIES	number right _____ × 4 equals _____ points	
RETENTION	number right _____ × 2 equals _____ points	
COMPLETION	number right _____ × 3 equals _____ points	
DEFINITIONS	number right _____ × 2 equals _____ points	

(Total points: 100) **total** _____ points

MAIN SENTENCE   Each of these sentences appears in the text. Which one best describes or best summarizes the content of the passage? _____

1. If you look at Steve now, you can see that he rides really low, which cuts down the wind resistance and makes him seem like one with his horse.

2. After losing on his first four mounts, he took a 4-year-old named Illiterate out for the featured $25,000 eighth race.

3. Cauthen is now in the third "kiss" stage of his stunning apprenticeship.

GENERALITIES   Based on the passage, which of the following generalities seem justifiable? _____ and _____.

1. Cauthen has horse racing in his blood.

2. None of the owners want Cauthen because he is so young.

3. Weight is a serious problem with Cauthen.

4. For a while, Cauthen has a weight advantage in races.

RETENTION   Based on the passage, which of the following statements are True (T), False (F), or Not answerable (N)?

1. _____ Cauthen's first winner paid more than $60.

2. _____ Cauthen is considered an ordinary jockey.

3. _____ By the time this article was written, Cauthen had won almost 250 races.

4. _____ Riding in New York is a hot and muggy business.

5. _____ Cauthen's birthday is May 1.

6. _____ Cauthen discounted films of races.

7. _____ Cauthen will earn almost $2 million in his first season.

8. _____ Baeza was Cauthen's first winning mount.

9. _____ Larry Snyder is a rider Cauthen admires.

10. _____ Apprentices ride with a seven-pound allowance until they are forty years old.

11. _____ Cauthen has been to only one Kentucky Derby.

12. _____ Cauthen weighs ninety-five pounds.

13. _____ King of Swat will never run again.

14. _____ Cauthen has an agent.

15. _____ Cauthen could not stay up to watch a television special on him.

16. _____ Cauthen competed with Larry Snyder several times.

17. _____ There are some seven thousand certified jockeys.

18. _____ Cauthen's family owns nothing, but lives in a trailer.

19. _____ Cauthen grew up in Kentucky.

20. _____ Cauthen has never raced at Aqueduct.

COMPLETION Choose the best answer for each question.

1. _____ Cauthen is amazed at the attention he: (a) missed.   (b) got in New York.   (c) got from Cordero.   (d) shifted to his mounts.

2. _____ Cauthen has been accepted as a(n):   (a) owner.   (b) real friend.   (c) beginner.   (d) race-rider.

3. _____ A bale of hay costs about: (a) $100   (b) $20   (c) $2.50   (d) $1.75

4. _____ Saran wrap kept his: (a) mount steady.   (b) gear on.   (c) head on the stripe.   (d) feet warm.

5. _____ Kisses in racetrack terminology refer to: (a) luck.   (b) losses.   (c) weights.   (d) wins.

6. _____ Many jockeys almost commit suicide by: (a) losing too much.   (b) forcing mounts.   (c) risking themselves.   (d) starving themselves.

DEFINITIONS   Choose the best definition for each italicized word.

1. _____ his weight *lingered:*   (a) remained (b) changed (c) grew (d) dwindled

2. _____ took on an *apprentice:*   (a) friend (b) pro (c) beginner (d) loser

3. _____ he *advised* Cauthen: (a) cautioned (b) sold (c) had (d) demanded

4. _____ Bold Forbes *outgamed* Honest Pleasure: (a) lost to (b) raced (c) set a limit on (d) defeated

5. _____ more *readily* than I: (a) slowly (b) easily (c) stubbornly (d) fiercely

6. _____ *emitting* screams: (a) smothering (b) having (c) letting out (d) sparing

7. _____ *in excess of* a million: (a) under (b) through (c) with (d) over

8. _____ a *fledgling* rider: (a) new (b) weak (c) failing (d) real

9. _____ *stipulation:* no reducing: (a) impression (b) agreement (c) problem (d) fear

10. _____ he *bagged* twelve winners: (a) got (b) saw (c) took (d) fought for

11. _____ *potential* agents: (a) real (b) powerful (c) influential (d) possible

12. _____ an *available* horse: (a) failing (b) sour (c) accessible (d) cooperative

13. _____ *amazed* by the attention: (a) hurt (b) sent (c) surprised (d) helped

14. _____ a *full-fledged* jockey: (a) certified (b) big (c) overweight (d) winning

15. _____ his *abbreviated* season: (a) first (b) shortened (c) last (d) next

30 *BARRY LOPEZ*

The Wolf Kill

Only recently have we begun to realize that it is not to our advantage to exterminate the wolf. Wolves are social animals who are part of an important, complex system of interdependences. By studying wolves, biologists can learn about the development of social systems, and can see that the wolf's relationship to its environment is critical to keeping the wilderness population under control.

No one knows how wolves pick out the animal they will try to kill. Biologists suspect that acting on certain cues from the prey the wolves spot the older, weaker members of the herd and concentrate their killing there. They also kill "surplus young." This is orderly and contributes to the "balance of nature." However, it's not the rule; and since the old, the weak, and the very young are the ones least capable of eluding the wolf the suggestion is simply tautological.

In recent years at least three ideas have surfaced to suggest that what passes between wolves and their prey is more complex and less deterministic. Hans Kruuk, working with hyenas in Africa, documented a surplus kill phenomenon. Hyenas, under certain conditions of extreme darkness, killed more animals than they could possibly eat. (Kruuk found the same true of foxes and black-headed gulls in dense fog in England.) Kruuk believed surplus killing was the result of a short circuit; the natural sequence of events (predator attacks, prey flees, predator pursues) was upset because the animals couldn't see each other clearly. The hyenas' "urge to kill" wasn't shut off, and so they simply went on killing. Dave Mech, the American authority on wolves, saw surplus killing by wolves in northern Minnesota in 1969; he speculated that unusually deep snows prevented deer from escaping, and this triggered killing by a resident pack far beyond its needs.

A second piece in the puzzle was suggested ten years ago by William Pruitt, who discovered by accident that wolves signal their prey—caribou in this case—if they are intent on attacking. In the absence of such a signal, caribou browse at ease. Prey also signal their predators; the antelope flashes his white rump, a deer suddenly bolts. With both predator and prey signaling each other there is the possibility of a conversation.

A third phenomenon suggests how little we know about predatory behavior in general. Mech has shown that at least one wolf pack in his Minnesota study concentrates its killing in a different area of its territory each year, allowing the prey population elsewhere to recover.

Other phenomena, some worn and familiar, some recently discovered, take on new meaning. Wolves in hot pursuit of a deer bleeding from its wounds will suddenly break off and let the animal go. Why? One caribou in a small herd may leave off fleeing and present himself to pursuing wolves in what appears to be an altruistic sacrifice. What is happening?

Biologists deal easily with the physical aspects of death but are loath to discuss it in a sociological context. This is odd, since the same biologists agree that one of the most intriguing things about the wolf is its social behavior. The behavior of the pack is comparable in its complexity, cooperation, and exchange of information to a Paleolithic hunting group. The scraps of information gathered by the biologists who have actually seen wolves kill prey indicate that their selection is neither arbitrary nor capricious. Indeed, the kill itself may represent a response to something more complex than the simple need to eat.

I think wolves kill the way Paleolithic hunters killed—by paying close attention to the movement of game herds and by selecting individual animals on the basis of various cues. The killing is by mutual agreement. This exchange between predator and prey might be called the conversation of death.

Wolves are the most elusive social animals in the Northern Hemisphere. They are rarely seen; major studies of wolves in the wild are complex, expensive, and can be counted on the fingers of both hands. All that is known about the wolf—its social organization, biology, ecology, behavior—has been learned in the past thirty-five years, with the perfection of aerial observation techniques and the development of the radio collar as an aid in tracking.

The wolf has long had a reputation as a wanton, innately evil creature, a sort of terrestrial shark. It runs down large ungulates, slashing at their hams, ripping their flanks, tearing at their heads until the animals weaken enough to be thrown to the ground; then it may rip open the abdominal cavity and begin eating before the animal is actually dead. Yet where the shark is a peabrained loner the wolf has proved to be a sophisticated social animal with at least three systems of intra- and interpack communication: vocal, postural, and olfactory. He coordinates hunts, plans ambushes, peaceably shares food, plays with his young, courts his mate, and joins other wolves to howl in what one scientist calls "the jubilation of wolves." Following the publication of Aldo Leopold's classic

Game Management and a pioneering study of wolves by the late Adolph Murie in 1944, it was accepted that the function of wolves in the scheme of things was to "cull" their prey, to keep it from overpopulating an area, overbrowsing it, and starving to death. But no one knew how they did it, or why.

Beginning in the winter of 1959, Dave Mech spent more than 400 hours over a period of three years in a tiny plane suspended over the 210 square miles of Isle Royale in Lake Superior, looking for wolves. During that time, when the snow conditions provided a contrasting background and the lack of deciduous growth allowed for increased visibility, Mech observed encounters between wolves and their major prey species, the moose.

Of the 160 moose Mech saw from the air on Isle Royale and judged to be within range of hunting wolves, twenty-nine were ignored, eleven discovered the wolves first, and eluded them, and twenty-four refused to run and were left alone. Of the ninety-six that ran, forty-three got away immediately, thirty-four were surrounded but not harmed, twelve made successful defensive stands, and seven were attacked. Of these seven, six were killed, and one was wounded and abandoned.

Today, seventeen years later, Mech is more than ten years into a study of wolves in northern Minnesota, where the last wolf population in America outside Alaska is concentrated. He has watched them track, chase, and kill their primary prey species, the white-tailed deer. Mech knows the physics of how wolves kill and he knows something about why they kill, but he still does not know why one animal in a herd is killed and another goes free.

Postmortem examination of prey on Isle Royale and in other studies showed that wolves did select primarily the very young, the old, and the injured and diseased. However, the observation can be reversed: it can be said that these three groups "gave" themselves to the wolf in ritual suicide, or that the animals fell victim because they were ill-equipped to escape.

Vulnerable prey animals apparently "announce" their condition to wolves by subtleties of stance, peculiarity of gait, rank breath, or more obvious signs of visible infection. Frequently wolves "test" a herd by making it run. The Nunamiut Eskimo, who live on the Arctic slope with wolves, have observed that hundreds of animals may be chased, many lackadaisically, before a burst of speed brings one down. The Nunamiut think a wolf can bring down any caribou it chooses, so if it's just tagging its prey they assume it's playing, testing, or perhaps waiting for a return signal from an individual caribou.

There is logic to the biologists' cull theory. The aged, diseased, and injured announce themselves and the wolf dispatches them. The young are cropped to control the size of the herds and perhaps to eliminate inferior or maladaptive combinations of genes at the outset. But the drive to make the facts conform to a theory of nature in the balance is based on at least one sweeping assumption: that wolves look for moose only to kill them. Testing prey might also be a deadly form of recreation.

Wolves will also attack an animal and then halt the chase for an hour to take a nap. One wolf may insist on attacking a certain individual while the rest of his pack will refuse. A pack on the hunt may investigate fresh moose tracks less than one minute old, pick up some subtle cue there, and not pursue.

It has long been held that wolves employ hunting strategies. They are reputed to lie low in the grass, switching their tails from side to side like metronomes to attract curious but swift antelope close enough to jump them. They herd buffalo onto lake ice, where the huge animals lose their footing. On occasion wolves employ what seems to be a conscious strategy, sending one or two individuals out to herd prey into an ambush. They vary their tactics, adapting to the terrain and to the type of prey. They prefer to attack mountain sheep from above and to work a swamp in a line-abreast formation. They may split up to skirt both sides of an island in a frozen lake and then precipitously flush the game driven toward the island's tip. They use man-made roads to conserve energy and facilitate ambushes. All this is strategy, but it is not necessarily killing strategy.

Once begun, the wolf's chase of a prey animal may last only a few seconds, go on for miles, or carry on intermittently for days. However, the pathology of death is consistent. First, there is massive damage to the animal's hips, breaking its stride; then slashing, crushing, and tearing, causing bleeding and inducing trauma; then harassment, tiring the animal; and, finally, disembowelment, causing death. With larger animals one wolf may grab the nose and hang on while the others undercut the animal and mob it to get it off its feet. Smaller animals, such as sheep, can be ridden down by a single wolf with a neck or head hold. Adult moose are often left to stiffen and weaken from their rump wounds and then killed. Once an animal is wounded and has taken its death stand, one or two wolves may harass it—make it exert itself, keep it bleeding—while the others rest or play. The pack may even depart, leaving one or two animals on a death watch. Yet some of the wounded survive. They have effectively announced their desire to live, as the others might have signaled their readiness to succumb.

The outcome of the hunt is usually settled in the first moment, the moment of eye contact between the animals. Mech writes, "The wolves and the deer remained absolutely still while staring at each other, 100 feet apart, for 1-2 minutes. . . . Suddenly the deer bolted, and instantly the wolves pursued."

The deer cannot stand at bay and fight off wolves as a caribou or moose can. It has no choice but to run. But with large ungulates, the outcome of the stare is less predictable. Immediately after a one-minute stare the moose may simply walk away, or the wolves may turn and run, or the wolves may charge and kill the animal in less than a minute. This hard stare is frequently used by wolves to communicate with each other and to take the measure of strangers. (Other animals, such as the gorilla, use a stare to communicate also.) What transpires in those moments of staring between predator and prey is probably a complex exchange of information regarding the appropriateness of a chase and a kill. This encounter is the conversation of death.

The conversation falters noticeably when wolves encounter domestic stock, animals that have had the language of death bred out of them. The domestic horse, a large animal as capable as a moose of cracking a wolf's ribs or splitting its head open with a kick, will almost always panic and run. It will always be killed. When a wolf wanders into a flock of sheep and sees them running into each other, flipping over on their backs like turtles and panicking, there is chaos. The wolf who has initiated a prescribed ritual has received nothing in return; he has met with ignorance in an animal with no countervailing ritual of its own. So he wounds and kills in anger.

When a wolf "asks" for an animal's life he is opening a formal conversation that can take any number of turns, including "no" and "yes," and can proceed either ritually or personally from there. It does not exclude play, play that can be lethal to the uninitiated; and it may encompass humor although the encounter itself is not humorous. It may be compared to encounters between the war parties of Plains Indians, who had their own ritualized and idiosyncratic ways of fighting, dying, and laughing.

Paleolithic cultures in general tended to stress that there is nothing wrong with dying. This idea was rooted in a very different perception of ego: a person was simultaneously indispensable and dispensable (in an appropriate way) for the good of fellow beings. At a more primitive level, exactly the same principle operates between wolves and their prey.

The moose's death is something that is mutually agreeable. The moose may be constrained to die because he is old or injured, but there is still the ritual and the choice. There is nobility in such a death. The wolf grows strong eating an animal that knows how to die with its whole heart; he wastes away on the flesh of animals that do not know either how to live or how to die. In just the same way Indians were reluctant to have anything to do with cattle. They would not eat them, raise them, or milk them, because there was no power in cattle.

When Robinson Jeffers wrote, "What but the wolf's tooth whittled so fine/ the fleet limbs of the antelope," he was telling, I think, only half the story. Predator and prey grow stronger together by means of a series of tests, through all the years of their lives, tests that pit them against each other at both psychological and physiological levels, tests that weed both culturally and genetically.

Wolf and moose seem to be far better at interspecies communication than we are. There is no reason why they should be confined to the antiquated, almost Newtonian system of behavior that we have devised for them. We should not be afraid—but we are, and profoundly so—to extend to the wolf and the moose the physical and metaphysical variables we allow ourselves. It is not man but the universe that is subtle.

LENGTH: 1800 WORDS

30   The Wolf Kill

SCORING: Reading time: _____ Rate from chart: _____ W.P.M.

MAIN SENTENCE   number right ____ × 4 equals ____ points

GENERALITIES   number right ____ × 4 equals ____ points

RETENTION   number right ____ × 2 equals ____ points

COMPLETION   number right ____ × 3 equals ____ points

DEFINITIONS   number right ____ × 2 equals ____ points

(Total points: 100) **total** ____ points

MAIN SENTENCE   Each of these sentences appears in the text. Which one best describes or best summarizes the content of the passage? _____

1. Paleolithic cultures in general tended to stress that there is nothing wrong with dying.

2. It is not man but the universe that is subtle.

3. No one knows how wolves pick out the animal they will try to kill.

GENERALITIES   Based on the passage, which of the following generalities seem iustifiable? _____ and _____.

1. Wolves are as savage and as murderous as humans.

2. Paleolithic hunters ran amuck when hunting in dense fog.

3. Wolves do not kill their prey for no reason.

4. A balance between predator and prey is built into nature.

RETENTION   Based on the passage, which of the following statements are True (T), False (F), or Not answerable (N)?

1. ____ The wolf and the moose seem able to communicate.

2. ____ Like the wolf, the fox and the black-headed gull are predators.

3. ____ Predators never kill more than they can eat.

4. _____ Predator and prey seem to have a conversation of death.

5. _____ American Indians would not eat cattle.

6. _____ Wolves are still easy to find and track.

7. _____ Wolves are good hunters even though they do not plan ahead.

8. _____ The wolf always hunts in a predictable way.

9. _____ Interestingly enough, the wolf pack works cooperatively in hunts.

10. _____ After a hunt, wolves fight with one another over the food.

11. _____ The "cull" theory explains why there is no overpopulation of prey.

12. _____ Surplus killing may be caused by a kind of visual short circuit.

13. _____ Wolves always kill the animals they stalk.

14. _____ The shark is a peabrained loner.

15. _____ Wolves sometimes "crop" different geographical areas for prey.

16. _____ Dave Mech is studying wolves in northern Minnesota.

17. _____ Eskimos have heard about wolves, but they have never seen any in action.

18. _____ Large prey have difficulty defending themselves on frozen lakes.

19. _____ An animal's breath can signal the fact that it is "ready" to die.

20. _____ Biologists avoid speaking of the sociology of death.

COMPLETION   Choose the best answer for each question.

1. _____ The author says that testing helps predator and prey: (a) die. (b) control an area. (c) grow stronger together. (d) size each other up.

2. _____ Indians felt cattle had no: (a) power.   (b) milk.   (c) luck. (d) defenses.

3. _____ The wolf kill is a ritual activity except in the case of: (a) other predators.   (b) birds.   (c) insane animals.   (d) domestic prey.

4. _____ One important form of communication is the: (a) wig-wag system.   (b) hunt.   (c) stare.   (d) community romp.

5. _____ The outcome of the hunt is usually settled in the: (a) chase. (b) field.   (c) most appropriate way.   (d) first moment.

6. _____ One important aid in scientists' tracking the wolf is the: (a) luminous collar.   (b) footprint.   (c) broken twig.   (d) radio collar.

DEFINITIONS Choose the best definition for each italicized word.

1. _____ Indians were *reluctant:* (a) killed (b) slow (c) stubborn (d) unwilling

2. _____ it will always *panic:* (a) cry (b) sing (c) lose control (d) run off

3. _____ *nobility* in death: (a) satisfaction (b) fear (c) grossness (d) greatness

4. _____ the *appropriateness* of a chase: (a) cause (b) craving (c) rightness (d) fear

5. _____ the *domestic* horse: (a) savage (b) tamed (c) biggest (d) native

6. _____ what *transpires* then: (a) dies (b) crosses over (c) happens (d) demands

7. _____ the conversation *falters:* (a) weakens (b) falls (c) stops (d) improves

8. _____ *precipitously* flush the game: (a) eventually (b) in some cases (c) after all else has failed (d) suddenly

9. _____ they *vary* their tactics: (a) plan (b) change (c) intensify (d) assume

10. _____ they *employ* a strategy: (a) use (b) have (c) want (d) need

11. _____ a form of *recreation:* (a) play (b) farming (c) sexual activity (d) dying

12. _____ *conform to* a theory: (a) have (b) fit (c) insist on (d) refute

13. _____ they are *elusive* animals: (a) deadly (b) small (c) difficult to find (d) subtle

14. _____ he *speculated* about them: (a) guessed (b) looked at (c) crowed (d) screamed

15. _____ a system he *devised:* (a) denied (b) saw (c) invented (d) rejected

31 *LOREN EISELEY*

The Hidden Teacher

Loren Eiseley, a scientist for whom the world is itself a huge classroom, recognizes that the universe is filled with teachers. The work of insects, the habits of animals, the persistence of plants—all can teach us about the mysteries of the universe.

Sometimes the best teacher teaches only once to a single child or to a grownup past hope.

—ANONYMOUS

The putting of formidable riddles did not arise with today's philosophers. In fact, there is a sense in which the experimental method of science might be said merely to have widened the area of man's homelessness. Over two thousand years ago, a man named Job, crouching in the Judean desert, was moved to challenge what he felt to be the injustice of his God. The voice in the whirlwind, in turn, volleyed pitiless questions upon the supplicant— questions that have, in truth, precisely the ring of modern science. For the Lord asked of Job by whose wisdom the hawk soars, and who had fathered the rain, or entered the storehouses of the snow.

A youth standing by, one Elihu, also played a role in this drama, for he ventured diffidently to his protesting elder that it was not true that God failed to manifest Himself. He may speak in one way or another, though men do not perceive it. In consequence of this remark perhaps it would be well, whatever our individual beliefs, to consider what may be called the hidden teacher, lest we become too much concerned with the formalities of only one aspect of the education by which we learn.

We think we learn from teachers, and we sometimes do. But the teachers are not always to be found in school or in great laboratories. Sometimes what we learn depends upon our own powers of insight. Moreover, our teachers may be hidden, even the greatest teacher. And it was the young man Elihu who observed that if the old are not always wise, neither can the teacher's way be ordered by the young whom he would teach.

For example, I once received an unexpected lesson from a spider.

It happened far away on a rainy morning in the West. I had come up a long gulch looking for fossils, and there, just at eye level, lurked a huge yellow-and-black orb spider, whose web was moored to the tall spears of buffalo grass at the edge of the arroyo. It was her universe, and her senses did not extend beyond the lines and spokes of the great wheel she inhabited. Her extended claws could feel every vibration throughout that delicate structure. She knew the tug of wind, the fall of a raindrop, the flutter of a trapped moth's wing. Down one spoke of the web ran a stout ribbon of gossamer on which she could hurry out to investigate her prey.

Curious, I took a pencil from my pocket and touched a strand of the web. Immediately there was a response. The web, plucked by its menacing occupant, began to vibrate until it was a blur. Anything that had brushed claw or wing against that amazing snare would be thoroughly entrapped. As the vibrations slowed, I could see the owner fingering her guidelines for signs of struggle. A pencil point was an intrusion into this universe for which no precedent existed. Spider was circumscribed by spider ideas; its universe was spider universe. All outside was irrational, extraneous, at best, raw material for spider. As I proceeded on my way along the gully, like a vast impossible shadow, I realized that in the world of spider I did not exist.

Moreover, I considered, as I tramped along, that to the phagocytes, the white blood cells, clambering even now with some kind of elementary intelligence amid the thin pipes and tubing of my body—creatures without whose ministrations I could not exist—the conscious "I" of which I was aware had no significance to these amoeboid beings. I was, instead, a kind of chemical web that brought meaningful messages to them, a natural environment seemingly immortal if they could have thought about it, since generations of them had lived and perished, and would continue to so live and die, in that odd fabric which contained my intelligence—a misty light that was beginning to seem floating and tenuous even to me.

I began to see that among the many universes in which the world of living creatures existed, some were large, some small, but that all, including man's, were in some way limited or finite. We were creatures of many different dimensions passing through each other's lives like ghosts through doors.

In the years since, my mind has many times returned to that far moment of my encounter with the orb spider. A message has arisen only now from the misty shreds of that webbed universe. What was it that had so troubled me about the incident? Was it that spidery indifference to the human triumph?

If so, that triumph was very real and could not be denied. I saw, had many times seen, both mentally and in the seams of exposed strata, the long backward stretch of time whose recovery is one of the great feats of modern science. I saw the drifting cells of the early seas from which all life, including our own, has arisen. The salt of those ancient seas is in our blood, its lime is in our bones. Every time we walk along a beach some ancient urge disturbs us so that we find ourselves shedding shoes and garments, or scavenging among seaweed and whitened timbers like the homesick refugees of a long war.

And war it has been indeed—the long war of life against its inhospitable environment, a war that has lasted for perhaps three billion years. It began with strange chemicals seething under a sky lacking in oxygen; it was waged through long ages until the first green plants learned to harness the light of the nearest star, our sun. The human brain, so frail, so perishable, so full of inexhaustible dreams and hungers, burns by the power of the leaf.

The hurrying blood cells charged with oxygen carry more of that element to the human brain than to any other part of the body. A few moments' loss of vital air and the phenomenon we know as consciousness goes down into the black night of inorganic things. The human body is a magical vessel, but its life is linked with an element it cannot produce. Only the green plant knows the secret of transforming the light that comes to us across the far reaches of space. There is no better illustration of the intricacy of man's relationship with other living things.

The student of fossil life would be forced to tell us that if we take the past into consideration the vast majority of earth's creatures—perhaps over ninety per cent—have vanished. Forms that flourished for a far longer time than man has existed upon earth have become either extinct or so transformed that their descendants are scarcely recognizable. The specialized perish with the environment that created them, the tooth of the tiger fails at last, the lances of men strike down the last mammoth.

In three billion years of slow change and groping effort only one living creature has succeeded in escaping the trap of specialization that has led in time to so much death and wasted endeavor. It is man, but the word should be uttered softly, for his story is not yet done.

With the rise of the human brain, with the appearance of a creature whose upright body enabled two limbs to be freed for the exploration and manipulation of his environment, there had at last emerged a creature with a specialization—the brain—that, paradoxically, offered escape from specialization. Many animals driven into the nooks and crannies of nature have achieved momentary survival only at the cost of later extinction.

Was it this that troubled me and brought my mind back to a tiny universe among the grass-blades, a spider's universe concerned with spider thought?

Perhaps.

The mind that once visualized animals on a cave wall is now engaged in a vast ramification of itself through time and space. Man has broken through the boundaries that control all other life. I saw, at last, the reason for my recollection of that great spider on the arroyo's rim, fingering its universe against the sky.

The spider was a symbol of man in miniature. The wheel of the web brought the analogy home clearly. Man, too, lies at the heart of a web, a web extending through the starry reaches of sidereal space, as well as backward into the dark realm of prehistory. His great eye upon Mount Palomar looks into a distance of millions of light-years, his radio ear hears the whisper of even more remote galaxies, he peers through the electron microscope upon the minute particles of his own being. It is a web no creature of earth has ever spun before. Like the orb spider, man lies at the heart of it, listening. Knowledge has given him the memory of earth's history beyond the time of his emergence. Like the spider's claw, a part of him touches a world he will never enter in the flesh. Even now, one can see him reaching forward into time with new machines, computing, analyzing, until elements of the shadowy future will also compose part of the invisible web he fingers.

Yet still my spider lingers in memory against the sunset sky. Spider thoughts in a spider universe—sensitive to raindrop and moth flutter, nothing beyond, nothing allowed for the unexpected, the inserted pencil from the world outside.

Is man at heart any different from the spider. I wonder: man thoughts, as limited as spider thoughts, contemplating now the nearest star with the threat of bringing with him the fungus rot from earth, wars, violence, the burden of a population he refuses to control, cherishing again his dream of the Adamic Eden he had pursued and lost in the green forests of America. Now it beckons again like a mirage from beyond the moon. Let man spin his web, I thought further; it is his nature. But I considered also the work of the phagocytes swarming in the rivers of my body, the unresting cells in their mortal universe. What is it we are a part of that we do not see, as the spider was not gifted to discern my face, or my little probe into her world?

We are too content with our sensory extensions, with the fulfillment of that ice age mind that began its journey amidst the cold of vast tundras and that pauses only briefly before its leap into space. It is no longer enough to see as a man sees—even to the ends of the universe. It is not enough to hold nuclear energy in one's hand like a spear, as a man would hold it, or to see the lightning, or times past, or time to come, as a man would see it. If we continue to do this, the great brain—the human brain—will be only a new version of the old trap, and nature is full of traps for the beast that cannot learn.

It is not sufficient any longer to listen at the end of a wire to the rustlings of galaxies; it is not enough even to examine the great coil of DNA in which is coded the very alphabet of life. These are our extended perceptions. But beyond lies the great darkness of the ultimate Dreamer, who dreamed the light and the galaxies. Before act was, or substance existed, imagination grew in the dark. Man partakes of that ultimate wonder and creativeness. As we turn from the galaxies to the swarming cells of our own being, which toil for something, some entity beyond their grasp, let us remember man, the self-fabricator who came across an ice age to look into the mirrors and the magic of science. Surely he did not come to see himself or his wild visage only. He came because he is at heart a listener and a searcher for some transcendent realm beyond himself. This he has worshiped by many names, even in the dismal caves of his beginning. Man, the self-fabricator, is so by reason of gifts he had no part in devising—and so he searches as the single living cell in the beginning must have sought the ghostly creature it was to serve.

LENGTH: 1900 WORDS

31   The Hidden Teacher

SCORING:	Reading time: _____ Rate from chart: _____ W.P.M.

MAIN SENTENCE   number right _____ × 4 equals _____ points

GENERALITIES   number right _____ × 4 equals _____ points

RETENTION   number right _____ × 2 equals _____ points

COMPLETION   number right _____ × 3 equals _____ points

DEFINITIONS   number right _____ × 2 equals _____ points

(Total points: 100) **total** _____ points

MAIN SENTENCE   Each of these sentences appears in the text. Which one best describes or best summarizes the content of the passage? _____

1. Many animals driven into the nooks and crannies of nature have achieved momentary survival only at the cost of later extinction.

2. The human brain, so frail, so perishable, so full of inexhaustible dreams and hungers, burns by the power of the leaf.

3. Man, the self-fabricator, is so by reason of gifts he had no part in devising— and so he searches as the single living cell in the beginning must have sought the ghostly creature it was to serve.

GENERALITIES   Based on the passage, which of the following generalities seem justifiable? _____ and _____.

1. Humans' keen senses limit them as the spiders' do the spiders.

2. The most important things we have to learn are archaeological.

3. Humans will never be free until they understand their own nature.

4. Our apparent limitlessness may be another form of specialization.

RETENTION   Based on the passage, which of the following statements are True (T), False (F), or Not answerable (N)?

1. _____ Eiseley went to the Far West to study spiders.

2. _____ Oddly enough, the orb spider does not spin a web.

3. _____ Job was much younger than Elihu.

4. _____ Orb spiders are rather small.

5. _____ Eiseley regarded the web as the spider's universe.

6. _____ Plants make our oxygen.

7. _____ Most of the earth's creatures have become extinct.

8. _____ Eiseley does not feel that humans and spiders have much in common.

9. _____ Humans have broken through boundaries that control other forms of life.

10. _____ Spiders seem to understand that humans exist.

11. _____ Phagocytes live inside Loren Eiseley.

12. _____ Consciousness depends on the presence of oxygen.

13. _____ No other form of life has flourished on earth longer than humans.

14. _____ Specialized creatures perish with the environment that created them.

15. _____ The human brain depends on plants.

16. _____ Prehistoric humans had nothing to do with caves.

17. _____ Eiseley says the earth may be 1 million years old.

18. _____ Oxygen is carried to the brain by the lime in our bones.

19. _____ The salt in sea water is like the salt in our blood.

20. _____ The telescope at Mount Palomar looks into a gigantic distance of space and time.

COMPLETION   Choose the best answer for each question.

1. _____ Job heard: (a) a voice in a whirlwind. (b) several teachers. (c) a child ministering in the sands. (d) the answer to his prayers.

2. _____ The ghostly creature we "search for" is—in spider terms—like: (a) a moth. (b) a pencil. (c) humans. (d) the long trail of history.

3. _____ Eiseley says that if we continue as we are, our great brain will simply become a: (a) fossil. (b) trap. (c) spider. (d) new web.

4. _____ At heart, humans are searchers for some transcendent realm: (a) in

space.   (b) in history.   (c) beyond themselves.   (d) beyond the blue
horizon.

5. _____ Eiseley saw from the spider's reaction that all creatures live in: (a)
their own universes.   (b) solitude.   (c) fear.   (d) special situations.

6. _____ The spider was a symbol of: (a) vain striving.   (b) limitlessness.   (c) humanity in miniature.   (d) the fear we all have of the
unknown.

DEFINITIONS   Choose the best definition for each italicized word.

1. _____ its *menacing* occupant: (a) fearful   (b) huge   (c) threatening   (d) lurking

2. _____ *enabled* two limbs to be freed: (a) saw   (b) permitted
(c) helped   (d) had

3. _____ brought the *analogy* home: (a) science   (b) hurt   (c) comparison   (d) thing

4. _____ mind's *ramifications:*   (a) limits   (b) range   (c) depths
(d) branching out

5. _____ intelligence *amid* the pipes: (a) within   (b) outside   (c) between   (d) off

6. _____ *cherishing* a dream: (a) having   (b) valuing   (c) ruining
(d) becoming

7. _____ a *version* of the trap: (a) sort   (b) dislike   (c) fear   (d) variation

8. _____ see his wild *visage:*   (a) face   (b) friend   (c) wolf   (d) sight

9. _____ beckons like a *mirage:*   (a) sultan   (b) mirror   (c) illusion
(d) portent

10. _____ in the *dismal* caves: (a) earliest   (b) hunting   (c) big   (d) gloomy

11. _____ generations had *perished:*   (a) remained   (b) come   (c) died
(d) failed

12. _____ *formidable* riddles: (a) religious   (b) hard   (c) awesome   (d) the
worst

13. _____ one *aspect* of education: (a) kind   (b) friend   (c) look   (d) phase

14. _____ there *lurked* a spider: (a) was   (b) looked   (c) waited   (d) had
been

15. _____ a web *tenuous* even to me: (a) harmful   (b) slender   (c) full
(d) heavy

32 *EDITORS OF* U.S. NEWS & WORLD REPORT

Should Prisons Punish, Not Reform, Criminals?

One of the most serious controversies in modern penology has to do with whether criminals can be rehabilitated. Those who say yes demand that prisons reform their inmates. Those who say no demand that prisons punish them. The swing now is away from reform and toward punishment.

There's a revolution going on inside prisons. It's not the kind that will mean a new spate of prisoner riots. It's a revolution in the way prisons are run and the purposes they serve.

What's causing this change is a growing disillusionment with what once was viewed as a main task of prisons: the rehabilitation, or reform, of criminals.

New studies are challenging the effectiveness of rehabilitation programs, charging that they don't work. Too many inmates have come out of prisons just as committed to crime as when they went in, or even more so. And crime rates have continued to soar.

Many prison experts, joined by citizens who are fed up with rising crime, now have concluded that the rehabilitation system is "bankrupt." It is not really reforming criminals.

Prisons, as a result, are beginning to turn from reform to punishment as their primary purpose.

The latest evidence of the change in thinking that is occurring came on August 10 [1975]. After a three-and-a-half-year study, an official report branded as "a failure" New York City's multimillion-dollar program of trying

SHOULD PRISONS PUNISH, NOT REFORM, CRIMINALS? "Big Change in Prisons, Punish—Not Reform." Reprinted from *U.S. News & World Report,* August 25, 1975. Copyright 1975 U.S. News & World Report, Inc.

to rehabilitate criminals and develop alternatives to prison sentences. Actually, the report warned, such efforts may be adding to the problem instead of reducing crime.

Last February, it was announced that the federal penal system would no longer stress rehabilitation as its primary goal for prisons. Norman Carlson, director of the Federal Bureau of Prisons, gave this explanation: "The unfortunate truth of the matter is that we don't know very much about the causes or cures for crime. For a long time we said we did—or kidded ourselves that we did. But I think a new sense of reality is now sweeping over the entire criminal-justice system of this country."

This "new sense of reality" puts more importance on mere confinement of criminals. Even if it doesn't deter crime, the idea is, it will cut crime by getting criminals off the street.

With this shift will come some significant changes. Among other things, there will be changes in the nature of the sentences given to criminals.

As experts see the future, sentences will become more punitive, surer, more swiftly imposed, more definite in length. Parole boards will have less power to decide when prisoners are released. In some cases, parole may be abolished. Probation may be used less often as an alternative to prison. And certain types of criminals, particularly the career and violent offenders, will be dealt with more harshly.

As a result, it is predicted, more criminals will be going to prison. That will mean more prisons must be built, because current facilities are already full. Construction costs, high and rising, may run as much as $40,000 per prisoner.

Prisons of the future will probably be smaller and nearer to urban areas than today's prisons.

All this predicted change does not mean that rehabilitation programs will be abandoned completely. In federal prisons, Mr. Carlson says, they will be offered only on a voluntary basis.

In the past, prisoners in most penal systems had no choice. They were required to take part in programs such as education, vocational training or psychological counseling. Criminals were viewed as "sick." And it was seen as a prison's job to "cure" them.

Spurred by the new evidence against rehabilitation, several states are considering following the lead of federal prisons. Some may go further.

Under an Illinois plan, not only would programs be voluntary, but a prisoner's progress at rehabilitation would have no bearing on his release date. If he took advantage of programs it would only be because he truly wanted to help himself.

Currently, parole boards release a prisoner when they decide he's been rehabilitated. Prisoners have become wise to this, and "acting" rehabilitated has become common among inmates. "It's turned prisons into drama schools," says Hans Mattick, a noted criminologist and former assistant jail warden. The move to "unhook" rehabilitation progress from a prisoner's release date has two immediate consequences.

First, it requires a frank admission that prisons will no longer be seen as places to help people. "They'll be places to isolate, to punish," says Norval Morris, a well-known criminologist and dean of the University of Chicago Law School.

Second, it necessitates a rethinking of the kind of sentences judges should impose on a convicted defendant. Most States now are using some variation of the "indeterminate sentence," with a minimum and a maximum, say 10 to 20 years. And when a prisoner is released depends on when he's judged to have been rehabilitated.

Prisoners have charged that the indeterminate sentence has been used as a club by prison officials to keep prisoners in line.

One alternative to the indeterminate sentence is the "flat sentence." David Fogel, executive director of the Illinois Law Enforcement Commission, has a plan that calls for fixed, definite prison terms. For example, Mr. Fogel says, a murderer might get 25 years. In heinous or in extenuating circumstances, the plan allows for some flexibility, but not much, say 20 per cent either way. Also, there would be no parole. But if prisoners caused no trouble they would get a day off their sentence for every day they're "good."

A side effect of the plan would be to reduce disparity in sentences—make them more nearly equal for all convicted of similar crimes. Disparity, along with the indeterminate sentence, is a prime cause of prisoner resentment.

Maine recently adopted the "flat sentence" approach, California is close to approving it, and 26 states have made contact with Mr. Fogel, expressing an interest in his plan.

Because the power to grant parole, like the indeterminate sentence, is geared to rehabilitation, it, too, will change, prison experts say. Parole boards are expected to lose power or be abolished as states change their sentencing systems.

The argument over how to handle criminals is far from new. It goes back at least 200 years. It was then that well-meaning Quakers proposed the idea of a "penitentiary." At that time, it was a novel idea. The penitentiary was to be an alternative to mutilation, execution, banishment, slave labor or dungeons—then the sanctions commonly used against lawbreakers.

In penitentiaries, criminals were to be isolated to contemplate their crimes and eventually to become reformed through meditation. It seldom worked out that way. But the penitentiary system was born. And still held by many is the idea that man's nature is such that he can be reformed in a penitentiary.

Even among Quakers, views have shifted in recent years. In 1971, the Working Party of the American Friends Service Committee published a book concluding that the penitentiary system has not worked and that "this reformist prescription is bankrupt." That was the beginning of the big change in attitudes on rehabilitation. Other events speeded up the change.

In 1974, reported crime in the U.S. went up 17 per cent over the previous year, the largest increase in 14 years. The then-Attorney General, William Saxbe, cited the rise as evidence that rehabilitation is a "myth." Large numbers of the crimes were found to be committed by repeaters who had served prison terms.

Then, last spring, the attack on rehabilitation was intensified by a major study that criticized its value. Robert Martinson, a sociologist from the City College of New York, published his findings on 231 rehabilitation programs that had operated between 1945 and 1967. He concluded: "With few and isolated exceptions, the rehabilitative efforts that have been reported so far have had no appreciable effect on recidivism."

In other words, his finding was that such programs had not deterred most criminals from returning to crime.

The Martinson findings were no surprise to criminologist Mattick, who says the failures of rehabilitation belie "a view that crime is a lower-class phenomenon." He explains: "Society says, 'If only the criminal had a job, could read and was mentally healthy, he'd be O.K., like us—middle class.' But the Watergate criminals were literate, had jobs and weren't crazy. We've just been working under a warped sense of reality."

Too often, Mr. Mattick says, we put a mugger in a wood-shop course and all we get when he's through is a mugger who can cut wood.

Since 1967, the Law Enforcement Assistance Administration [LEAA], a federal agency that funds projects aimed at cutting crime, has spent or committed 1.3 billion dollars on programs to improve correction systems. Mr. Martinson's critics say many of these projects show great promise.

These critics also argue that the reason rehabilitation has not worked may be because the destructive atmosphere of most prisons makes reform impossible. Under more humane conditions, they say, programs would do their jobs.

Prison authorities have backed off on one point, though, as a result of studies such as Mr. Martinson's. They now admit that rehabilitation doesn't work for everyone. "We've been reluctant to admit that in the past," says Vernon Housewright, president of the American Association of Wardens and Superintendents. "But it seems clear now that some prisoners are just beyond hope. They're mean, vicious people. About all we can do with them is keep them locked up, away from the public."

That, really, was all Mr. Martinson was saying in his study: that nothing works for everybody, there are no panaceas. Some programs do have limited success, partly because they have dedicated personnel, partly because the prisoners in them would have succeeded anyway. They were winners to start with.

One attitude that seems to be catching on in the wake of the rehabilitation disappointment is that it's best to use the "least restrictive" means of punishing a criminal. Among means being tried are short sentences, correction within the criminal's home community, early parole, or release from prison during the day for work or school. None may prevent crime more effectively than long, harsh prison sentences. But, say some prison experts, studies have shown they do no worse.

One advantage is that such programs are cheaper. This economic considera- tion is becoming more important as prisons face spiraling fuel and maintenance costs. It is estimated it currently costs about $10,000 a year to keep a person locked up in a traditional prison.

Additionally, the "least restrictive" approach is seen as having a secondary effect of helping to keep criminals from becoming hardened and hostile and from picking up crime techniques, as often happens in a regular prison.

The disillusionment with rehabilitation programs has also prompted many to urge a harder line against crime. Even some liberals, now embarrassed by their past advocacy of rehabilitation programs, are backing a tougher stand.

Mandatory sentences are being urged for violent offenders, harsher sen- tences for those convicted repeatedly. In his recent crime message, President Ford supported such measures. And he launched a federal program to crack down on "career criminals." The LEAA will fund projects to help prosecutors convict professionals who make careers of crime. LEAA Administrator Richard Velde says such criminals are often not caught because they are too clever or too experienced. And, if arrested, they often "beat the rap" by using continuances and other ploys in court.

James Q. Wilson, a Harvard professor, suggests that probation should be used less as an alternative to prison. He favors putting most offenders in prison, if only for a short time. Even if this does not prove a stronger deterrent to crime, he argues, it cannot help having an effect on the crime rate by getting more criminals off the streets.

This tougher approach will swell prison populations. Even without a crackdown, it is estimated there will be 240,000 prisoners in state and federal institutions by 1985, compared with about 204,000 at the latest count.

Many prison authorities don't think the public realizes what a tougher stand on crime will cost in increased spending. "We can't even afford to be 'soft on crime,'" jokes William Leeke, director of South Carolina's prison system, lamenting the shortage of funds his overtaxed system already faces.

Some extreme hard-liners are expected to call for scrapping all rehabilitation programs, arguing they are a waste of money. "What they're talking about is a return to 'warehousing' prisoners," says Raymond Procunier, the head of California's Adult Authority, the state's parole agency. "That can only bring violence and riots."

Some may also use the confusion created by the attack on rehabilitation to renew their call to "tear down the prison walls," abolish prisons.

Neither the extreme hard-liners, nor those who would abolish prisons, are expected to prevail. But it seems likely that other reformers will use the debate over rehabilitation as an opportunity to impose some changes that were being advocated before the recent controversy began.

A particularly significant group of reformers is the new breed of prison administrators who come from academic backgrounds rather than from the ranks of custodial officers.

They argue that, in de-emphasizing rehabilitation, the U.S. should take a more rational look at the whole system of criminal justice.

Among changes reformers are expected to urge with new vigor are: "coed" prisons, conjugal visits for prisoners, more women and minority guards to help relieve guard-prisoner tension, pay for prisoners, and decriminalization of so-called "victimless crimes," such as drunkenness, prostitution, gambling and drug addiction. Many claim these crimes, which clog up already overcrowded courts and prisons, could be dealt with better outside the criminal-justice system.

"It seems ironic," says Mr. Carlson, "but all this talk of de-emphasizing rehabilitation, which was supposedly a humane approach to prisons, will probably wind up making prisons more humane."

What the revolution now under way adds up to, at least as most authorities see the future, is this: More criminals will go to prison, perhaps for longer terms. But they are likely to serve their time in less-crowded institutions, under more "civilized" conditions. And they will know where they stand.

All this will happen, experts predict, because society appears ready to abandon the idea that criminals can be reformed in prisons.

LENGTH: 2200 WORDS

32   Should Prisons Punish, Not Reform, Criminals?

SCORING: ·   Reading time: _____ Rate from chart: _____ W.P.M.

MAIN SENTENCE	number right _____ × 4 equals _____ points	
GENERALITIES	number right _____ × 4 equals _____ points	
RETENTION	number right _____ × 2 equals _____ points	
COMPLETION	number right _____ × 3 equals _____ points	
DEFINITIONS	number right _____ × 2 equals _____ points	

(Total points: 100) **total** _____ points

MAIN SENTENCE   Each of these sentences appears in the text. Which one best describes or best summarizes the content of the passage? _____

1. Large numbers of the crimes were found to be committed by repeaters who had served prison terms.

2. Mandatory sentences are being urged for violent offenders, harsher sentences for those convicted repeatedly.

3. Prisons, as a result, are beginning to turn from reform to punishment as their primary purpose.

GENERALITIES   Based on the passage, which of the following generalities seem justifiable? _____ and _____.

1. Prisoners do not like prison.

2. Rehabilitation programs have not proved successful.

3. Parole boards see a great deal of good acting.

4. Mandatory sentences have been normal in prisons.

RETENTION   Based on the passage, which of the following statements are True (T), False (F), or Not answerable (N)?

1. _____ The federal penal system still stresses reform.

2. _____ If punishment is stressed in prison, parole boards will grow stronger.

3. _____ An official report concluded that New York City's rehabilitation system had failed.

4. _____ There are at least 2 million prisoners in the United States.

5. _____ Confinement actually deters crime.

6. _____ A tough policy on criminals will increase the prison population.

7. _____ Even the Quakers have gone back on their original ideas about prisons.

8. _____ Two hundred years ago, punishment for crime was milder than it is today.

9. _____ The Illinois plan has mandatory rehabilitation for all prisoners.

10. _____ It costs only $2000 a year to keep a prisoner locked up.

11. _____ The Quakers originally thought that meditation would reform prisoners.

12. _____ Sentences for the same crime can vary considerably.

13. _____ Rehabilitation efforts, however, have cut down the number of repeat offenders.

14. _____ One advantage of the "least restrictive" measure is that it is cheaper than jailing a criminal in a traditional prison.

15. _____ The view that crime is a lower-class phenomenon is disputed in this article.

16. _____ Actually, it has never been proposed that criminals are sick.

17. _____ The flat sentence contrasts with the indeterminate sentence.

18. _____ Jailing more criminals will have no effect on the crime rate.

19. _____ There have been no careful studies of rehabilitation programs.

20. _____ The argument over how to handle criminals is very new.

COMPLETION Choose the best answer for each question.

1. _____ Most states now use a variation of the: (a) indeterminate sentence. (b) rehabilitation formula. (c) fixed-plea system. (d) life sentence.

2. _____ Advocates of rehabilitation admit that it does not work, but they blame the: (a) wardens. (b) society. (c) prisons themselves. (d) lack of money available.

3. _____ Abandoning rehabilitation forces us to admit that prisons: (a) cannot work. (b) will not govern themselves. (c) are a farce. (d) do not help people.

4. _____ A prime cause of prisoner resentment is: (a) disparity of sentencing. (b) poor food. (c) parole board whimsy. (d) a sense of not belonging.

5. _____ Under an Illinois program, rehabilitation would be voluntary and would not: (a) work. (b) count toward release. (c) lead to a job after release. (d) invalidate parole.

6. _____ If every criminal has to serve some time, the prisons: (a) will disappear. (b) can fold up. (c) will swell. (d) can continue as is.

DEFINITIONS Choose the best definition for each italicized word.

1. _____ it *deters* crime: (a) isolates (b) sees (c) discourages (d) elaborates

2. _____ reluctant to *admit:* (a) confess (b) hit (c) come to (d) clarify

3. _____ effect on *recidivism:* (a) sin (b) crime (c) returns (d) monstrosity

4. _____ develop *alternatives:* (a) hopes (b) studies (c) failures (d) choices

5. _____ there are no *panaceas:* (a) pains (b) curealls (c) certainties (d) sleuths

6. _____ results *belie* the possibilities: (a) stymie (b) misrepresent (c) study (d) cure

7. _____ new *spate* of riots: (a) outburst (b) condition (c) approach (d) feeling

8. _____ growing *disillusionment:* (a) disengagement (b) facing reality (c) involvement (d) disinterest

9. _____ *rehabilitate* criminals: (a) punish (b) reform (c) "warehouse" (d) stop

10. _____ the *economic* considerations: (a) financial (b) worst (c) next (d) social

11. _____ *lamenting* the shortage of funds: (a) correcting (b) seeing (c) complaining of (d) having to put up with

12. _____ sentences are *punitive:* (a) weak (b) seemly (c) punishment (d) punishing

13. _____ *spurred* by evidence: (a) stunned (b) ridden (c) urged (d)
startled

14. _____ attack was *intensified:* (a) defeated (b) striven (c) emphasized (d) doubled

15. _____ prisons are not *humane:* (a) human (b) kindly (c) stolid (d)
beguiling

33 *THOMAS HOGE*

Will There Be a New Ice Age?

Several Ice Ages already have occurred in the earth's history, with glacier's moving down over the earth's surface and then slowly receding. Although we have become convinced that Ice Ages are phenomena of the past, examination of recent weather patterns suggests that we may be in for a future Ice Age—and it may be starting now.

Weather satellites fanning across the Northern Hemisphere report the permanent snow and ice caps mantling the North Pole have shown an ominous increase in the past few years. If scientists read these signals correctly, we may be heading for a global cool-off that could spell widespread tragedy. It could even be the first signal of another Ice Age, like the one that brought glaciers deep into North America before it retreated some 10,000 years ago. Or perhaps we could experience a cold snap like the "Little Ice Age" that caused death and widespread misery in the 17th century.

One respected scientific body forecasts that droughts, floods and plummeting temperatures will probably cause major crop failures in the next decade.

"If national and international policies do not take such failures into account, they may result in mass deaths by starvation . . ." is the grim conclusion of a meeting of experts in climatology, agricultural economics and political science called by the International Federation of Institutes for Advanced Study (IFIAS).

WILL THERE BE A NEW ICE AGE? "Another Ice Age?" by Thomas Hoge. *The American Legion Magazine,* December 1976. Copyright 1977, The American Legion Magazine, reprinted by permission.

With ominous forecasts already on record for a shrinking world food supply, such crop failures could be devastating.

A study of the weekly maps of the National Oceanographic and Atmospheric Administration says the snow and ice found the year round in the coastal mountains of British Columbia and in such Asian ranges as the Himalayas increased by 12 per cent in 1971 and have remained at the new level.

A closer look shows that strange things have been happening to the weather around the world in the past few years, both in the northern and southern sectors of the globe.

Canada, for instance, suffered the coldest winter in memory in 1972. A disastrous frost hit Brazil recently, virtually wiping out its vital coffee crop. Americans feel the chill every week at the supermarket.

Reports from Arctic regions say ice floes clogging the seas off Greenland and Iceland have done more damage to shipping and fishing than at any time since the 17th century. Then it began when a Norse colony in Greenland became isolated and perished as the Arctic ice pack gradually engulfed their encampment. And it was apparently still in force a century later. Meterologist Nigel Calder says in his book "The Weather Machine" that during the American Revolution, British soldiers were able to slide their guns across the ice from Manhattan to Staten Island.

English farmers have been complaining for some years about a shorter growing season, and a recent check of the records proved them right. Because of a gradual change of the Gulf Stream, England's growing season is nine to ten days shorter than it was in 1950.

Untold thousands, tens of thousands of Africans have died of famine in droughts gripping the area south of the Sahara. The southern rim of the arid Sahara appears to be creeping into the populated, famine-struck Sahel. The U.S. Agency for International Development says that over the past 50 years, 250,000 square miles of arable land have been "forfeited" to the Sahara's expanding southern edge.

Killing droughts also have wreaked havoc throughout the Middle East, India, Southern Asia and North China. Half a world away, they struck Central America.

A recent United Nations survey shows that the world's desert areas are spreading. Man will pay for it in higher food prices and political turmoil. The survey by the U.N. Environmental Program shows that "desertification" now amounts to about 6.7 per cent of the earth's surface, an area larger than Brazil.

Calder in his book notes that thousands of deaths in Africa over the past few years have been the result of only a moderate change in climate. He suggests that the effects of a major climatic change would be roughly comparable to the casualties in a nuclear war.

While vast areas of Africa, the Middle East and Latin America were drying up, the Midwestern United States, the Philippines and Italy were engulfed two years ago by raging floods that were rated the worst in centuries. And in 1976, storm-lashed waters swept across Western Europe causing the worst havoc in decades. Last spring floods covered wide areas of North Dakota.

An unprecedented rash of tornadoes has rampaged across the United States in the past few years, with more than a thousand recorded in 1973 alone. It was said to be worst in 1974 when these awesome twisters ripped through a 12-state area. On April 3 of that year, 70 of these killers plowed paths of devastation through the Midwest and South. That same year, in one savage outburst, a thunderstorm front raced from Colorado to Ohio in a matter of hours, spawning tornadoes that destroyed or damaged nearly 20,000 homes, business houses and farm buildings. The storm killed more than 320 persons and injured some 3,700. The weather abated somewhat in 1975, then started up again. Weather Bureau experts are reluctant to draw conclusions. Statistical data can be misleading, they emphasize, particularly since tornado reports cannot always be confirmed.

But farmers in Meade, Ks., still talk in awed tones about howling, 60-mile winds that blackened the skies early this year and kicked up dust to a height of 11,000 feet. Spongy heaps of black topsoil drifted beside barbed wire fences and filled roadside ditches. It was a scene reminiscent of the choking dust bowl of the 1930's.

The 1976 drought has significantly reduced the winter wheat crop. It has also forced premature slaughter of cattle, a move that threatens to diminish meat supplies and boost prices. Droughts also hit California this year, hurting the fruit and nut crops and dealing a blow to the daily industry in that state.

Such climatic changes are even more disturbing in light of the world's already unstable food stores. World grain reserves are down to less than one month's supply, compared with a two-month stockpile in 1972. This has prompted a leading climatologist to sound a warning.

"There is very important climatic change going on right now," says Reid Bryson, director of the Institute of Environmental Studies at the University of Wisconsin. "This has been the most abnormal period in at least a thousand years." If the change continues, Bryson warns, "it will affect the whole human occupation of the earth."

In fact, this outspoken observer of weather danger signals believes that the changes now taking place are so severe that up to one billion people—one quarter of the global population—could starve to death.

A Soviet climatologist, quoted by Calder, goes still further. He says that if the polar ice sheets manage to edge a little closer toward the equator, we might find ourselves in the path of another full-fledged ice age. The entire globe would become encased in ice, he says, and life would eventually cease. (The impact on a northern nation such as the USSR could precipitate untold reactions.) All this suggests the threat of an ice age may not be bizarre.

Bryson says weather ships patrolling the lonely waters of the North Atlantic report an average dip in temperatures of two degrees Fahrenheit. That doesn't seem like much, but Bryson noted in an interview that "the difference between the present time and an ice age is only six degrees Centigrade" which is 10^4/s degrees Fahrenheit. Considering the fact that a dip of one degree Centigrade on a global scale has taken place in two decades, trouble could be coming.

A recent study of the last Ice Age which began 18,000 years ago has unearthed the hitherto unknown fact that it was the cause of droughts.

The study known as CLIMAP (Climate Long-Range Investigation Mapping and Prediction) was carried on at Columbia University. The climate of 18,000 years ago was reconstructed from evidence in the sediments on land and at sea and in the Greenland ice layers laid down at that time. Contrary to longstanding assumptions, the study showed that it snowed very little during the Ice Age. When the ice sheets began to form, the survey revealed, they spread rapidly, but their effect on atmospheric circulation was such that the world became increasingly arid. In fact, the study disclosed that global precipitation 18,000 years ago was 15 per cent lower than today.

Unfortunately, government policies on grain reserves and agriculture in general have, until recent years, proceeded on the premise that a relatively warm and stable climate was normal and could be expected to last indefinitely. This rosy picture was based on the experience of the first half of the 20th century when, despite some setbacks, climatic conditions were generally benign for agriculture in the great "breadbasket" of North America and many other countries as well.

When grandpa used to say the weather was more rugged back in his day he wasn't just spinning yarns. Meteorological records show that winters really were colder before 1900 than they were in the first half of the 20th century. There was a gradual warming trend to about 1950 when the thermometer began to drop and it has continued downward.

Climatologists tell us we may be heading into a cold snap that might linger for years. How long, no one seems to know. Investigations by British meteorologist Hubert Lamb indicate that, in the past, cool spells usually lasted for between 100 and 150 years. The minimum, he said, was 40 years. But this is not taking into account the specter of another Ice Age. That would be a very different ball game.

Most think that the weather is something going on outdoors right now. But local weather is in fact a product of conditions that existed many years ago and perhaps thousands of miles away. Whether rain or sunshine beats down on you today may depend on what was happening in the sea off Japan last week, in the Indian Ocean last month, in the frozen waters off Iceland last winter and in the polar ice sheets a century ago.

LENGTH: 1480 WORDS

33   Will There Be a New Ice Age?

SCORING: Reading time: _____ Rate from chart: _____ W.P.M.

MAIN SENTENCE   number right _____ × 4 equals _____ points

GENERALITIES   number right _____ × 4 equals _____ points

RETENTION   number right _____ × 2 equals _____ points

COMPLETION   number right _____ × 3 equals _____ points

DEFINITIONS   number right _____ × 2 equals _____ points

(Total points: 100) **total** _____ points

MAIN SENTENCE   Each of these sentences appears in the text. Which one best describes or best summarizes the content of the passage? _____

1. All this suggests the threat of an ice age may not be bizarre.

2. A recent United Nations survey shows that the world's desert areas are spreading.

3. Climatologists tell us we may be heading into a cold snap that might linger for years.

GENERALITIES   Based on the passage, which of the following generalities seem justifiable? _____ and _____.

1. The earth's weather goes through long cycles of change.

2. Seventeenth-century climatologists did not help us understand what we needed to know.

3. No one believed the older people who said it was colder in their youth.

4. Changes in climate beget changes in politics.

RETENTION   Based on the passage, which of the following statements are True (T), False (F), or Not answerable (N)?

1. _____ Canada's fiercest winter in memory was in 1972.

2. _____ Local weather conditions are governed by local preconditions.

3. _____ The most recent warming trend ended around 1950.

4. _____ The Sahara is a desert that grows.

5. _____ In 1973, one of the worst years for tornadoes, fewer than one hundred occurred in the United States.

6. _____ The nineteenth century, according to this passage, saw a "Little Ice Age."

7. _____ Fortunately, the world's food supply is expanding.

8. _____ Brazil has recently been hit by a disastrous frost.

9. _____ The Ice Age was actually only 6° C. colder than today.

10. _____ The last Ice Age began 18,000 years ago.

11. _____ Luckily, droughts are not connected with Ice Age conditions.

12. _____ Statistical information is usually quite reliable.

13. _____ If a new Ice Age comes, up to 1 billion people may die.

14. _____ A new Ice Age will increase tourist traffic to equatorial countries.

15. _____ The "Blizzard of '88" was the result of a little Ice Age.

16. _____ Droughts have been widespread lately.

17. _____ Serious cooling of the earth will affect navigation with floating ice.

18. _____ Modern food planning has taken weather changes into account.

19. _____ If there is a new Ice Age, the Soviet Union will be one of the first countries affected.

20. _____ There is a full year's stockpile of world grain reserves.

COMPLETION   Choose the best answer for each question.

1. _____ Nigel Calder, author of *The Weather Machine,* is a: (a) meteorologist. (b) keen observer. (c) friend of the author. (d) worry-wart.

2. _____ The smaller winter wheat crop has caused a: (a) panic. (b) bit of speculative selling. (c) slaughter of cattle. (d) reorganization of crop stockpile planning.

3. _____ The reports of snow buildup in the North Pole were relayed by: (a)

Eskimos.   (b) dog-sledding explorers.   (c) the press.   (d) weather
satellites.

4. _____ A major climatic change will have effects similar to: (a) a great
diaspora.   (b) a revolution.   (c) what we have seen already.   (d) a
nuclear war.

5. _____ The British moved guns across the ice in: (a) Napoleon's time.   (b)
Greenland.   (c) the American Revolution.   (d) early fall in the
eighteenth century.

6. _____ The world's deserts now occupy an area as large as: (a) Ber-
muda.   (b) Africa.   (c) California.   (d) Brazil.

DEFINITIONS   Choose the best definition for each italicized word.

1. _____ it became *isolated:*   (a) colder   (b) frozen   (c) separated   (d)
deleted

2. _____ it could *precipitate* reaction: (a) cause   (b) rain   (c) sense   (d)
stifle

3. _____ may not be *bizarre:*   (a) funny   (b) reassuring   (c) sudden   (d)
weird

4. _____ *unearthed* new facts: (a) discovered   (b) brought   (c) sought
(d) maneuvered

5. _____ world became *arid:*   (a) fruitful   (b) wet   (c) alarming   (d) dry

6. _____ *climatic* change: (a) warm   (b) weather   (c) final   (d)
unsuspected

7. _____ *unstable* food stores: (a) unwelcome   (b) unreliable   (c) un-
well   (d) unfulfilled

8. _____ this *prompted* a warning: (a) on time   (b) early   (c) caused   (d)
recited

9. _____ the weather *abated:*   (a) gave up   (b) fouled   (c) subsided   (d)
acceded

10. _____ a *moderate* change: (a) slight   (b) mean   (c) average   (d) drastic

11. _____ land is *"forfeited":*   (a) lost   (b) sold   (c) ruined   (d) depressed

12. _____ political *turmoil:*   (a) advancement   (b) decision   (c) unrest   (d)
procedure

13. _____ droughts *wreaked* havoc: (a) saw (b) meant (c) dried up (d) inflicted

14. _____ *plummeting* temperatures: (a) recording (b) sensing (c) annoying (d) falling

15. _____ with *ominous* forecasts: (a) good (b) bad (c) threatening (d) baffling

34 *JIM KAPLAN*

Jim Dandy Gym

Some communities have high-school gymnasiums only because the law demands them. Some communities, however, regard the gym as a place for people who have a wide variety of interests. Jim Kaplan reports about a community in California that has invested itself in terms of imagination as well as money to create a gym that is truly outstanding.

San Rafael High School looks like the sort of place where old-fashioned physical education classes would be a staple. The building has a broad facade with high pillars and a long flight of steps leading to its entrance. The gym is gloomy, with wooden basketball backboards. But what is this? There is a coed volleyball game in progress. Outside, another group of boys and girls is scaling the gym wall in a rock-climbing class. And half a mile away other students are sailing in a canal.

This is a typical day of P.E. in San Rafael, a bedroom community of 44,000 situated 14 miles north of the Golden Gate Bridge. It has the country's most celebrated high school physical education program, one that offers 45 electives ranging from football to Frisbee, from team handball to tumbling, from *tai chi chaun* to boxing to yoga to self-defense. All classes are open to both sexes, and there is only the vaguest of dress codes. Even traditional educators are fascinated by all this, mainly because San Rafael High is accomplishing what every school would like to: not only is it offering the athletically gifted child a wide choice of activities, it is turning would-be spectators into athletes.

This does not happen everywhere. Twenty years of Presidents' fitness councils and the growth of women's sports and Jogging for Life notwithstanding, the U.S. is still mostly a nation of fans. According to every respected survey on the

JIM DANDY GYM   "Jim Dandy Gym" by Jim Kaplan from *Sports Illustrated,* November 15, 1976 © 1976 Time, Inc. Reprinted by permission.

subject, the majority of adult Americans do no regular exercise except walking. Meanwhile, deaths from cardiovascular diseases, which doctors have linked to sedentary life-styles, continue to mount.

Tomorrow's heart patients are not graduating from San Rafael High. "There's a carry-over effect," says John Donovan, assistant principal in charge of curriculum. "People who took scuba diving here are taking advanced courses elsewhere. Bikers and backpackers organize their own trips, and sailors continue sailing in college."

There are a number of reasons why San Rafael's P.E. program is so successful. Many students point to the relaxed dress code. Do clothes really matter as long as good courses are offered? "Yes," chorus four girls at sailing class. "My sister in junior high school hates P.E.," says junior Joanne Ashcroft. "Every day she comes home and throws her gym clothes on the bed." Students speak of gym uniforms as "monkey suits" and "prison garb," and describe the process of donning them—or "dressing out"—as torture. At San Rafael, shorts, sneakers and shirts are expected in most classes, but anything close will do.

"I found long ago that kids would come up with any excuse for not exercising, but it usually concerned dress," says Gym Instructor Bill Monti. "They didn't like to dress out because they were ashamed of their bodies. Legally, you can't impose a dress code unless you provide the uniforms, but I bet 90% of the schools in California have one anyway. It shouldn't be based on something so artificial, especially now, when kids see dress as a way of expressing themselves."

The San Rafael dress code was liberalized in 1970, three years before the school combined its men's and women's P.E. departments under a gym specialist named Marcia Arevalo. Previously, the departments had peered at each other across a sex gap as formidable as a gator-filled moat. When they fused and classes went coed, tensions eased.

To get the students as relaxed as the teachers, Monti and Arevalo prepared a questionnaire listing 99 possible P.E. courses, including boccie, yoga, fly-casting and even spectator sports. The boys voted heavily for activities like scuba diving; the girls leaned toward horseback riding, archery and tennis. The five-woman, six-man P.E. department has been adding electives ever since.

"People ask me how we can teach 45 sports with a budget of $6,000," Arevalo says. "We try to be creative. At first, we begged, borrowed and stole. Outsiders offered help, and teachers went to clinics. Some groups gave us equipment such as boats. Fencing and scuba equipment, which is expensive, we split with our sister school, Terra Linda, which has about the same number of electives under a more traditional format."

Most students are required to take one 55-minute P.E. course a day. In the ninth grade there is a core program in which pupils learn basic team games, develop coordination and agility through individual sports, and find out about their bodily capabilities through tests. Electives start in the tenth grade. There are semester-long courses in gymnastics, rock-climbing, sailing and modern dance, and six-week programs in other areas. Grading is 60% on attendance and participation. There are few failures.

The most dramatic successes often have been pupils who had been considered unathletic. "I'm probably the least competitive member of my family, but I take volleyball twice a day," says one coed. "It takes my mind off everything." A classmate, breathing easily after a rock-climbing drill in which he clambered up a 15-foot wall using just knobs, ledges, rocks and sidewalls—but no ropes—said, "I only do competitive sports for fun. I hunt and fish most of the time, and rock-climbing seems to go along."

While most electives strain the muscles, others, such as Frisbee, strain credulity. "Frisbee can be taught," says Arevalo. "We make it interesting by creating golf courses. There are skills involved, and, of course, it's a lifetime sport. We're interested in the whole person."

By every significant criterion—skills, teamwork, self-control, sex roles—rock-climbing is probably the most interesting course. "We originally drew people who didn't want to be involved with team sports," says Monti, a San Rafael graduate who started the course upon his return as a teacher in 1963. "In fact, it's more of a team sport than any other because it can involve life and death. It teaches stress and responsibility."

Monti has since branched out into sailing, and rock-climbing now is taught by Bill Ranney, who squeezes in his classes when he is not coaching the swim team, climbing mountains, taking pictures and training for walking races. "We have almost as many girls as boys now," he said. "At first there were just boys. I tried to recruit girls with a poster showing you can do it and still be cute. It's important to have girls, because they're more flexible."

As Ranney spoke, a coed was casually dangling from a rope halfway up the 30-foot gym wall. She was a member of Ranney's advanced class, which on that day had been told to work on direct-aid climbing, rappelling and traversing. The students not only understood the terms but also knew how to perform the maneuvers, because they had studied about them for 4½ months before attempting them. Now they climb local slopes and gym walls, and on rainy days use a simulated slope in the wrestling room.

"I go to a camp where they do a little rock-climbing, but nothing like this," said the girl. "We do mountaineering, rescue work and first aid. It's really safe, if you go by the rules. You need strength, agility and flexibility.

"I've taken two semesters of sailing and two of rock-climbing, and I may get into scuba diving. I also take volleyball, softball and badminton. These courses may not help my studies, but they're too good to pass up. San Rafael is the best thing that ever happened to P.E."

And the 23 varsity teams are not suffering because of it. "One program doesn't rule out another," says Basketball Coach Mike Diaz. "We had 353 of our 2,009 students out for extramural sports in 1972; that has increased to about 500 now." According to Football Coach Bob Muster, the fact that he has lost only half a dozen players to injuries during the last three years is the result of his players' P.E. sessions in weights and aerobic running during the off-season.

The major change in extramurals—coed teams—is less related to P.E. than to Title IX. Yet it somehow seems appropriate that, in addition to several girls on the boys' swim and tennis teams, there has been a female wrestler at San Rafael. A junior varsity regular at 127 pounds last year, Dana McCoy lost the six matches she wrestled (three others were forfeited to her), but surprised almost everyone by surviving every first period—and three entire matches—without being pinned. She also made points by being, in Arevalo's words, "tall, slender and very attractive—not the way you might picture a female wrestler."

It would be heady indeed to leave San Rafael on the quintessentially reformist idea of coed wrestling, but that would ignore some problems. Teachers who have undergone traditional training elsewhere have complaints about the free-form decision-making at the school. The scuba program once was suspended when the equipment was stolen. And most distressing to the physical education department, despite the excellence of its program, even San Rafael has not been able to eliminate all the old objections to mandatory gym classes. The school board last year used a local-option clause in a new state law to make P.E. optional for juniors and seniors.

The law was designed to force schools to improve unsatisfactory P.E. programs, to make their gym classes attractive enough so that students will attend voluntarily. Critics of the law fear that physical education programs may be dropped as economy measures instead. Whether good programs will also suffer is problematical. Forty-two percent of the seniors at San Rafael quit P.E. when the course was made optional for them on an experimental basis. However, Arevalo points out, "A lot of students told me they liked P.E., but they wanted half days in school. Although we could have lost potentially 500 or 600 students when the new law came to pass, we only lost 100."

Defenders of the law point to an Oregon study demonstrating that good P.E. programs will maintain their enrollments after an initial drop-off. This only begs the question of whether P.E. should be optional in the first place. Should English and math be optional when *they* are poorly taught?

Some San Rafael school board members argued that P.E. is not a lifetime requirement and that kids 16 to 18 stay in shape on their own. Rebutting for the minority, board member Gale Fisher said, "This is the last chance to get children involved for life in physical education. The physicians on the President's council agreed unanimously that kids should take P.E. all the way through school. It's wonderful to educate a marvelous brain, but if that brain is in a dead body at age 40, it isn't doing much good."

LENGTH: 1910 WORDS

34   Jim Dandy Gym

SCORING: Reading time: _____ Rate from chart: _____ W.P.M.

MAIN SENTENCE	number right _____ × 4 equals	_____ points
GENERALITIES	number right _____ × 4 equals	_____ points
RETENTION	number right _____ × 2 equals	_____ points
COMPLETION	number right _____ × 3 equals	_____ points
DEFINITIONS	number right _____ × 2 equals	_____ points

(Total points: 100) **total** _____ points

MAIN SENTENCE   Each of these sentences appears in the text. Which one best describes or best summarizes the content of the passage? _____

1. The most dramatic successes often have been pupils who had been considered unathletic.

2. Tomorrow's heart patients are not graduating from San Rafael High.

3. San Rafael High School looks like the sort of place where old-fashioned physical education classes would be a staple.

GENERALITIES   Based on the passage, which of the following generalities seem justifiable? _____ and _____.

1. Math and English programs should follow this example.

2. Sexual integration has been beneficial to the San Rafael program.

3. The wide variety of choice in athletics has not hurt the P.E. program.

4. The biggest boost to the program was an expanded budget.

RETENTION   Based on the passage, which of the following statements are True (T), False (F), or Not answerable (N)?

1. _____ San Rafael is a bedroom community.

2. _____ The P.E. program at San Rafael became coed only last year.

3. _____ The department was made coed, but it is still run by a man.

4. _____ San Rafael has more than twenty varsity sports.

5. _____ San Rafael seems to be emphasizing sports for life.

6. _____ Tensions mounted after the P.E. department became coed.

7. _____ Dress codes do not have much effect on a P.E. program.

8. _____ The students at San Rafael High generally dress casually.

9. _____ The new P.E. program has not had an impact on extramural sports.

10. _____ The San Rafael program even teaches Frisbee.

11. _____ There are about two thousand students at San Rafael High.

12. _____ P.E. is now optional for juniors and seniors at San Rafael.

13. _____ According to Presidents' fitness councils, most adult Americans overexercise.

14. _____ San Rafael's P.E. department even offers a semester course in dance.

15. _____ The coed regulation in P.E. does not mean that extramural teams have to be coed.

16. _____ A semester-long course in P.E. (sailing, for instance) cannot be repeated.

17. _____ Apparently, rock-climbing has proved to be one of the most popular sports.

18. _____ In general, girls are more flexible than boys.

19. _____ Many students who quit P.E. at San Rafael said they liked it.

20. _____ The San Rafael program is being studied by schools all over the country.

COMPLETION   Choose the best answer for each question.

1. _____ The San Rafael program is turning spectators into: (a) fanatics. (b) big-time players. (c) athletes. (d) real fans.

2. _____ Forty percent of the grading in the courses seems to be on: (a) participation. (b) skill and achievement. (c) whether one dresses out. (d) personality.

3. _____ Many of the students who dropped out of P.E. wanted: (a) more sports they liked. (b) nothing at all. (c) to sleep. (d) half days in school.

4. _____ Most students at San Rafael have P.E.: (a) two hours a day. (b)

one hour a week.   (c) fifty-five minutes a day.   (d) three hundred minutes a week.

5. _____ Kaplan says the most interesting course taught at San Rafael is probably: (a) rock climbing.   (b) scuba diving.   (c) canoeing.   (d) yoga.

6. _____ Aerobic running seems to have helped: (a) Marcia Arevalo.   (b) the football team.   (c) with coed integration.   (d) the program survive as it has.

DEFINITIONS   Choose the best definition for each italicized word.

1. _____ dull classes are a *staple:*   (a) main ingredient   (b) trial   (c) fact   (d) nail

2. _____ *vaguest* of dress codes: (a) worst   (b) smallest   (c) slightest   (d) best

3. _____ *rebutting* for the majority: (a) hitting   (b) talking   (c) seeing   (d) contradicting

4. _____ *cardiovascular* diseases: (a) heart   (b) lung   (c) permanent   (d) breathing

5. _____ *donning* suits: (a) cleaning   (b) putting on   (c) having   (d) scuba diving

6. _____ *elective* courses: (a) important   (b) unrequired   (c) novel   (d) political

7. _____ an experimental *basis:*   (a) foundation   (b) style   (c) sport   (d) problem

8. _____ *fused* the classes: (a) ruined   (b) saw   (c) established   (d) joined

9. _____ traditional *format:*   (a) shape   (b) pattern   (c) style   (d) habitat

10. _____ *optional* courses: (a) sudden   (b) unrequired   (c) good   (d) casual

11. _____ a significant *criterion:*   (a) standard   (b) judgment   (c) fable   (d) problem

12. _____ *mandatory* gym classes: (a) workable   (b) customary   (c) required   (d) labored

13. _____ a *forfeited* match: (a) uncontested   (b) struggling   (c) formidable   (d) good

14. _____ *coed* sports: (a) men's (b) women's (c) children's (d) men's and women's

15. _____ a *significant* move: (a) unexpected (b) powerful (c) sudden (d) important

SECTION V

Vocabulary Preview

The following words come from the six reading selections in Section V. Study the list carefully, pronouncing the words aloud if possible. Conceal the definitions with a card or your hand and test your command of the meanings of the words.

afflict, *verb*   to harm or hurt; to trouble
affluent, *adj.*   comfortable; rich
amass, *verb*   to accumulate; to gather
anarchy, *noun*   confusion; lack of government
antagonist, *noun*   enemy; opponent
apparatus, *noun*   device; machine or mechanism
archives, *noun*   place for keeping records
armistice, *noun*   truce; end of fighting
arrested, *adj.*   stopped; put an end to; held back
assayed, *adj.*   evaluated
avocation, *noun*   hobby
banished, *adj.*   sent away
bestow, *verb*   to give as a gift
bona fide, *adj.*   genuine; authentic
capital, *noun*   money; wealth
chivalry, *noun*   good manners; noble behavior
comprise, *verb*   to make up; to contain
condescended, *verb*   acted superior to
conferred, *verb*   gave; bestowed
consanguinous, *adj.*   related by blood
contiguous, *adj.*   touching; very close to

converging, *verb*   moving toward a meeting point

credence, *noun*   belief of something

creditably, *adv.*   deservedly; meritoriously

cum laude, *adj.*   with honor

debauchery, *noun*   corruption

debilitation, *noun*   weakness

degenerate, *verb*   to decay; to deteriorate

discretion, *noun*   good judgment; tact

divert, *verb*   to turn away; to send in a new direction

dyspepsia, *noun*   indigestion

embodiment, *noun*   representation; personification

empathy, *noun*   sympathy; feeling for

ensue, *verb*   to follow after; to result

entice, *verb*   to lure; to stimulate

equivocation, *noun*   ambiguous statement or position

exploits, *noun*   deeds; acts

feasibility, *noun*   possibility

fervently, *adv.*   passionately; intensely

feted, *adj.*   honored; celebrated

fidelity, *noun*   faithfulness; loyalty

foster, *verb*   to encourage; to support

gerontological, *adj.*   pertaining to old age

glean, *verb*   to collect; to gather

glutted, *adj.*   filled to excess

hereditary, *adj.*   related to one's heritage; related to genetic or other
  inheritance

homilies, *noun*   sermons; lectures

humility, *noun*   modesty

imperceptibly, *adv.*   not noticeably; invisibly

imposition, *noun*   obligation; burden

inadvertent, *adj.*   unintentional

inaugurated, *adj.*   begun; started

infringe, *verb*   to trespass; to violate

ingenuity, *noun*   cleverness; imagination

integral, *adj.*   relating to the whole; significant to the whole

irony, *noun*   sarcasm; unlikely outcome of events

irremediable, *adj.*   not fixable; incurable

irreversible, *adj.*   permanent; not capable of being reversed

judicial, *adj.*   showing good judgment; relating to law or justice

lassitude, *noun*   weakness; fatigue

mired, *adj.*   stuck in

notoriety, *noun*   state of being well-known for bad things

nurture, *verb*   to encourage; to look after; to feed and help grow

pace, *verb* to set a speed for; to establish a rate

pacifist, *noun* person opposed to war

philanthropy, *noun* charitable actions; love of fellows

physiology, *noun* study of life processes

piscine, *adj.* fishlike

posturing, *verb* assuming an artificial manner

prescience, *noun* foresight; knowing about things before they happen

procreative, *adj.* relating to reproduction and creation

proficiency, *noun* skill

progeny, *noun* offspring; descendants

prolong, *verb* to continue or keep going

propagation, *noun* reproduction

propulsion, *noun* forward movement

protuberant, *adj.* bulging; sticking out

provisions, *noun* food; supplies

radically, *adj.* basically; deeply; extremely

renowned, *adj.* well-known

resolve, *noun* determination; firmness

restraint, *noun* control; ability to hold back

retarded, *adj.* held back; slowed

retraction, *noun* taking back of something—usually a statement

reverent, *adj.* respectful

rigor, *noun* strictness; severity

rueful, *adj.* regretful; unhappy

scoff, *verb* to mock at; to jeer

senescent, *adj.* relating to age; beginning senility

shirked, *verb* avoided; got out from

sinister, *adj.* evil

stigma, *noun* mark of disgrace; stain

stipulated, *verb* specified; required

substantiate, *verb* to back up; to support

subvert, *verb* to overthrow; to undermine and ruin

surmising, *verb* supposing; guessing

surreptitiously, *adv.* secretly; underhandedly

syndrome, *noun* pattern; group of characteristic symptoms

taciturnity, *noun* silence (of a person); nontalkative state

transactions, *noun* dealings; occurrences

tribulations, *noun* sufferings; trials; troubles

unsolicited, *adj.* not asked for; unrequested

veritable, *adj.* true; genuine; real

verities, *noun* eternal truths

withering, *verb* shriveling; drying up

Complete the following sentences, using the correct words from the list.

1. The heat and lack of food made Joe a victim of _____.

2. The _____ nature of the experiment means that once the propulsion begins it cannot be terminated.

3. Frank may be a pacifist, but his _____ in boxing is formidable.

4. The king _____ in the battle, but his progeny were cowards.

5. The party began peacefully, but soon _____ into a brawl.

6. Pat showed discretion when she voted to _____ good relations with Cuba.

7. The anarchist diverted us with obvious _____ and other time-worn clichés.

8. The committee began by scoffing at me, but ended by _____

   _____ on me the grand prize.

9. Margi _____ the situation carefully before speaking.

10. The government did all it could to _____ the pacifist rally in the park.

11. My friend's wounded expression gave credence to the fact that she had

    suffered many _____ that had prolonged her pain.

12. The plant began by blooming, but ended by _____.

13. Dave used very sinister means to _____ such a fortune.

14. George's first suggestions were in support of a strong central government,

but soon he reversed himself and supported total _____

_____.

15. One's progeny are always _____.

16. Pellegrino was an _____ part of the whole scheme.

17. My cousin gained _____ for constant debauchery and irreverence.

18. Yet, when he reformed, he made a _____ to avoid further stigma.

19. As it was, he died a calm and remarkably _____ man, considering that he had once been a beachcomber.

20. Edna _____ nurtured the escaped prisoner back to health.

21. Susan could not relate to strong people, but she had great _____

_____ for those weaker than she.

22. We thought Jean knew nothing about mountain climbing, but, ironically,

she showed more _____ than we did.

23. Because of her famous novels and plays, she was _____ all over the world.

24. I thought Mandy would be my strongest supporter, but she ended up by

being a profound, although chivalrous, _____.

25. We wondered if there was any _____ of getting the job done by Monday.

35 *O'DONALD MAYS*

The Nobel Prizes

The Nobel Prizes, which honor achievement in six fields of human endeavor, have become justifiably famous. Each year they are awarded to men and women from a wide range of nations. This selection tells about the history of the Nobel Prizes, and names some of its more eminent recipients.

"The conquests of scientific research," said Alfred Nobel, ". . . wake in us the hope that microbes, the soul's as well as the body's, will gradually be exterminated and that the only war humanity will wage in the future will be war against these microbes."

These idealistic words, spoken by a practical man devoted to service and philanthropy in his own lifetime, explain why Nobel, one of the world's wealthiest men in his day, determined to leave the greater part of his estate for annual prizes to those who have "conferred the greatest benefit on mankind."

Three-quarters of a century after the Nobel Prizes were instituted, 440 men and women—drawn from more than 30 nations and from every continent—have received the cherished awards. While the value of the prize is now approximately $155,000, most recipients would gladly settle for the honor alone which the awards bestow upon them. Nobel's will specified that the annual prizes should be awarded in the fields of physics, chemistry, physiology or medicine, literature, and "for the best work for fraternity between nations . . ."—or peace.

The advanced nations of the world, with their highly developed cultures, have taken the lion's share of the prizes. The United States alone has seen 120 of its citizens honored, representing over 27 per cent of the total. British recipients number 69, while Germany has had 59, France 41, and Sweden 21. Other

---

THE NOBEL PRIZES   "The Prizes of Alfred Nobel" by O'Donald Mays. *The Rotarian,* September 1976. Reprinted by permission.

countries whose citizens have earned 10 or more Nobel Prizes are the Soviet Union, Switzerland, The Netherlands, Austria, Denmark, and Italy. Yet the poorer and the smaller nations figure more and more prominently in the annual prize-giving. India, Guatemala, and Vietnam now take pride in recipients.

The Nobel Prizes came into being in 1901, five years after the death of Alfred Nobel. His will had clearly laid down provisions for the annual awards, but the estate was contested and it took five years to settle the differences and organize the procedure for selecting the winners. Although his father had gone bankrupt twice, Alfred Nobel proceeded to amass one of the world's greatest fortunes. There is some irony in the way in which he made it. By the time of his death in 1896, this peace-loving man had invented dynamite, blasting gelatin, and a host of other explosives and explosive devices; he held 355 industrial and scientific patents and his industrial empire sprawled over more than a dozen nations. Nobel fervently believed the advances in communication and scientific progress growing out of his inventions would draw the nations of the world closer together. Now tunnels could be quickly blasted beneath mountains separating nations, and canals could be dug linking contiguous countries. He was distressed when wars erupted and his explosive devices were put to sinister uses.

One of those who may have influenced Nobel toward instituting a prize for peace was Bertha von Suttner, an Austrian who served as his secretary for a brief period and who already had earned a reputation as a champion of peace. Nobel was also influenced by the pacifist views of Percy Bysshe Shelley, the great English poet.

Of frail health all his life, Nobel was a shy, retiring character who preferred solitude to the gay life of the 1890's. His biographer, Eric Bergengren, quotes the inventor's choice of privacy in nature "among trees and bushes, silent friends who respect the state of my nerves." Whenever possible, he rejected honors and honorary degrees, retorting: "I am not aware that I have deserved any notoriety and I have no taste for its buzz."

Nobel's will revealed an estate worth about $71 million (U.S.) today; the will also stipulated that the fortune should be invested in "safe" securities so as to insure continuity of the annual awards. The Nobel Foundation has done a superb job of preserving the original capital and raising the value of the prizes to its present respectable figure of $155,000. The Foundation's formula: investments (book value) comprise stocks (42.4 per cent), mortgage loans (47.1 per cent), and real estate (10.5 per cent).

Almost a full year is required to screen the hundreds of candidates for the annual prizes, select the winners, and stage the presentations. There is a committee for each of the five prizes, four of which sit in Sweden and one (that for the peace prize) in Norway. When the prizes were started in 1901, Norway and Sweden were a united kingdom; after their separation into independent countries in 1905, the original arrangements were left intact. The Swedish Royal

Academy of Sciences selects the winners of the physics and chemistry prizes, the teaching staff of the Caroline Institute's Faculty of Medicine chooses the recipient of the prize for physiology or medicine, and the Swedish Academy picks the winner of the literature award. A special "Nobel Committee" of the Norwegian Parliament (The Storting) chooses the peace prize winner. Nominations must be in by February 1 of each year, awards are announced in October or November, and on December 10—the anniversary of Nobel's death—the prizes are awarded.

How is a candidate nominated? The rules vary from committee to committee, but generally speaking, candidates must be suggested either by Swedish or internationally renowned authorities in the five fields. Candidates may also be suggested by former Nobel Prize recipients. A person who believes himself or herself to be prize material will automatically be disqualified if he or she proposes himself or herself—even if already a world figure.

Elaborate ceremonies take place both in Stockholm and Oslo on the day of presentation in the presence of the kings of the two nations. Recipients receive, in addition to checks, handsome diplomas and medals in gold. The winners have by this time become "Nobel laureates" and usually give a "Nobel lecture" during their stay in Stockholm or Oslo. A social highlight is a banquet in the Golden Hall of Stockholm's city hall for the winners who received their awards in the Swedish capital; the peace prize winner is similarly feted in Oslo.

As many as three people may share a Nobel Prize in any one field, and this frequently happens with the awards in physics, chemistry, and physiology/medicine. This usually occurs when a team of scientists or medical researchers jointly achieve a breakthrough in their fields, making it impossible to single out one individual. The literature prize, on the other hand, generally goes to one person. The peace award can be given to organizations as well as to individuals; indeed, 10 organizations have been so honored, including the International Red Cross on three occasions. The peace prize is usually withheld during wartime. Two United States Presidents, Theodore Roosevelt (1906) and Woodrow Wilson (1919), have won the peace prize, as have also five U.S. secretaries of state: Elihu Root (1912); Frank B. Kellogg (1929), Cordell Hull (1945), George C. Marshall (1953), and Henry Kissinger (1973).

In 1969 a new prize in economic science was instituted by the Swedish Central Bank at its tercentenary. Although the value of the prize is the same as the Nobel awards and it is given at the same time, and in honor of Alfred Nobel, it is not considered to be a Nobel Prize in the strict sense because it was not stipulated in Nobel's will. Since it was inaugurated, the economics prize has been awarded to five U.S. citizens, twice to British citizens, and once each to residents of Sweden, Norway, The Netherlands, and the Soviet Union.

Have winners of the Nobel Prize truly reflected the world's best minds? Arbitrary decisions are always disputed, however carefully and thoroughly the screening committees may do their homework. Yet a list which includes Rudyard Kipling, Pearl Buck, John Steinbeck, Ernest Hemingway, John Galsworthy, and Pablo Neruda can hardly be said to neglect the best writers of this century. And in the realm of science and medicine, who can complain of awards made to Marie Curie, Albert Einstein, Sir Alexander Fleming, and Enrico Fermi?

LENGTH: 1360 WORDS

35   The Nobel Prizes

```
┌─────────────────────────────────────────────────────────────────────┐
│ SCORING:    Reading time: _____ Rate from chart: _____ W.P.M. │
├─────────────────────────────────────────────────────────────────────┤
│        PURPOSE        number right _____ × 4 equals _____ points      │
│                                                                       │
│        GENERALITIES   number right _____ × 4 equals _____ points      │
│                                                                       │
│        RETENTION      number right _____ × 2 equals _____ points      │
│                                                                       │
│        COMPLETION     number right _____ × 3 equals _____ points      │
│                                                                       │
│        DEFINITIONS    number right _____ × 2 equals _____ points      │
├─────────────────────────────────────────────────────────────────────┤
│                  (Total points: 100) total _____ points               │
└─────────────────────────────────────────────────────────────────────┘
```

PURPOSE   Which of the following phrases best expresses the purpose of the passage? _____

1. to show how important the Nobel Prizes have been to the modern world.

2. to help convince us to work hard and become eligible for a Nobel Prize.

3. to inform us about the background and stipulations of the Nobel Prize.

GENERALITIES   Based on the passage, which of the following generalities seem justifiable? _____ and _____.

1. Citizens of small nations as well as those of large nations seem to have a good chance of winning the prizes.

2. Political considerations have become more and more important to the prizes.

3. The prizes seem to have honored worthy people over the years.

4. Nobel's lifework may have done more harm than his prizes have done good.

RETENTION   Based on the passage, which of the following statements are True (T), False (F), or Not answerable (N)?

1. _____ There were no Nobel Prizes in the nineteenth century.

2. _____ Nobel made a great deal of money because of his father's bankruptcies.

3. _____ Norway and Sweden were one country when Nobel died.

4. _____ The peace prize was apparently the first one Nobel thought of.

5. _____ Only one person can receive the literature prize in any one year.

6. _____ These days all the prizes are awarded in Sweden.

7. _____ A winner is described as a Nobel Laureate.

8. _____ The International Red Cross has been nominated for the peace prize.

9. _____ A contestant either nominates himself or herself or is nominated by someone else.

10. _____ Cordell Hull once won the peace prize.

11. _____ Alfred Nobel himself won the first prize awarded.

12. _____ The prizes are awarded on the anniversary of Nobel's death.

13. _____ Ironically, Nobel disdained most honors.

14. _____ In addition to a medal, winners receive a diploma.

15. _____ As many as ten people can share a Nobel Prize in one field.

16. _____ Americans have won almost 30 percent of all prizes given so far.

17. _____ The Soviet Union is the only country close to the United States in number of prize winners.

18. _____ No Russian has ever won the literature prize.

19. _____ Presidents of countries are ineligible for Nobel Prizes.

20. _____ The Nobel Foundation has more than $70 million in investments.

COMPLETION   Choose the best answer for each question.

1. _____ The newest award given through the Nobel Foundation is for: (a) physical chemistry. (b) space research. (c) physics. (d) economics.

2. _____ The Norwegian Parliament is called the: (a) "Father" of the awards. (b) most explosive house of government in the world. (c) Storting. (d) "Nobel" Parliament.

3. _____ The Nobel Foundation does not invest in: (a) stocks. (b) real estate. (c) municipal bonds. (d) mortgage loans.

4. _____ One country definitely named as having a Nobel Prize winner is: (a) Vietnam. (b) Sierra Leone. (c) Ireland. (d) Singapore.

5. _____ The poet named as an important influence on Alfred Nobel is: (a) Keats. (b) Kipling. (c) Shelley. (d) Shakespeare.

6. _____ Nobel was deeply distressed when his inventions: (a) backfired. (b) were used in sinister ways. (c) never bore fruit. (d) succeeded so well.

DEFINITIONS   Choose the best definition for each italicized word.

1. _____ it was *stipulated* in the will: (a) remanded for cause (b) mentioned explicitly (c) simply hinted at (d) specifically argued against

2. _____ How is a candidate *nominated?*: (a) named for consideration (b) eliminated (c) entitled (d) assigned a committee

3. _____ the arrangements were left *intact:* (a) undistributed (b) without being dismantled (c) ultimately unfinished (d) worse than before

4. _____ the rules *vary:* (a) are constant (b) change (c) stink (d) remain

5. _____ pacifist *views:* (a) opinions (b) insights (c) eyesores (d) inventions

6. _____ one prize was *withheld:* (a) awarded (b) stifled (c) avoided (d) unawarded

7. _____ *recipients* get a medal: (a) nominees (b) friends (c) winners (d) losers

8. _____ microbes are *exterminated:* (a) killed off (b) shut down (c) removed bodily (d) isolated in Petri dishes

9. _____ what the awards *bestow on* them: (a) confer on (b) imply for (c) have in (d) imply for the future

10. _____ the will *specified:* (a) said (b) named (c) made explicit (d) put in

11. _____ devoted to *philanthropy:* (a) humankind (b) doing good (c) himself (d) earth

12. _____ *annual* awards: (a) national (b) large (c) yearly (d) periodical

13. _____ to *screen* candidates: (a) discourage (b) indict (c) choose (d) review

14. _____ undeserving *notoriety:* (a) fame (b) pain (c) insistence (d) knowledge

15. _____ link *contiguous* countries: (a) strife-torn (b) touching (c) similar (d) explicitly friendly

36 *MICHAEL KERNAN*

Fiftieth Anniversary of the Rocket

Only a little more than fifty years ago, Robert Goddard launched the first liquid-propellant rocket into the air. It shot up less than fifty feet. Few people watching that event could have believed that in less than half a century a rocket would take men to the moon and back.

March 16, 1926: Near a cabbage patch on Effie Ward's farm in Auburn, Massachusetts, three men and a woman, bundled against the cold, stood watching a curious apparatus of steel tubing somewhat like a jungle gym. One man approached the thing with a blowtorch on a long pole and touched it off. A sudden roar, which continued for about ten seconds, and it began to move—almost imperceptibly at first; then, gaining speed, it took off from the frame, zoomed 41 feet up, arched, plunged, and hit the frozen ground 184 feet away.

Robert Hutchings Goddard had brought the world perceptibly nearer the space age—which finally arrived 31 years later—by launching the first rocket using a liquid propellant.

A modest man who mostly kept his soaring dreams to himself, Goddard was to live and work in relative obscurity until his death in 1945 two months before his 63rd birthday. Only three months before he died, as World War II wound down, Wernher von Braun and the German scientists under him who had developed the V-2 long-range ballistic missile at Peenemünde came over to the Americans. When American intelligence officers asked him for details about the German rockets, one of the engineers suggested that they ask Dr. Goddard—of whom they had barely heard—about the principles. The design of a rocket built by Goddard in 1939 had, as he himself observed, essentially the same features as the German V-2 of 1944.

Even then, recognition was not forthcoming, though Goddard had developed the forerunner of the World War II bazooka and demonstrated it to the Army a few days before the armistice in 1918, and had developed liquid-propellant jet-assisted takeoff during World War II. There were 214 patents filed and issued in his name, ranging from the significant features of the modern rocket (in 1914) to an oscillator that anticipated the radio tube.

His monograph written for the Smithsonian Institution—his first backer and for years his only one, supplying most of his research funds from 1917 to 1929—was titled "A Method of Reaching Extreme Altitudes." In it he speculated that Man might send a payload to the moon with a multistage rocket. Goddard's speculations on moon flight attracted wide attention, but they were only a small part of that 1919 paper. Unknown to the public were four unsolicited reports Goddard made for the Smithsonian in which he spelled out his dreams of interplanetary flight. They were kept secret at his request, and not published until 1970.

Some of his ideas were summarized two years earlier, however, by Frederick C. Durant III, assistant director for astronautics at the National Air and Space Museum, who has written extensively on Goddard. The ideas are remarkably familiar to a follower of space exploits of the past few decades. According to Durant, the first (1920) report alone discusses manned and unmanned space probes, photography of the moon and planets, gyro-stabilization, flight-path corrections by small rocket motors, solar-powered electric propulsion, tracking of spacecraft, a reentry heat shield—and the advantages of liquid hydrogen and oxygen as ideal propellants. By the third paper he was including a 1,200-pound manned "observation compartment" in his designs, while in the fourth he discusses the advantages of electron and ion rocket engines.

The *New York Times,* which in 1920 editorially scoffed that the inventor lacked "the knowledge ladled out daily in our high schools," printed a retraction 49 years later while Apollo 11 cruised toward the moon: "It is now definitely established that a rocket can function in a vacuum. The Times regrets the error."

By 1960 the federal government acknowledged that it had infringed on Goddard's patents for the liquid-propellant engine used in the Atlas, Thor, Jupiter, Redstone and Vanguard rockets. It settled for a million dollars, and Goddard's widow gave half to the Daniel and Florence Guggenheim Foundation, which had financed almost all of his research between 1930 and 1941 in Roswell, New Mexico.

Today, the monuments have been built, the books have been written, and fame has come to this representative of the great solitary tinkerer-inventors who are so much a part of America's legend.

But one thinks back to that day 50 years ago at Aunt Effie's farm. It was a

Tuesday. Goddard met his machinist, Henry Sachs, at the physics shop of Clark University in Worcester, where he had been teaching physics for 12 years, and the two men drove to nearby Auburn, to Pakachoag Hill, with two tanks of liquid oxygen casually laid between them on the seat of the coupé and trailer jouncing behind.

The rocket weighed 5¾ pounds empty and 10¼ pounds loaded with gasoline and liquid oxygen. The previous December, it had lifted its own weight in the static testing rack, hanging in the air for 27 seconds, and now it was to be cast loose.

The advantages of liquid propellants over the ancient gunpowder-type solid fuel were that it was more powerful and could be metered and controlled. A major problem was directing the two liquids (oxygen and gasoline) into the combustion chamber. This posed great technical difficulties, because oxygen remains a liquid only below −297 degrees F. As it vaporizes, it creates pressure in the oxygen tank. Goddard used this pressure to force both propellants into the combustion chamber.

These two liters of liquid oxygen were the last that Linde Air Products Company in Worcester would be able to provide until April. So there was no room for mistakes. All morning the two men erected the apparatus, the two-foot-long motor on top, the fuel tanks below (they were to be reversed a few months later), ten feet of tubing connecting them, one line for gasoline, the other for oxygen. The sheet steel came from England. Valves and nozzles had to be designed and handmade as the project developed.

Noon came and went. Percy Roope, assistant professor of physics at Clark, arrived with Esther, Goddard's young wife. Mrs. Goddard was to operate the movie camera, which ran seven seconds.

At the farmhouse, Effie Ward ("She was right out of a book," Mrs. Goddard recalled) offered a last cup of hot malted milk, and the little group headed outdoors again, pulling on mittens and buttoning coats to the neck. It was 2:30 p.m.

Thirty feet away, turning a handle on an oxygen cylinder, Goddard let oxygen into the rocket. At liftoff the hose would pull free and a valve would shut on the rocket. The launch was simple: a blowtorch was used to heat an igniter filled with black powder above the motor, and when that started to burn, valves were opened, releasing gasoline and liquid oxygen into the combustion chamber. The last chore was to ignite a little alcohol burner under the liquid oxygen tank to speed its vaporizing.

Goddard and Roope stepped behind a protective sheet iron barricade. Sachs set off the black powder with his blowtorch, lit the burner and raced back to join them. Mrs. Goddard's camera, which had been recording all this, ran down.

A sharp bang. A white blast from the nozzle. A long pause, a lazy movement upward, then acceleration.

"Even though the release was pulled," Goddard reported in his notes the next day, "the rocket did not rise at first but the flame came out, and there was a steady roar. After a number of seconds it rose, slowly until it cleared the frame, and then at express train speed, curving over to the left, and striking the ice and snow, still going at a rapid rate.

"It looked almost magical as it rose, without any appreciably greater noise or flame. . . ."

The flight was 2½ seconds long.

One person of whom it made a believer was Mrs. Goddard. Before that day, she said, the whole business had seemed somewhat abstract. Seeing it go up, she could finally share his excitement and elation.

"He didn't say much," she recalled, "but you ask any inventor about his invention when it works for the first time, and there's just nothing like it."

They were worried about the reaction of neighbors, but there was none. "It was real noisy, but only for a few seconds," she said. The problem was to arise three years later, when a rocket burned up and set small fires in the field, and frantic phone calls by neighbors brought policemen up the hill looking for the remains of a plane crash.

Soon after that, the state fire marshal decided Aunt Effie's farm was too close to civilization, and banished Goddard's rockets from Auburn, ultimately resulting in the move to New Mexico.

Mrs. Goddard, who still lives in the family home in Worcester, did remember an audience for the early rocket shots, however.

"There were woods around the field," she said, "and after a rocket went off those trees would erupt little boys. Two dozen of them. The woods were alive with them. Sneaked up there to watch. When we had a fire, they'd come out and help stamp out the embers."

It was a shame, she added, that Bob Goddard never lived to see the moon rockets whose feasibility he had predicted with such prescience—not merely predicted, but demonstrated—at a time when the world's other space pioneers were still working equations on paper.

Percy Roope, today living in retirement in California, remembers that launch clearly. Especially he remembers Dr. Goddard's immediate reaction:

"He was calm, he always was quiet and cool. But you could tell he was really excited. He flushed up a bit. . . . Afterward we went back and had coffee and talked about it."

Roope lives very close to Vandenberg Air Force Base, a center for rocket missile tests and experiments.

"Oh yes," he observed quietly, "I see 'em going by every so often. . . ."

LENGTH: 1750 WORDS

36   Fiftieth Anniversary of the Rocket

SCORING: Reading time: _____ Rate from chart: _____ W.P.M.

PURPOSE	number right _____ × 4 equals _____ points	
GENERALITIES	number right _____ × 4 equals _____ points	
RETENTION	number right _____ × 2 equals _____ points	
COMPLETION	number right _____ × 3 equals _____ points	
DEFINITIONS	number right _____ × 2 equals _____ points	

(Total points: 100) **total** _____ points

PURPOSE   Which of the following phrases best expresses the purpose of the passage? _____

1. to suggest ways in which individuals may help the progress of science.

2. to show that the work of individual inventors sometimes has a powerful influence on later developments.

3. to show how teams of experts are needed to achieve scientific breakthroughs.

GENERALITIES   Based on the passage, which of the following generalities seem justifiable? _____ and _____.

1. German scientists recognized Goddard's achievement sooner than Americans did.

2. Effie Ward had a keen understanding of what inventors really needed.

3. There were very few sources of financial support for Goddard's early work.

4. Our entire space program depended on inventors like Dr. Goddard.

RETENTION   Based on the passage, which of the following statements are True (T), False (F), or Not answerable (N)?

1. _____ Wernher von Braun and his colleagues deserted the German side before the war ended.

2. _____ Goddard's first liquid-propellant flight was only 2½ seconds long.

3. _____ Mrs. Goddard's film of the flight was studied by the United States government.

4. _____ The Goddard home is in New Mexico.

5. _____ The rocket was launched with a match.

6. _____ Goddard's first liquid-propellant flight was in Auburn, Massachusetts.

7. _____ There were no telephones in the neighborhood of the launching.

8. _____ Dr. Goddard survived his wife by only a year.

9. _____ A fire set by a later rocket experiment was thought to be caused by a plane crash.

10. _____ Dr. Goddard had no official position at Clark University.

11. _____ The German V-2 rocket was a long-range ballistic missile.

12. _____ One of the liquids used for propelling the rocket was gasoline.

13. _____ Hot malted milk is also a liquid propellant.

14. _____ Oxygen becomes liquid at −150° F.

15. _____ Neighbor boys used to watch the experimental launchings.

16. _____ Percy Roope was a professor of physics at Clark.

17. _____ Mrs. Goddard was excited about the rocket project from the very first.

18. _____ No one is alive, according to the article, who saw the first launching.

19. _____ The United States government tests rockets in California.

20. _____ The first launch, as described, was virtually soundless.

COMPLETION   Choose the best answer for each question.

1. _____ One of the organizations that gave Goddard financial support was: (a) the National Science Foundation. (b) Yale University. (c) the Smithsonian Institution. (d) the Auburn Foundation for Science.

2. _____ In 1920 the *New York Times* declared that a rocket could not travel in: (a) parabolas. (b) a vacuum. (c) the ionosphere. (d) defiance of gravity.

3. _____ Goddard's later papers on rocketry anticipated: (a) modern discoveries. (b) the problems von Braun had. (c) space travel and

multistage rockets.　(d) the unusual political implications of space-shuttle diplomacy.

4. _____ From the time Goddard's rocket was launched in 1926, to the space shot to the moon was only:　(a) eleven years.　(b) twenty years.　(c) thirty-one years.　(d) forty-nine years.

5. _____ Goddard's speculations about flights to the moon were made public in:　(a) the *New York Times*.　(b) 1919.　(c) *National Geographic*.　(d) 1970.

6. _____ One weapon Goddard developed and demonstrated in 1918 was the:　(a) armored tank.　(b) high-ignition bomb.　(c) electron ray.　(d) bazooka.

DEFINITIONS　Choose the best definition for each italicized word.

1. _____ it moved *imperceptibly:*　(a) silently　(b) suddenly　(c) fiercely　(d) slightly

2. _____ a curious *apparatus:*　(a) machine　(b) phenomenon　(c) thing　(d) modality

3. _____ the world was *perceptibly* nearer:　(a) somewhat　(b) noticeably　(c) now　(d) in some senses

4. _____ the *feasibility* of the plans:　(a) probability　(b) possibility　(c) ability　(d) applicability

5. _____ they were *essentially* the same:　(a) more or less　(b) precisely　(c) at times　(d) basically

6. _____ to *operate* the camera:　(a) stop　(b) start　(c) run　(d) open

7. _____ oscillator that *anticipated* the radio tube:　(a) made obsolete　(b) came before　(c) looked like　(d) struck out against

8. _____ print a *retraction:*　(a) accusation　(b) libel　(c) statement explaining the issues　(d) statement taking back certain views

9. _____ four *unsolicited* reports:　(a) unwanted　(b) unasked for　(c) unanswered　(d) unplanned and therefore spontaneous

10. _____ *solitary* tinker-inventors:　(a) lone　(b) cold　(c) arrested　(d) unique

11. _____ they *infringed on* his patents:　(a) went back on　(b) insisted on　(c) violated　(d) ultimately incapacitated

12. _____ follower of space *exploits:* (a) shots (b) travels (c) adventures (d) ships

13. _____ the government *acknowledged* its actions: (a) admitted (b) suddenly took a hard look at (c) hid (d) saw the foolishness of

14. _____ they recognized Goddard's *prescience:* (a) intelligence (b) commitment to his work (c) anticipation of ideas to come (d) awareness of flight in general

15. _____ his rockets were *banished* from Auburn: (a) shot (b) sent away (c) executed (d) identified as being

37 *LYNWOOD MARK RHODES*

The Real American Cowboy

There is probably no more distinctive a figure in American history than the cowboy. Europeans often think that he still exists as he used to and that much of America is like the plains and cattle-lands he once roamed. He's been so idealized that it is sometimes difficult to recognize what he was really like.

Swaggering, self-confident, tall-in-the-saddle, he is one of the most distinctive and durable figures in American history. His hey-day lasted only from the end of the Civil War until the mid-1880's, and in that brief span no more than 40,000 of his breed rode the cattle trails across the Great Plains.

"It would be . . . difficult to imagine a replacement for him," says historian William Savage, Jr. Only the cowboy, that lanky man on horseback, "has captured and held the imagination of the American people with an interest undiminished by time."

Yet, no folk hero in our history has ever been so misunderstood or unfaithfully represented as the real, dyed-in-the-wool cowboy.

And most of them were just that—boys between the ages of 18 and 25.

Some were mustered-out Union veterans. Far more were former Rebels, especially Texans. Even a few sailors exchanged the sea for the arid plains, in time remodeling their favorite chantey of "O, bury me not in the deep, deep sea" to go "O, bury me not on the lone prairie." Still others were penniless immigrants, moneyed Easterners (including future President Teddy Roosevelt, who went to North Dakota to learn to rope and ride in 1883), rangeland drifters and men on the dodge from the law. And, contrary to Hollywood, nearly one cowboy in three was either Mexican, Indian or black — most of the latter former slaves.

THE REAL AMERICAN COWBOY   *The American Legion Magazine,* September 1976. Copyright 1977, The American Legion Magazine, reprinted by permission.

Whatever his race or color, a cowboy's job was simply more tiring than heroic, more boring than romantic. He was a hired hand—"a dirty, overworked laborer who fried his brains under a prairie sun" that might reach 100° in the shade on a summer noon, or "rode endless miles in rain and wind to mend fences or look for lost calves" during a "blue norther" that could drop the thermometer 50° in a day. His hours were long, usually 18 a day, seven days a week; his pay a measly $25 to $40 a month with "found," as room and board were called; and his common educational level was lower grade school.

Exposure to the elements in cattle country brought on pneumonia, second only to being dragged by a horse as the leading cause of cowboy deaths. Yet such tribulations were part of the game and, if mentioned at all, turned up in his rueful ballads. He sang of loneliness ("I'm a poor lonesome cowboy and a long way from home"), of death, ("I spied a young cowboy wrapped up in white linen, as cold as the clay"), of life's harsh realities ("I wash in a pool and wipe on a sack; I carry my wardrobe all on my back"). But in the 1870's, men took to punching cattle "as a preacher's son takes to vice," according to one colorful old-timer.

Not that our movie and TV image of the cowboy entirely lacks truth. Most cowboys *were* the tall, silent type. In fact, taciturnity was a way-of-life, especially at meals. About the only time tongues ran free was in swearing. "Cowboy talk," says historian William Forbis, "assayed somewhere around one-third profanity and obscenity, which was directed at horses and cattle or used as the salt and pepper of ordinary speech."

The upshot was an underlying, rough humor that helped the cowboy endure while carrying himself with a sort of vinegary pride laced with bravado and exaggeration. An Englishman visiting a ranch unknowingly tweaked the peppery quirk when he inquired of a cowpuncher, "Is your master at home?" The range rider looked at him levelly and replied, "The son of a bitch hasn't been born yet." There was no humor, however, in the reverent feelings he reserved for women—at least, the nice-girl portions of womankind.

"He made love on almost a seasonal schedule, as though in a rut" with cattle-town prostitutes, says historian Paul Horgan, but his longing for storybook love was so great that it was unreal, a chivalry-type love that put a virtuous female "on a pedestal from which she could be worshipped but not touched." For marriage was a mode of life that most cowboys had to shun since they were always on the move and their pay was too low to support a family in any case. Still, they yearned for the company of "good" women and a lonesome cowboy would travel miles, by one account, "just to sit on a porch for an hour or two and watch some homesteader's red-faced daughter rock her chair and scratch her elbows—and not a smack or a hug."

The nearest living being he could turn to with affection was his horse.

Few cowboys actually owned one. The ranch they worked for supplied their mounts from its remuda or common pool of horses. It was usually a stocky, sturdy pony, descended from the ornery Spanish mustang, which made it a natural-born animal with endurance, stamina and—best of all—"cow sense" in controlling cattle, "as sensitive as a suitor to their changing moods." Beyond that, it was his daylong companion and helper, obeying his orders as it took him in and out of danger.

"My horse," said a cowboy in his domesticated old age, "was something alive, something friendly and true . . . and for him I had a profound feeling. I sometimes think back on my remarkable horses in much the same way that I think back on certain friends that have left me. Many a time I have divided the water in a canteen with a horse. I went hungry sometimes, but if there was any possible way of getting food for my horse or if there was a place to stake him, even though I had to walk back a mile after putting him to graze, I never let him go hungry."

Which was quite a tribute since the real cowboy was strictly a riding man and detested walking, even for short distances. About the farthest he condescended to walk was from the corral to the bunkhouse. He might gripe about a chore, but he shirked nothing—if it could be done on the back of a horse where he was master of his fate. But unhorsed, says "Teddy Blue" Abbott, himself an old cowhand, "was like a man overboard at sea, prey to anything the plains had to offer." It was the dread a cowboy feared most. As cowhand Jo Mora put it, a cowboy dismounted was "just a plain, bowlegged human who smelled horsey at times, slept in his underwear and was given to boils and dyspepsia."

The truth is, he normally wore long johns unless it was too hot; a stout cotton flannel shirt; tight-fitting trousers sewn with coarse yellow thread or of dark wool fortified with buckskin that stayed up by themselves since suspenders chafed him and he rarely wore a belt; a cloth or leather vest unbuttoned to prevent sweating but "with deep pockets where he kept his Bull Durham tobacco;" and a bandanna of tough silk around his neck which he used for everything from a mask to filter out trail dust to a tourniquet in case of rattlesnake bite.

On his boots, which might cost more than $50 a pair—two months' wages—he wore spurs of silver or iron whose jinglebobs made a sound that was music to his ears. At work, he also donned a pair of bullhide, seatless leggings of Spanish origin called *chaparreras*—later Americanized to "chaps"—that reached from ankle to groin, buckled or tied at the waist, and shielded him against thorny thickets and rope burns. And he always wore a hat—Wide brimmed to protect him from sun and wind, the crown dented into a pyramid or flattened, it was his proudest, most personal possession. A cowboy so hated to be without his hat that Western etiquette allowed him to wear it when he sat down to a meal indoors. Sometimes, he even wore it to bed.

The standardized Levi's, boots with decorative hand-stitching and beautifully crafted Stetsons came later. But when fully outfitted at the zenith of the cowboy era in 1876, a cowpuncher's head-to-toe garb "identified him as distinctly as a knight's armor identified its owner." He still led a hulluva life, though—and that's putting it mildly.

His home was a bunkhouse, often just a shack made from weatherboard or cottonwood logs. It was stifling in summer, numbing in winter. Cowboys "might spruce up their quarters with a coat of whitewash on the walls, maybe a real wood floor over the dirt, buffalo robes or wolfskins for the bunks and perhaps a crude fireplace," but no one ever got rid of an instantly recognizable feature all bunkhouses shared: a distinctive aroma.

They smelled to high heaven—a nose-twitching composite, according to a gasping account, "of sweaty men, dry cow manure, the licorice in chewing tobacco plugs, old work boots, and the smoke from lamps that burned coal oil or even tallow rendered from the generous supply of skunks that scavenged around the ranches." Clothes were "hung on the floor," supposedly "so they wouldn't fall down and get lost." Cowpuncher Charlie Siringo recalled an iron-clad rule his bunkhouse pals made "that whoever was caught picking gray backs [lice] off and throwing them on the floor without first killing them should pay a fine of ten cents for every offense."

Yet, astonishingly enough, some cowboys found the bunkhouse atmosphere downright homey and, in later years, more than one got a lump in the throat remembering the twangy choruses of "There's an Empty Cot in the Bunkhouse Tonight" that his guitar-strumming buddies sang.

If comfort came far down on any list of necessities, it was because a ranch's primary purpose was the care and well-being of cattle, not people. The critter that cowboys watched over and worried about was the longhorn that evolved from cattle brought to the Americas by Spanish *conquistadores*.

There never was enough sleep for the weary cowhands and rarely enough water for the cattle on the parched prairies where less than 15 inches of rain might fall in a year. Andy Adams in his classic, "The Log of a Cowboy," once noticed a heat-crazed herd deliberately walk into the sides of the horses. "For the first time," he wrote, "a fact dawned on us that chilled the marrow in our bones—the herd was going blind" from lack of water.

Indians constantly tried to beg or steal cows. Settlers drove the herds from their fields with guns. And a clap of thunder, a bolt of lightning, a coyote's yelp, a horse's whinny could set off a stampede.

Cowboys tried to slow the charge by flailing their slickers in the faces of the leaders or firing their guns to the stampeders' ears. After three or four terrifying hours, the cattle usually began to circle, then mill. This was one of the most dangerous times for cowhands. With the herd jammed so closely together, a trapped horseman might be jostled from his mount. At the end of one stampede, horrified cowboys came upon "the remains of a comrade who had fallen to the ground beneath the circling crush of hooves. Nothing was left but a gun butt."

In the worst stampede in history, in July 1876, a big herd plunged into a gully near the Brazos River in Texas. When it was over 2,000 steers were either dead or missing.

With luck, a day's drive generally averaged about ten miles. But "folks didn't really drive cattle," an old puncher explained, "they moved 'em." A few dominant steers always took the lead early on a trail drive and stayed out front like pied pipers, the other cows following instinctively. Except that there were dozens of rivers to cross and it was a rare crossing that went smoothly.

Cows mired in quicksand; panicked and drowned in deep water; the lead steer might decide not to jump in or, once in, turn back. Worse yet, "cattle would not swim if they could not see the opposite bank; neither would they swim with the sun in their eyes," writes historian Joe Frantz. A cowboy tells of one crossing when a herd massed in midstream, swimming aimlessly in a circle. He stripped to his underwear, swam his horse to the mill and jumped "right into the cattle. They were so jammed together that it was like walking on a raft of logs. When I got the only real big steer in the bunch on the yon side, I mounted him and he pulled for the shore." The herd followed. It was quite a feat. Cowboys hated deep water; many could not swim at all.

The drive ended each afternoon about 5 o'clock when the herd neared the site chosen by the trail boss for the night's bed-ground. "I do not know of anything more satisfying," mused a cowboy years later, "than seeing cattle come in on their bed-ground at night so full and contented that they grunt when they lie down," chewing their cud from grazing on the buffalo and grama grass that covered the plains.

He could have added that their diet was as monotonous as a cowboy's. A chuckwagon cook kindled a fire for supper with brush or dried cow manure, dubbed "prairie coal," collected during the day ("getting the stuff required gloves; there was a scorpion under almost every cow chip") and inevitably ladled up the same meal every night—"prairie strawberries" as the boys called beans, fried bacon that passed under the name of "overland trout," cornbread, sorghum molasses, and always coffee. A cowboy drank a quart or more a day "boiled from whole beans" but, as one said, "you would hesitate if judging from appearance, whether to call it coffee or ink."

On rare occasions, the cook butchered a young cow to make "the gourmet dish known as sonofabitch stew for which there were nearly as many recipes as there were range cooks."

After supper, the men swapped yarns, rolled cigarettes, and fell asleep listening to their buddies on the first watch singing hymns—"Ole One Hundred" was a favorite—or sentimental lullabies to calm the herd. The cows usually stirred only once during the night—if all went well—when they rose at 11 o'clock to lie down in a new position. But there were four guard changes through the night.

No matter that a cowboy licked horse sweat from a saddle when the chuck wagon ran out of salt, or that he got a paltry $100 in hard wages in return for three or four months of dust, thirst, blisters, cold and danger. What counted was "the glorious oasis" at trail's end, "a place to get a bath and a haircut, a woman and a bottle of 'Kansas sheep dip,' " as he called his rot-gut whiskey.

"Money and whiskey flowed like water down hill," an eyewitness said of the rip-roaring sprees in Abilene, Dodge City, Newton, Wichita and other Kansas cattle-towns. Eager haberdashers outfitted him in new clothes, at hastily marked-up prices; and saloons enticed him with gambling games of poker, faro and monte. He paired off with the bar girls—a "calico queen" or a "painted cat"—to pound the dance floor for hours "with Indian yells" and foot-stomping shenanigans. Or he made a beeline for the red-light districts where lusty prostitutes with names like Hambone Jane, Big Nose Kate, the Galloping Cow and Squirrel Tooth Alice hung out in "quarters like cattle stalls." An occasional cowboy passed up the hoopla. "Attended Sabbath school this A.M. and . . . it was the most pleasant hour I spent since leaving home."

It's true that most cowboys painted the towns red, letting off steam with liquor and a compulsion to shoot up the streets with blazing Colt revolvers. But the lawless tag history pins on every cowhand as a sharp-shooting hombre with a gun who, in the words of western scholar Walter Prescott Webb, "wears it low and pulls it smokin' " doesn't jibe with the facts. He admittedly had courage with a six-shooter or in the face of one, for the law of the West permitted a gun in protecting one's life, but "the average cowboy was not a gunman, nor had he a notch in his gun," says historian Joe Frantz. "His occupation was tending cattle" and that took up most of his time. Many a cowboy didn't even tote a gun in his regular duties or, if he did, used it "to kill a rattlesnake, to finish off a horse that had a broken leg or to turn aside a stampede."

We forget, points out William Savage, that the eight-inch barreled Colt weighed two and a quarter pounds—not including its ammunition—and when "fully loaded was a rather heavy piece of iron to fire accurately." It wasn't likely to hit where aimed beyond 25 to 30 yards. A more deadly weapon was his Winchester rifle, but he didn't even take it far because "a large firearm was awkward to hand-hold and when carried in a saddle scabbard, it rubbed against his horse, producing sores" or could easily snag his reins or lariat.

Live and—with exceptions—let live was his philosophy more often than not. Homer Grigsby, a cowhand for many years, admitted that he "never saw a gun drawn on another man except by a feverish greenhorn who had heard that courage in the West was proved with a Colt." His hung-head confession is closer to the truth than commonly supposed. "There is a good deal of exaggeration about us cowboys," said one puncher at the time. "We're not near so bad as we're painted. We like to get up a little racket now and then, but it's all play." As time passed, upright citizens even outlawed that by forbidding firearms within city limits. Dodge City managed to hold out the longest, well into the mid-1880's, boasting that it was "The Beautiful, Bibulous Babylon of the Frontier," yet none of the cattle-towns ever truly surpassed the first of the boomtowns—Abilene.

It was here that Americans discovered the cowboy first displaying for a national audience "those extremes of temperament that make a hero." Here he first stood on a chute and forced steers into rail cars with a prod that gave him a lasting nickname—cowpoke. Here he first strutted down wooden sidewalks, "his spurs jingling loudly, suggesting fatality like a rattlesnake's rattling." Here he sowed his wild oats and, as one cowhand later owned up, "I regret to say I also sowed all the money I made right along with the oats." For here, after a few days of frolic and debauchery, he started back home in a cheap new suit "the color of which we never knew" until the next sunup, but usually dead broke from "a poker hand that swallowed his whole wad" and only memories about "the way we drank and gambled and threw the girls around. . . ."

And here, in Kansas, he became a legend.

William (Buffalo Bill) Cody almost singlehandedly transformed the cowboy into a larger-than-life figure with his "Wild West" show in 1884. Aided by a New York pulp writer called Ned Buntline, Cody took a handsome, six-foot five-inch Texas cowpuncher named William Levi (Buck) Taylor, dressed him up in fancy chaps, and billed him as "King of the Cowboys." Taylor thus became the first bona fide cowboy matinee idol. Dime novels, romanticized reports of Western travelers, silent movies, talkies, then television, did the rest, adding to the grand illusion by providing "erstwhile cowgirls with moxie," trail-hardened cowhands who blushed at the slightest mention of sex, and a zesty man of brawn who carried his action on his hips, shooting more and talking less but always using his Colt "on the side of good, thwarting evil with a hail of righteous lead that punctuated his drawled homilies." It was the stuff that dreams are made of.

Cowboys cooperated in forever fixing these ideas of their glamorized life in America's imagination by continuing to move through their sweaty, dirty jobs with a posturing pride. One cowhand, when asked on the witness stand why he killed a neighbor, thought for a moment, shrugged his shoulders and answered, "Because he was a thief, an outlaw, and just a little slow." Humility simply wasn't part of a cowboy's character. "If one man dismounted to talk, the other also stepped down from his horse so they could meet eye-to-eye on equal terms," according to the code of the West.

But it was the expansion of the railroads, a glutted cattle market, the disastrous winter blizzards of 1885-86, a changing taste for more tender beef, and—all important—barbed wire that literally fenced the cowboy in, pulling up short by 1892 one of the most colorful eras in American history.

Even so, he needs no apologies, nor a debunking. He wasn't a saint and he didn't pretend to be. "The American cowboy," sums up Joe Frantz, "has carved a niche—niche nothing, it's a gorge—in American affection as a folk hero." And, today, if we nostalgically remember him not the way he was but the way we *think* he was . . . well, maybe the reason is that he was "the last American to live a life of wild freedom," self-reliant and less dependent on government and machines.

After all, it was the real cowboy who first tied the Great Plains together—not by rescuing a beautiful damsel in distress and riding off into the sunset with his arm about her waist, but by driving an estimated 5.5 million cantankerous longhorns up from Texas between 1867 and 1887. Not by being the lithe, perfect knight in Owen Wister's "The Virginian," but by being himself—brash and arrogant, dirty and saddle-sore, bold and courageous. "A lot of sunshine put that squint in his eyes," says western chronicler Ramon Adams, "and a lot of prairie wind tanned his face."

LENGTH: 3650 WORDS

37 The Real American Cowboy

```
┌─────────────────────────────────────────────────────────────────────┐
│ SCORING:    Reading time: _____ Rate from chart: _____ W.P.M. │
├─────────────────────────────────────────────────────────────────────┤
│         PURPOSE        number right _____ × 4 equals _____ points       │
│                                                                         │
│         GENERALITIES   number right _____ × 4 equals _____ points       │
│                                                                         │
│         RETENTION      number right _____ × 2 equals _____ points       │
│                                                                         │
│         COMPLETION     number right _____ × 3 equals _____ points       │
│                                                                         │
│         DEFINITIONS    number right _____ × 2 equals _____ points       │
├─────────────────────────────────────────────────────────────────────┤
│              (Total points: 100) total _____ points                    │
└─────────────────────────────────────────────────────────────────────┘
```

PURPOSE Which of the following phrases best expresses the purpose of the passage? _____

1. to show historical facts can become romantic legends.

2. to show that cowboys really earned every bit of "legend" they got.

3. to help establish a valid portrait of the western cowboy.

GENERALITIES Based on the passage, which of the following generalities seem justifiable? _____ and _____.

1. The movie portrait of the cowboy is much closer to reality than not.

2. Even many former cowboys became sentimental about their past way of life.

3. The cowboy was an inevitable part of the expansion of the United States.

4. Economic and geographic conditions "created" the cowboy.

RETENTION Based on the passage, which of the following statements are True (T), False (F), or Not answerable (N)?

1. _____ In all, there were probably no more than forty thousand original cowboys.

2. _____ Apparently, cowboys did not really sing cowboy songs.

3. _____ A cowboy's working day started at 8:00 A.M. and ended at 5:00 P.M.

4. _____ Living conditions were not so good, but food was really excellent.

5. _____ The leading cause of cowboy deaths was being dragged by a horse.

6. _____ One thing the cowboy was legendary for was not cursing.

7. _____ Most cowboys were the tall, silent type.

8. _____ Most cowboys could soon own their own horses.

9. _____ The unbuttoned leather vest prevented sweating.

10. _____ The cowboy's hat was his proudest personal possession.

11. _____ Longhorn steers evolved from Spanish cattle.

12. _____ Texans made the best and most legendary cowboys.

13. _____ More than two thousand steers were dead or missing after the worst stampede in history.

14. _____ Without cowboys for leaders, the steers on a trail drive always went in circles.

15. _____ The portrait of the cowboy "painting the town red" is false.

16. _____ The cowboys staunchly refused to patronize prostitutes.

17. _____ Few cowboys were fast, accurate shots with their Colts.

18. _____ Buffalo Bill's "Wild West Show" of 1884 made a "star" of the cowboy.

19. _____ The railroads and barbed wire helped end the era of the cowboy.

20. _____ The cowboy era lasted from about 1867 to 1887, just twenty years.

COMPLETION   Choose the best answer for each question.

1. _____ One reason the cowboy is a kind of culture hero is that he was the last of the Americans who lived: (a) hard and fast.   (b) amidst real danger.   (c) a life of independence.   (d) with and by the gun.

2. _____ One thing the cowboy never had enough of was: (a) sleep.   (b) whiskey.   (c) churchgoing.   (d) petticoat government.

3. _____ William Levi Taylor became the first: (a) casualty in the rail wars.   (b) cowboy matinee idol.   (c) rancher to use the railroad.   (d) of the singing cowboys.

4. _____ The first of the cowboy boomtowns was: (a) Salinas.   (b) Bibulous Babylon.   (c) Dodge City.   (d) Abilene.

5. _____ Prairie coal was actually: (a) sorghum molasses.   (b) scarce.   (c) cow dung.   (d) scorpion leavings.

6. _____ Apparently, some of the cowboys kept: (a) collections of pigeons. (b) in touch with their families. (c) careful journals. (d) up with the times.

DEFINITIONS Choose the best definition for each italicized word.

1. _____ he was a *durable* figure: (a) big (b) dumb (c) long-lasting (d) sweet

2. _____ a *taciturn* fellow: (a) polite (b) sturdy (c) silent (d) flashy

3. _____ the *arid* plains: (a) dry (b) vast (c) deadly (d) mysteriously quiet

4. _____ no one *shirked* a job: (a) lost (b) got (c) took on (d) avoided

5. _____ they had boils and *dyspepsia:* (a) arthritis (b) a fear of horses (c) indigestion (d) an awareness of their transience

6. _____ it *assayed* one-third profanity: (a) preferred (b) was evaluated at (c) soon became (d) never could reach the peak of

7. _____ horse with *stamina:* (a) endurance (b) friends (c) sickness (d) goods

8. _____ an *ornery* mustang: (a) native (b) tough (c) sweet (d) preposterous

9. _____ those cowboy *homilies:* (a) cabins (b) grits (c) sermons (d) historians

10. _____ *tribulations* were usual: (a) trials (b) days (c) distresses (d) poachers

11. _____ *undiminished* by time: (a) not lessened (b) not hurt (c) saved (d) seen

12. _____ *reverent* feelings for women: (a) pious (b) silly (c) neat (d) worshipful

13. _____ a *mode* of life: (a) style (b) necessity (c) result (d) encroachment

14. _____ he *donned* leggings: (a) gave up (b) put on (c) sat in (d) reached for

15. _____ a distinctive *aroma:* (a) feature (b) sight (c) problem (d) odor

38 *MERRILL LINDSAY*

The Hamilton — Burr Duel:
The Pistols Were Rigged

*Alexander Hamilton and Aaron Burr were two of the most powerful politi-
cians in America in the years immediately after the Revolution, and they
vied with each other for preeminence. Ultimately, they fought a duel that
resulted in Hamilton's death and Burr's exile. Merrill Lindsay explains that
the pistols were rigged in such a way as to give Hamilton an edge. But
events did not work out as planned.*

The sensational duel between Alexander Hamilton and Aaron Burr
has taken its place among American legends, along with Washington chopping
down the cherry tree. Hamilton, says the legend, brilliant former Secretary of the
Treasury and driving force of the Federalist Party (who sought a strong central
government), was ruthlessly gunned down by Burr, Vice President under Jefferson and later tried for treason because of his mad plan to set up a Mississippi
Valley empire. Hamilton, mortally wounded in the shoot-out, gasped that he
had never intended to fire. The truth is, the pistol in Hamilton's hand did indeed
shoot harmlessly high, its ball striking a tree behind Burr, 12 feet up. Hamilton
has always come across as the good guy, tragically slain. Burr has always worn
the black hat.

Until recently, few have questioned this legend. And no one has looked at an
important piece of surviving evidence—the pistols with which the duel was
fought.

THE HAMILTON–BURR DUEL: THE PISTOLS WERE RIGGED   "Pistols Shed Light on Famed Duel" by
Merrill Lindsay. Copyright 1976 Smithsonian Institution, from *Smithsonian* Magazine, November
1976.

Let us explore a few facts. Burr came of illustrious parentage: his father was the second president of Princeton (then the College of New Jersey), his mother the daughter of Jonathan Edwards. In the Revolution, young Aaron was a gallant officer under General Benedict Arnold during the disastrous march on Quebec; later saved his brigade during the battle of Long Island; later still served creditably at Valley Forge and Monmouth. In politics he won the same number of votes as Jefferson for the Presidency, became Vice President upon decision by the House of Representatives. One edition of the *Encyclopaedia Britannica* notes, "His fair and judicial manner as president of the senate, recognized even by his bitterest enemies, helped to foster traditions in regard to that position. . . ." He was "generous to a fault, and was intensely devoted to his wife and daughter."

Hamilton, illegitimately born on one of the Leeward islands in the Caribbean, rose to prominence during the Revolution when he served as an artillery officer under Washington and also as aide-de-camp to the Commander in Chief. He married into the powerful Schuyler family and played a major role in forming a nation rather than a confederation of states.

Historians have pointed out that Hamilton, who hated Jefferson, hated Burr more and threw his lot against Burr and the Federalists in their preference for Burr's Presidency. Hamilton also contributed, along with his father-in-law, General Philip Schuyler, to Burr's defeat in his bid for the governorship of New York in 1804, the year of the fateful duel.

No one talks about the very real financial conflict between the two. Hamilton had played a major role in founding the Bank of New York and the Bank of the United States, which for a time enjoyed a virtual monopoly. Burr had an interest in the Manhattan Company, which had been set up to supply clean drinking water to the city of New York. Burr obtained a charter from New York State for the new water company. That company's charter included a clause giving it the right to engage in "moneyed transactions." So the Manhattan Company opened its first bank in competition with Hamilton in 1799, and on the day before its opening, Hamilton's brother-in-law, John B. Church, an experienced dueler who had killed his man in England, insulted Burr. The insult was deliberate, obviously planned and issued in front of Burr's friends. Burr, who could not have relished fighting Church, felt required to challenge him. The duel was fought with Church's pistols. Burr had a button shot off his coat. Church was unharmed.

Five years later, in 1804, a letter in the Albany *Register,* signed by an upcountry clergyman, referred to Hamilton's "despicable opinion" of Burr. Burr demanded satisfaction. Hamilton chose to fight with Church's pistols.

The pistols that Hamilton provided had concealed hair triggers—what a modern target shooter would call a single-set trigger. Church had bought the pair in London. By using them, Hamilton could surreptitiously set his hair trigger without anyone's noticing. This would give Hamilton a theoretical advantage by allowing him to shoot very quickly with a tiny, half-pound squeeze on the trigger. Burr's gun had the same trick trigger, but Burr probably didn't know it. He would fire with the ordinary 10- or 12-pound pull.

Although Hamilton owned a fine pair of correct English dueling pistols, he elected to borrow the trick pair from Church.

With his pistol, the hair trigger set, Hamilton, I maintain, booby-trapped himself that morning of July 11, in Weehawken. Tensely, the two men faced each other. As Hamilton lowered the gun on its target, he was holding a little too tightly and accidentally fired before he had Burr in his sights. Burr squeezed hard and slow and put an aimed shot into Hamilton. The lead .54 caliber ball found Hamilton's liver and killed him within 36 hours.

I have booby-trapped myself many times shooting target guns with single- or double-set triggers, and my only excuse was the tension of a competitive match. Even though no one was pointing a loaded pistol at me, I squeezed too hard too soon and blew my hopes by throwing away a shot, high in the sky.

It is hard to know the intent of the dying Hamilton, who said that he had no intention of shooting Burr. He was either trying to make Burr out to be a cruel scoundrel which he succeeded in doing, or he was trying to divert attention from the pistols, realizing that they would do him no credit if the trick were found.

Actually, the Church pistols have several unusual characteristics which should have disqualified them for use in duels. They have not only concealed set triggers, but weighted bronze fore-ends, adjustable front and rear sights and a .54 caliber bore. While some of these features could be found on a cased pair of gentleman's pistols, none of them would appear on a proper set of dueling pistols.

The caliber for duelers had been established at .50—big enough to do plenty of damage. Proper dueling pistols do not have adjustable sights. Dueling with pistols usually required you to bring your arm down and pull the trigger when your index finger was pointed at your antagonist. You were not to take cold-blooded aim and drill your quarry through the left nipple.

How can we be sure that these pistols are indeed the ones with which Burr killed Hamilton? The bank Burr founded, which is now the Chase Manhattan, has done research in the archives and documents connected with this bit of history. A bank publication establishes that these pistols were used in three duels. The first, as noted, was between Church and Burr. The second was between Hamilton's son Philip and a J. G. Eckhardt—and Philip Hamilton was killed.

After the third and final duel, the pistols were returned to Colonel John B. Church by Hamilton's second, Nathaniel Pendleton. Colonel Church's great granddaughter, Mrs. Mary Helen Church Gilpin, has written about the subsequent history of the pistols:

"John B. Church purchased a large tract of land in Allegheny County in western New York and built the first stone house west of the Allegheny River, calling it Belvedere. In 1805 his son Philip, my grandfather, married the daughter of General Walter Stewart and brought his bride to the old homestead, and it was there that my father, Richard, was born in 1824, his death occurring in 1911. I, too, was born at Belvedere in 1872, and it was in this historic old place on the Genesee River that the pistols and the many interesting letters were kept for three generations."

During the Civil War, Richard Church organized a volunteer company and, owning no side arm of his own, he had one of the Burr-Hamilton pistols converted to percussion from the original flint. Fortunately, only one of the pistols was converted. In 1930, Colonel Church's granddaughter sold the two cased pistols to the Chase Manhattan Bank, where they have resided either in the bank's museum or vaults ever since. It was on the occasion of the U.S. Bicentennial anniversary that David Rockefeller, Chairman of the Board, generously gave permission to the U.S. Bicentennial Society of Richmond, headed by historian Virginius Dabney, to remove the pistols from the vault and have them reproduced. The reproductions, which have been made with complete fidelity to the original surviving flintlock, were made under my supervision by the Italian gunsmith, Walter Agnoletto, who restores ancient arms for museums all over the world.

We had to take the original pistol completely apart to authenticate the reproduction. It was when we removed the lock from the stock that the long-kept secret of the concealed hair trigger came to light.

LENGTH: 2430 WORDS

38 The Hamilton — Burr Duel: The Pistols Were Rigged

SCORING: Reading time: _____ Rate from chart: _____ W.P.M.

PURPOSE	number right _____ × 4 equals _____ points
GENERALITIES	number right _____ × 4 equals _____ points
RETENTION	number right _____ × 2 equals _____ points
COMPLETION	number right _____ × 3 equals _____ points
DEFINITIONS	number right _____ × 2 equals _____ points

(Total points: 100) **total** _____ points

PURPOSE   Which of the following phrases best expresses the purpose of the passage? _____

1. to try to set the record straight about who was the villain in the duel.

2. to show how unreliable dueling pistols could be.

3. to indicate the way modern research depends on accidents.

GENERALITIES   Based on the passage, which of the following generalities seem justifiable? _____ and _____.

1. Duelists were not to aim carefully, but to shoot relatively quickly at their opponents.

2. History has treated Aaron Burr as a less worthy person than Alexander Hamilton.

3. Coming from sharply different backgrounds weighed heavily on each man.

4. The basis of the duel was the fact that Burr almost became president.

RETENTION   Based on the passage, which of the following statements are True (T), False (F), or Not answerable (N)?

1. _____ Alexander Hamilton was a bastard.

2. _____ The duel took place in New York City.

3. ____ Hamilton's son died in a duel using the same pistols his father later used.

4. ____ Aaron Burr was an experienced duelist before he met Hamilton on the field.

5. ____ The pistols were a gift to the Chase Manhattan Bank.

6. ____ Hamilton was born in New Jersey.

7. ____ Neither Hamilton nor Burr served in the army.

8. ____ Hamilton and Burr were actually businessmen in competition with each other.

9. ____ The bank Hamilton headed failed soon after his death.

10. ____ The pistols in question were purchased by John Church in America.

11. ____ Hamilton once was the Secretary of the Treasury.

12. ____ Aaron Burr actually received the same number of votes for the presidency as Thomas Jefferson, but he lost to Jefferson anyway.

13. ____ Hamilton married into a powerful American family.

14. ____ Technically, Hamilton was ineligible to be president of the United States.

15. ____ The rigging of the pistols gave Hamilton a theoretical advantage.

16. ____ The normal bore for a dueling pistol was no larger than .50 caliber.

17. ____ Burr immediately would have known about the hair trigger.

18. ____ Both the pistols were originally percussion types.

19. ____ Chase Manhattan Bank has a museum.

20. ____ After Hamilton's death, dueling was made illegal in the United States.

COMPLETION   Choose the best answer for each question.

1. ____ Burr's father was a: (a) minister. (b) noted general. (c) college president. (d) revolutionary architect.

2. ____ The pistols used in the duel had a: (a) burr-trigger. (b) fur-trigger. (c) modified flint-pull trigger. (d) single-set trigger.

3. ____ Burr's Manhattan Company was chiefly responsible for: (a) New York City's water. (b) running the city government. (c) trading with other nations. (d) lending money to major corporations.

4. ____ Hamilton owned, for a time, a virtual monopoly in: (a) weapons. (b) shipping. (c) western land. (d) banking.

5. _____ Lindsay explains that the danger with a hair-trigger is: (a) that it will not fire. (b) that it fires erratically. (c) in the weight of the pull. (d) the possibility of firing too soon.

6. _____ Proper dueling pistols do not have: (a) adjustable sights. (b) weights of any sort. (c) a specific trigger. (d) identifiable caliber bores.

DEFINITIONS   Choose the best definition for each italicized word.

1. _____ an *illustrious* son: (a) model (b) dangerous (c) worthless (d) famous

2. _____ *fidelity* of reproduction: (a) cost (b) loan (c) accuracy (d) validity

3. _____ he served *creditably:* (a) soon (b) on loan (c) with honor (d) when he could

4. _____ rose to *prominence:* (a) notice (b) the occasion (c) estate (d) his level

5. _____ the *fateful* duel: (a) Greek (b) deadly (c) poor (d) dramatic

6. _____ sight your *quarry:* (a) prey (b) horsecart (c) pistol (d) friend

7. _____ the *subsequent* history: (a) real (b) authorized (c) unreliable (d) later

8. _____ to *divert* attention: (a) sense (b) include (c) turn aside (d) call up

9. _____ *surreptitiously* set the trigger: (a) secretly (b) shrewdly (c) efficiently (d) significantly

10. _____ research in the *archives:* (a) records (b) museums (c) halls of ivy (d) vaults

11. _____ at your *antagonist:* (a) second (b) own person (c) friend (d) enemy

12. _____ a cruel *scoundrel:* (a) thug (b) schemer (c) villain (d) fighter

13. _____ a fair and *judicial* manner: (a) courtly (b) superficial (c) sensational (d) just

14. _____ helped *foster* traditions: (a) encourage (b) stifle (c) illegitimate (d) new

15. _____ to *authenticate* the reproductions: (a) scale down (b) fabricate (c) try to establish (d) confirm

39 *T. H. BELL*

Is Discipline Education's Missing Link?

Education has often concerned itself with discipline, but it has not always concerned itself with the kinds of discipline T. H. Bell describes here. By discipline Bell does not mean corporal punishment but the values that underlie what he might call character.

Discipline and moral values, I am convinced, are the keys to responsible citizenship. I fear that responsible citizenship is withering in our land, and in many other parts of the world as well. We must all raise our voices for a more disciplined society through more disciplined education.

By discipline in education I do not mean punishment, control, restraint. I mean commitment. I mean high standards and academic rigor. I mean sacrifice in the name of excellence.

We are drifting away from discipline in our schools, colleges, and universities. We must make new commitments to it in education and in our life as citizens. Discipline makes us productive, affluent, strong, enlightened, and free. Take away discipline and you have decay, decline, anarchy, and abandonment of truth.

Thomas Jefferson, in his first inaugural address, asked:

"Would the honest patriot, in the full tide of successful experiment, abandon a government which has so far kept us free and firm, on the theoretic and visionary fear that this government, the world's best hope, may by possibility want energy to preserve itself?"

IS DISCIPLINE EDUCATION'S MISSING LINK?   "Discipline: Education's Missing Link" by T. H. Bell. *The Rotarian,* December 1976. Reprinted by permission.

I fear that we in the United States have come almost to the point where we must answer *yes* to Jefferson's question. Academic test scores, voter registration figures—almost all the indexes we have—point to the kind of citizen lassitude Jefferson feared.

What are some of the signals that discipline is sagging in our education system?

Testimony at a special Congressional hearing on violence and vandalism in the schools left an impression that many of our secondary schools are gripped by hopelessness and despair. Key witnesses implied that student assaults and violence could not be corrected—that school authorities could not cope with the situation.

An article in a well-known publication recently reported that more than 40 percent of the graduating class of a reputable university had graduated with honors or *cum laude,* implying that standards had slipped at this institution and that its academic rigor had declined.

And here are some of the warnings we have received that undisciplined education bears only the rotting fruit of undisciplined, apathetic citizenship:

The overall voting record is lower in the U.S. than in most other democracies. Voters between 18 and 21 years old had the worst voting record of any age group in both 1972 and 1974.

The Yankelovich Survey, a study of young men and women financed by a number of foundations, found in 1967 that some 35 percent of Americans aged 16 to 26 considered patriotism an important value. Six years later, in 1973, the figure had dropped to 19 percent.

The National Commission on the Reform of Secondary Education analyzed hundreds of handbooks on "Student Rights and Responsibilities," published by schools and state departments of education. More than 99 percent dealt with student *rights.* Fewer than 1 percent even mentioned *responsibilities.*

The Council of Chief State School Officers—U.S. state superintendents or commissioners of education—concluded at their 1974 annual convention that "recognizing the need for a new level of citizenship education may be the most important action this council can take at this time."

I agree, and I set up in the U. S. Office of Education a task force to make recommendations on citizenship education in the schools. The actual carrying out of its recommendations is left to state and local educators at their discretion. As Commissioner I could not impose a plan on them; however, I had a responsibility to lead and I exercised that responsibility.

Others share my concern and are taking active steps to nurture and encourage citizenship education and responsible participation in civic affairs. The American Bar Association, for example, supports a national clearinghouse on "Youth Education for Citizenship," and the National Endowment for the Humanities helped finance a program for the first 12 grades focusing on such concepts as participation, justice, and responsibility. A National Task Force on Citizenship Education, supported by private foundations, is examining new concepts and teaching methods for responsible citizenship. Its report is available to educators and the general public.

I strongly suspect that much of the trouble in schools is a response to boredom. A more disciplined society would give young people a more disciplined, demanding, and therefore far more stimulating environment. There is more to learn than ever before, and our youth are more talented and able than they have been ever before.

I do not imply that education should disregard learning problems. If there is any place where discipline must be constantly mellowed by compassion, it is in schools and colleges. We must always allow for individual differences. We must stand up for the rights of minorities. Equality of opportunity must begin with education if we are to apply this principle to all facets of living. We must have compensatory education for the disadvantaged. Those with learning problems need and deserve the extra effort and expense to meet their needs. Teachers should be charitable and kind in applying rules and standards to students deserving of a break. But at the same time, we may be spreading classroom charity over too many students who need and deserve more challenge.

Disciplined education does not need to be a mindless, authoritarian system that drives more than it leads, punishes more than it persuades. Without abandoning compassion and empathy, we can have a no-nonsense program that calls for mastery of reading, mathematics, spelling, and other basics. Too many students are getting by from one grade level to another without this mastery. We know vastly more than ever before about *how* to teach the bottom 25 percent; we should apply what we know. Not all children will attain a high level of proficiency in reading and mathematics. But we can't live with the high percentage of students who in some large urban school systems fail to reach an *acceptable* level.

A school system committed to disciplined standards of excellence in teaching and learning will take all measures possible to educate the bottom one-fourth of the student body. A few systems have demonstrated this capacity. What we need is a widespread resolve to reach a higher level of performance. We must help our youth find happiness and fulfillment through serious work in an atmosphere of reasonable standards that are sensibly, firmly, and consistently applied. Today's young men and women need to learn that the closest helping hand is at the end of their own arm. We need a strong, new, vigorous commitment to the old-fashioned work ethic. Let's teach that ethic in our schools. It will be the finest lesson our youth will ever learn.

When I speak to high school and college graduating classes, I sometimes pose a set of questions, and tell the graduates that if they can answer *yes* to all they can consider themselves to be educated persons. Among the questions:

Have you developed a clear set of standards and ideals to guide your life and your daily living?

A truly educated person lives by some abiding principles that are personally satisfying. It is good to be open and teachable and to let one's standards grow with true conviction and conversion to new thoughts. It is quite another matter, however, to agree with everyone and to lack strength of conviction. A very wise man once said, "He who trims himself to everybody will soon whittle himself away." Without being rigid, we all need a firm rooting in those basic principles that we hold to be genuine.

Have you educated your feelings, your spirit, and your inner soul? Have you learned to enjoy fine music, great art, good literature, the sounds and sights of nature?

A quality life calls for quality thoughts and feelings and an appreciation for the fine things around us. We can't consider ourself educated without these qualities.

Do you know *yourself,* and can you apply what you know to maintain your physical and mental health . . . can you control your appetites and passions?

It is of no avail to be an intellectual giant and a physical weakling! Most knowledgeable people know that exercise, proper nutrition, and adequate rest are essential to good health.

About mental health I ask: Do you live with reality? Are you positive in your thinking? Is your outlook uplifting and wholesome? Do you know how to be free and enjoy freedom?

Some people live as prisoners in a free land because they are slaves to their habits and to their fears and paranoiac outlook.

All these questions bear on self-discipline. A well-disciplined life is the only road to true happiness. It begins with an objective, disciplined education system, and it ends with more productivity and a richer life for individuals and people as a whole. Discipline means *more* freedom, not *less.*

Many educators believe that it is not the proper role of schools to teach moral standards and values. In their view, if we expose our youth to many concepts of behavior, each individual will arrive at those personal standards most acceptable to himself. Thus, to impose standards of conduct, dress, and speech is in many ways coercive. The conclusion is that there is not much room in a democratically managed institution for imposition of moral values or implied rules of conduct and behavior.

This view of morality and of personal human values leads us to let the so-called "felt needs" and demands of our students tell us how to run our schools. This in turn leads to "openness"—open admissions, open classrooms, and open grading—leaving the students free to simply elect a pass or fail grade rather than a "coercive" letter grade. We want students to feel free from "authoritarian" controls because such controls subvert a truly democratic society. This line of throught is at the heart of many of today's problems.

I consider such thinking nonsense, but many educators find it hard to oppose. If you teach morality and values, they ask, whose do you teach? They go on to conclude that if a school seeks out student views and "perceived needs," it will help their motivation. Concern for motivation is, of course, legitimate. It has led to some changes for the better. The problem is that it may be dominating our thinking about the entire education system.

Benefits from the pursuit of responsiveness, permissiveness, and neutrality on values have not been spectacular. We have reached an all-time high in truancy, disrespect, lack of commitment, and a host of other problems that will be with us until we abandon our moral and ethical neutrality.

Educators must assume more responsibility for moral development. We should avoid teaching religious precepts as such; that is the role of the home and the church. But our institutions of education should unapologetically teach a "quality" way of life—with moral values, a code of conduct, ethical standards. We don't have to be morally neutral. The universal verities of honesty, forthrightness, and unvarnished truthfulness must be reawakened in the classrooms.

Forcefully and without equivocation, schools should teach equality of opportunity, freedom from prejudice, honesty, respect for law. Our stand should be so strong, so clear, that we come across to the students as harboring no nonsense in this area. We need not be ashamed to teach great principles. Without them, we will teach only half of what students expect and deserve from us.

We in the United States have for a number of years been on a nationwide binge of permissiveness. Anything goes, we have been saying, because everything depends upon the individual's choice, taste, and personal appetite. But students don't want to be "liberated." They want to be challenged! Education must be committed to building self-confidence and ambition and ever-rising horizons in the mind and soul of youth. I quote Thomas Jefferson again:

"I know of no safe depository of the ultimate powers of the society but the people themselves, and if we think them not enlightened enough to exercise their control with a wholesome discretion, the remedy is not to take it from them, but to inform their discretion by education."

We have faced and conquered many problems, but new ones never stop coming up. Today many sorely challenge our technical ingenuity and our value system. Some, like unemployment, inflation, urban blight, and the energy shortage, are obvious. Others, not so obvious, are equally important and perhaps even more far-reaching in consequence—one especially, is the dropout of citizens from civic life. Self-government is on trial in the U.S. and elsewhere.

Only education can break the civic withdrawal syndrome and reinstall the values that make for responsible citizenship. Our formal school structure must play a lead role in this resurrection. But we also must realize that education doesn't begin or end at the schoolhouse door. Television and radio, newspapers, magazines, motion pictures, families, churches, and other institutions are in every sense integral parts of the education team.

There are indications that the tide is turning back in the direction of more citizenship education and participation. I intend to support and encourage this trend to the fullest in the hope that it will become a full-fledged international movement.

LENGTH: 2310 WORDS

39   Is Discipline Education's Missing Link?

SCORING: Reading time: _____ Rate from chart: _____ W.P.M.

PURPOSE	number right _____ × 4 equals _____ points	
GENERALITIES	number right _____ × 4 equals _____ points	
RETENTION	number right _____ × 2 equals _____ points	
COMPLETION	number right _____ × 3 equals _____ points	
DEFINITIONS	number right _____ × 2 equals _____ points	
	(Total points: 100) **total** _____ points	

PURPOSE   Which of the following phrases best expresses the purpose of the passage? _____

1. to establish special programs for scholastically gifted students.

2. to complain about the failure of permissiveness in education.

3. to promote new courses in citizenship in high school and college.

GENERALITIES   Based on the passage, which of the following generalities seem justifiable? _____ and _____.

1. The task force on citizenship education has been given special priority.

2. Bell assumes schools can help teach discipline and moral values.

3. Bell feels there is a general decline in discipline in America.

4. Bell feels academic test scores do not reflect discipline or moral values.

RETENTION   Based on the passage, which of the following statements are True (T), False (F), or Not answerable (N)?

1. _____ The government supports the national task force on citizenship education.

2. _____ Younger voters have the worst voting record in United States elections.

3. _____ Bell includes corporal punishment in his definition of discipline.

4. _____ A sense of commitment is of first importance to Bell.

5. _____ A high percentage of cum laude graduates displeases Bell.

6. _____ The government has refused to comment openly on Bell's proposals.

7. _____ The styles in education seem to run counter to Bell's wishes.

8. _____ Vandalism in schools can readily be brought under control.

9. _____ Other democracies seem to have a larger number of voters than the United States.

10. _____ "Open" education is not to Bell's liking.

11. _____ Bell agrees, however, that morality cannot be discussed in the classroom because it is too controversial.

12. _____ According to Bell, discipline increases freedom.

13. _____ Apparently, Bell feels a dress code might be good for schools.

14. _____ Bell is opposed to educators' seeking out students' needs.

15. _____ Bell feels schools should teach equality of opportunity and freedom from prejudice.

16. _____ Religious precepts should be taught in schools, Bell says.

17. _____ Most educators agree that moral values must be taught in school.

18. _____ Bell feels patriotism is an important positive value.

19. _____ Some people are slaves to their habits.

20. _____ This speech was given to the Thomas Jefferson Society.

COMPLETION Choose the best answer for each question.

1. _____ Discipline is said to make us: (a) coerced. (b) productive. (c) truthful. (d) moral.

2. _____ One of the Jefferson quotes definitely defends: (a) moral values. (b) education for life. (c) patriotism. (d) a serious challenge.

3. _____ One of the questions Bell asks graduating classes is whether they know: (a) their lessons. (b) who put them through school. (c) the name of their congressional representative. (d) themselves.

4. _____ One point of agreement is that schools know a great deal about how to educate the: (a) bottom 25 percent of students. (b) genius. (c) ordinary middle-class student. (d) above-average student.

5. _____ Truly educated people live by: (a) their wits. (b) some means of livelihood. (c) abiding principles. (d) the old-fashioned work ethic.

6. _____ Bell insists that educators take more responsibility for their students': (a) grades. (b) moral development. (c) personal attitudes. (d) capacity to achieve their academic dreams unaided.

DEFINITIONS   Choose the best definition for each italicized word.

1. _____ voter *lassitude:* (a) power (b) time (c) fatigue (d) ripeness

2. _____ citizenship is *withering:* (a) disappearing (b) losing (c) drying up (d) increasing

3. _____ the civic-withdrawal *syndrome:* (a) pattern (b) guilt (c) sets (d) house

4. _____ *integral* parts of the team: (a) big (b) small (c) new (d) important

5. _____ educational *verities:* (a) problems (b) truths (c) aids (d) failures

6. _____ codes are an *imposition:* (a) help (b) fear (c) need (d) restriction

7. _____ our technical *ingenuity:* (a) prowess (b) skill (c) cleverness (d) might

8. _____ no one could *cope:* (a) deal with (b) mean (c) see (d) impose on

9. _____ at the educators' *discretion:* (a) suggestion (b) meaning (c) last explanation (d) judgment

10. _____ *nurture* citizenship: (a) foster (b) nature (c) rupture (d) injure

11. _____ *subvert* democracy: (a) have (b) head off (c) change (d) ruin

12. _____ student *proficiency:* (a) grief (b) skill (c) reluctance (d) uproar

13. _____ drifting toward *anarchy:* (a) tyranny (b) no government (c) more government (d) modified socialism

14. _____ educators show *restraint:* (a) control (b) alarm (c) faith (d) stuff

15. _____ academic *rigor:* (a) foolishness (b) death (c) strictness (d) fields

40 *ALBERT ROSENFELD*

Extending Our Life Span

People have been guided by the Bible's assessment of a normal life span: three score and ten years. Science has done wonders in helping us live as long as the Bible promised: seventy years of age. But scientists now wonder if there is perhaps a way to extend that mark and make it possible for us to live indefinitely. Apparently, if the process of aging can be identified, such a possibility is feasible.

Human beings, like every other living thing, are designed to die. Evolution demands it. If accident or disease doesn't do us in first, we begin to deteriorate until one or more of our bodily systems fail. Medical advances of the last 50 years have increased our life expectancy—made it more probable that we will live out our life-span—but they have not yet increased the life-span itself.

Now half a dozen lines of promising—and converging—research suggest that in the next century we may learn how to alter that design so that our bodies do not self-destruct. We may learn to live, if not forever, then for centuries. The implications for society, as for individuals, are staggering.

Extending the human life-span will not happen all at once, but in a succession of small steps. Anti-aging drugs (including antioxidants) are already being tested, and it seems likely that even before we learn to extend life we will learn to prolong the years of good life.

True, nature programs us to survive—but only up to a point. That point is the production of offspring, and the rearing of those progeny to the realization of their own procreative capacities. It would appear that nature has an unflattering lack of concern for our preservation as individuals, except as instruments to

---

EXTENDING OUR LIFE SPAN   From *Prolongevity*, by Albert Rosenfeld. Copyright © 1976 by Albert Rosenfeld. Reprinted by permission of Alfred A. Knopf, Inc.

ensure the perpetuation of the species. Even that may be surmising too much. So many species have come and gone in the Earth's lifetime that we are well advised not to count on any guarantees, even for the human race.

The individual human life may be likened to one of NASA's planetary "fly-bys"—a comparison that has grown popular in gerontological circles. NASA has launched many space vehicles designed to fly by Venus, Mercury, Mars or Jupiter. If everything does not survive the trip in good enough condition to function properly when it arrives, then the whole effort has been wasted. So all systems are meticulously monitored all the way to the planet; the data that is sent back constitutes a treasury of new knowledge; the scientists and engineers are elated. But when the fly-by's task is done, the designers lose all further interest in the vehicle. It may go on out into space for a long time. Its instruments may even continue to function; but few give it a thought.

It is a reasonable analogy. Unlike the planetary fly-by, however, we are sentient vehicles, and *we* care about our individual fates, even if the designer no longer does. Moreover, we are intelligent, and have been accumulating sufficient knowledge about our own workings to give us hope that we can now begin to modify what was formerly irremediable.

We have had some limited success. In ancient Greece, when the average life expectancy was 22, that was enough to guarantee the propagation of the species. But we have gone on, over recent centuries, to raise this expectancy to the scriptural three score and ten. Now we know we can do even better, not only in terms of expectancy, but in extending the actual life-span. We can discover what keeps this fly-by from functioning after its official mission is complete; and we can perhaps restore those functions, or prevent their running down. If there is a self-destruct mechanism aboard—as many believe—we can find it, and abort or dismantle it.

A good place to start is with species that seem to exhibit such a self-destruct mechanism. The Pacific salmon, for example, is a powerful fish equipped to muscle its way like a decathlon champion through all obstacles. A veritable antigravity machine, it swims upstream against the rapids, jumps up and over waterfalls as it moves with undistractable compulsion to its spawning grounds. Once spawning has taken place, this magnificent embodiment of piscine strength, health and beauty—having discharged its procreative obligations—grows old with obscene suddenness. Senility sets in virtually overnight, and, within two weeks, the great fish is dead.

Some have speculated that the very coming-in-from-the-sea, the passage from salt water to fresh, somehow triggers the onset of senescence even as the salmon spends its last heroic energies running the obstacle course against gravity to its life-in-death rendezvous. Recent studies have shown that the totally preoccupied fish may quite literally starve to death, denying itself any nutritional refueling of its vanishing energies and at the same time rendering itself unable to produce the mucus that protects the gills which filter its oxygen; so it is deprived of oxygen as well as the nutrients it needs.

The change from salt water to fresh *could* be important in some varieties of salmon, inasmuch as such changes in environment do often trigger changes in biological activity, as Dr. Stewart Wolf, director of the Marine Biomedical Institute at the University of Texas Medical Branch at Galveston, points out. As one example, Wolf cites the case of a shark whose liver, under normal circumstances, resembles that of an alcoholic human's, yellow and full of fat. It manufactures only a trace of protein, causing a high concentration of urea in the bloodstream, which would represent advanced kidney failure in a human body. If that shark is moved from its customary saltwater habitat and put into fresh water, the urea levels quickly fall.

Nevertheless, O. H. Robertson, the British-born scientist who created the first blood bank, dismissed the likelihood that the mere change from salt water to fresh could wholly account for the multitudinous, simultaneous biological transformations which he observed taking place. He dismissed the idea because he found a breed of salmon called the kokanee—a dwarf blueback variety—that lived in landlocked lakes. They spent their lives in fresh water and never got out to sea at all, yet they underwent the same rapid degeneration after spawning as the migratory varieties. For this very reason, the kokanee proved to be Robertson's favorite experimental animal; it was easier to keep track of throughout its life cycle.

Robertson found that, in a process that probably began even before spawning, the salmon's pituitary enlarged, stimulating the adrenal cortex to grow many times its normal size—resulting in an enormous overproduction of steroid hormones. As others have noted, this strongly resembles what happens in Cushing's syndrome in human patients, where a great overbalance of glucocorticoids causes widespread and often severe symptoms, including fatigue, impotence, susceptibility to infection, and abnormal accumulation of fat. This violent hormonal disturbance could certainly account for many of the senescent changes that ensue at such an accelerated pace in the salmon.

What happens in Cushing's syndrome and in the senescent Pacific salmon is similar to what may happen in individual human cells. According to the controversial theory of W. Donner Denckla, this is what happens. As the organism ages, and the pituitary releases its "death hormones," the cell is prevented from taking up thyroxine for its vital metabolic needs. Though the glucocorticoids within the cell do not increase in quantity, they are in sudden oversupply when the thyroid hormone is not there to counterbalance their effects. As a consequence, the cell is afflicted with a kind of Cushing's syndrome in miniature, which could result in the disturbance of tissue-renewal processes. This would occur throughout the body, though the deterioration, subtle at the start (in puberty) and growing more pronounced only with further releases of the "death" hormone later in life, would proceed at a statelier pace than in the salmon.

Other findings have already shed a great deal of new light on the tragically accelerated events that highlight the last days of the salmon—findings that should lead to many human applications. For instance, Don Puppione of the Donner Laboratory of Medical Physics in Berkeley was astounded to discover that, just before spawning, the salmon's bloodstream contained 20 times the amount of fatty compounds—including cholesterol—found in normal human blood. Yet none of it seems to accumulate in the arteries!

In the salmon we seem to have occurring simultaneously the two diseases—both of them endocrine disorders—that most mimic aging in human patients: hypothyroidism (too little thyroid hormone) and hyperadrenocorticism (too much of the adrenal hormones, as in Cushing's syndrome). And they are without much doubt genetically programmed.

It was Eberhard G. Trams of the National Institute of Neurological Diseases and Stroke who especially concentrated on the brain and hormonal aspects of the salmon's senescence (and has continued to do so). He noted, as Robertson did but in more precise detail, the enlarged pituitary (three times as big in fresh water as in the ocean), the steroid overproduction, and other physiological changes. He also observed that the salmon died of "a complete metabolic shutdown," and that the increased production of adrenal steroid hormones seemed to inhibit antibodies, thereby leaving the fish more vulnerable to infection.

On the whole, the recent findings substantiate Robertson's in terms of hormonal causation, but it is now clearer that the process is already taking place during the entire time the salmon is journeying up-river. It could be that whatever impels the fish to undertake its amazing trip is the same trigger that sets in motion the decay processes—the compulsive behavior leading to the starvation leading to the glandular malfunctions in falling domino fashion.

But perhaps not. Hear, for instance, one more fish story—the steelhead trout's. The steelhead trout, like the salmon, comes in from the ocean and swims upriver to its spawning grounds, and also undergoes rapid degeneration. But Robert Van Citters of the University of Washington in Seattle discovered, some years ago, that the steelhead trout do not all die. Moreover, those that do survive and reach the ocean once more are somehow regenerated and rejuvenated! Terrible—presumably lethal—arterial damage simply disappears. Using radioactive tracers, Van Citters ascertained that some of the trout were able to spawn, degenerate and regenerate at least two or three times, apparently with no permanent damage. Rediscovering Van Citters' neglected work, Stewart Wolf is eager to do follow-up studies of the mechanisms that permit the trout's remarkable recovery. Can the trout teach us something about reversing human degenerative processes? Wolf is seeking support for the building of an artificial trout stream at or near UTMB's Galveston campus in order to pursue these investigations.

If the Pacific salmon and the steelhead trout represent nature's experiments—perhaps inadvertent—in accelerated aging processes, there is a fortunately rare human disease which serves as a similar gerontological model for similar reasons. The disease is progeria, which the *Journal of the American Medical Association* once headlined as "Nature's Experiment in Unnatural Aging." According to Franklin L. DeBusk of the University of Florida College of Medicine, who undertook an exhaustive survey of the literature, progeria occurs no oftener than once in eight million births in the United States, and he was able to find reports of only 60 cases of progeria, worldwide, as of April 1972.

There cannot be too many childhood diseases that are more tragic. Progeria victims often appear, for a period of anywhere from three months to three years, to be perfectly normal in every respect—just as height and weight may be normal at birth. But then disquieting signs begin to appear. Growth is retarded, and the progeric child, if he survives through his teens, never gets to be any bigger than a normal three-to-five-year-old. As soon as his telescoped childhood is over, other changes begin to take place. These have been described in several papers in the *Journal of the American Geriatrics Society* by William Reichel, chairman of the Department of Family Practice Program at the Franklin Square Hospital in Baltimore, who has made the study of progeria his lifelong avocation.

The typical progeric child begins to look frail and old as early as the age of three or four. He may start experiencing cardiac troubles as early as five, though often not until 10 or 15, and these troubles may include heart murmurs, atherosclerosis, elevated cholesterol levels, high blood pressure, angina pectoris, congestive heart failure—and finally the heart attack that is the most usual cause of death. The average life span of progerics is 12 to 18 years, though some have died as early as five (DeBusk reports those who died between five and seven were the victims of accidents, and that seven is the earliest death from "old age"), and some have survived to the age of 27. For the most part, though, it is an early teen-age death, after a long period of steady and irreversible debilitation and deterioration. The progeric is a dwarf, but with a head that is of normal size and therefore looks larger than normal compared to the stunted body. The skin is wrinkled and parchmentlike, also almost opaque, with virtually no fat under the skin and the blood vessels showing prominently. The hair is white and sparse—if any remains at all. The face is birdlike, the eyes protuberant, the nose hooked. In fact, progeria patients, as DeBusk points out, "bear an uncanny resemblance to one another." They are weak-limbed and stiff-jointed, and no medication or therapy has yet been found that will help them.

What perhaps renders their plight even more tragic, Reichel suggests, is the fact that they retain normal intelligence, hence are sensitive to the implications of their condition. "These children," DeBusk observes, "tended to be shy and aware of their unusual appearance. They were friendly, lively, witty and mischievous in the company of acquaintances, and they exhibited normal emotions, becoming happy, angry, and sad in the appropriate situation." Harvard's Dorothy B. Villee adds, in *Pediatrics,* that "Their major complaint is the social problems produced by the stigma of their appearance."

Though progeria undoubtedly mimics old age, its victims do not show all the signs of senescence (senile dementia is absent, for example), hence there are reservations about looking upon what happens as true aging. The similarities in symptoms could turn out to be nothing but coincidence. Reichel asks: "Is it truly a disease of accelerated aging? Does it in fact represent a genetic error? If so, is there one genetic mechanism regulating man's normal life-span? Or conversely: Is there a gene or group of genes whose purpose is to facilitate the incorporation of errors into a biological system? If so, does progeria represent an early activation of such a mechanism?" The questions must remain, for the moment, rhetorical.

Progeric children do not seem to have any gross chromosomal abnormalities. Though various studies have cast suspicion on the hormonal and immunological abnormalities of some progerics, the findings have not been consistent, and there exists no conclusive evidence that it is basically either a hormonal or an immunological disease. Reichel has found large accumulations of lipofuscin—the "aging pigment"—in the cells of progerics, as well as abnormalities in the connective tissue. Betty Shannon Danes of the New York Hospital-Cornell Medical Center has also reported that progeric cells have a lowered cloning efficiency, as well as a diminished capacity to duplicate their DNA or to divide normally (all those deficiencies logically go together, of course). And a Harvard team has turned up suggestive evidence of faulty DNA-repair mechanisms in progeric cells.

No one group of people seems to be singled out as progeria victims. The cases are spread over many nations, and the disease seems to afflict all races, males as readily as females. There are only three reports of more than one victim in a single family, and only one case that might have resulted from a consanguinous marriage. Thus, though progeria is suspected of being a genetic disease, much about it remains puzzling, and it has certainly not yet been proved to be hereditary.

There is a similar disease, however, which is known to be genetic—Werner's syndrome. Its onset does not occur until somewhere between 15 and 20 years of age, when most progeria victims are already dead. Some believe Werner's syndrome may be merely a later expression of progeria.

The Werner's victim also suffers from arrested growth, though of course not to the same extent as progerics. They are simply much shorter than average in stature, and they too become prematurely gray and bald. (Some of their otherwise normal relatives also turn prematurely gray.) They are prone to the earlier-than-usual arrival of diseases ordinarily associated with aging, such as diabetes melitus, atherosclerosis, heart disease, and cancer. They die of what looks like old age in their forties and fifties. Though Werner's syndrome is also rare, it occurs about twice as frequently as progeria.

What are we to glean from diseases such as these?

For one thing, whether we define them as "true" aging or not, there is no doubt that, in both diseases, widespread degenerative changes do take place at the level of both the individual cell and the total organism. Whatever it is that occurs brings on degenerative changes much sooner than would happen in the normal course of events, suggesting strongly that the occurrences are not due to simple wear and tear. The probability appears high that some internal timing mechanism is at work, whether it is identical to the clock of aging or not, and that it affects the entire organism; and, further, that the mechanism is somehow built into the individual's genetic information—perhaps as something added, perhaps as something missing, but in any event as something gone wrong. And the something wrong would seem to be in whatever mechanism regulates the onset and rate of deterioration. The defect could be in the molecular-genetic apparatus of the individual cell, passed on to all the body's cells by the original fertilized egg. Or it could be in the hypothalamic-pituitary controls of the endocrine system which affect all cells.

In progeria, it is quite clear very early in life that something has gone radically wrong with the child's development. In Werner's syndrome, it is equally clear that the something wrong has been postponed (if you compare it with progeria) *on program*. There are other devastating diseases, such as Huntington's chorea, which are genetically triggered late in life; but in the case of Werner's, what is triggered is a whole cascade of degenerative agelike changes. If these can be triggered genetically in Werner's victims, they can be triggered in "normal" individuals at more advanced ages—giving added credence to all genetic-clock theories of aging. The hope in these diseases, as in true aging (which is also, in that case, a genetic disease), is that if a program can be accelerated by accident, it can be slowed down—or reversed—on purpose.

LENGTH: 3410 WORDS

40   Extending Our Life Span

SCORING: Reading time: _____ Rate from chart: _____ W.P.M.

PURPOSE	number right _____ × 4 equals _____ points	
GENERALITIES	number right _____ × 4 equals _____ points	
RETENTION	number right _____ × 2 equals _____ points	
COMPLETION	number right _____ × 3 equals _____ points	
DEFINITIONS	number right _____ × 2 equals _____ points	

(Total points: 100) **total** _____ points

PURPOSE   Which of the following phrases best expresses the purpose of the passage? _____

1. to help us recognize that the life span of animals is established clearly in nature.

2. to show that the life cycle of fish can be remarkably similar to the life cycle of people, particularly regarding aging.

3. to suggest that the causes of aging may be in large measure genetic and therefore controllable.

GENERALITIES   Based on the passage, which of the following generalities seem justifiable? _____ and _____.

1. Age-related diseases like progeria imply that, like many other diseases, aging may someday be controlled by medicine.

2. The regenerative process of the trout really helps us understand how people can age profoundly "before their time."

3. One of the odd byproducts of biology is that we end up knowing more about the life cycles of fish than we do about the life span of humans.

4. Learning to control things often involves learning the causes of things.

RETENTION   Based on the passage, which of the following statements are True (T), False (F), or Not answerable (N)?

1. _____ Nature is not concerned about procreation.

2. _____ NASA's interest in fly-bys begins the moment the mission is over.

3. _____ In one kind of trout, lethal arterial damage seems to disappear when they return to salt water.

4. _____ The salmon is a veritable antigravity machine.

5. _____ Antioxidants would accelerate aging in humans.

6. _____ Progeria is peculiar to Caucasians.

7. _____ Researchers at Stanford are doing the most significant research in progeria.

8. _____ A genetic mechanism regulates the human life span.

9. _____ Progeria might be an early activation of a biological aging system.

10. _____ Progeria victims show the same senile dementia normal aging people show.

11. _____ Fortunately, progeria victims are not aware of their condition.

12. _____ Certain diseases are genetically triggered late in life.

13. _____ Progeric cells do not clone as well as normal cells.

14. _____ Lung failure is the chief cause of death of progerics.

15. _____ Werner's syndrome is like progeria, but it begins later in life.

16. _____ Progeria may be genetic, but few cases have occurred more than once in a family.

17. _____ There are no special journals for the study of aging.

18. _____ Progerics die in their teens; victims of Werner's syndrome die in their forties and fifties.

19. _____ Progeric infants and those subject to Werner's syndrome will never be able to be identified at birth.

20. _____ The hope is that if aging can be accelerated, then it can be retarded.

COMPLETION   Choose the best answer for each question.

1. _____ The salmon was observed in its efforts to return to: (a) the sea.   (b) the landlocked lakes of clear water.   (c) its spawning grounds.   (d) the place that will ultimately be its grave.

2. _____ The progeric child has a normal-sized: (a) spleen. (b) thyroid. (c) heart. (d) head.

3. _____ The major complaint of progeric children is: (a) that they will die. (b) that their appearance causes social problems. (c) much the same as that of Werner's syndrome patients. (d) what makes their study worthwhile.

4. _____ One of the conclusions that can be drawn from this research is that aging seems to: (a) arrive on a programmed schedule that may be encoded in our genes. (b) be one of those things, like death and taxes, that we will have to put up with. (c) be the same for fish as for humans. (d) have been as well understood in biblical times as today.

5. _____ The genetic-clock theory suggests that within the gene is locked: (a) a clue to aging. (b) a timing mechanism that starts the aging process. (c) the nucleus of the entire problem. (d) the secret of splenic divergence.

6. _____ The reason the article focuses on fish is that they exhibit: (a) a self-destruct mechanism. (b) both salt-water and fresh-water features. (c) some awareness of the aging process. (d) features of aging that cannot be duplicated in mammals or other land-based animals.

DEFINITIONS   Choose the best definition for each italicized word.

1. _____ *degenerative* changes: (a) good (b) creative (c) deteriorating (d) decorative

2. _____ the disease is *hereditary:* (a) transmissible (b) contagious (c) serious (d) part of a syndrome

3. _____ seems to *afflict* many people: (a) see (b) have (c) strike (d) eliminate

4. _____ the *stigma* of appearances: (a) mark (b) pain (c) looks (d) size

5. _____ *irreversible* change: (a) pointed (b) permanent (c) sudden (d) overt

6. _____ a sudden *debilitation:* (a) pain (b) headiness (c) weakness (d) fibrillation

7. _____ something *radically* wrong: (a) basically (b) infinitely (c) cruelly (d) oddly

8. _____ growth is *retarded:* (a) slowed (b) finished (c) weird (d) handicapped

9. _____ lifelong *avocation:* (a) study (b) help (c) hobby (d) problem

10. _____ findings *substantiate* the conclusions: (a) facilitate (b) disregard (c) have (d) prove

11. _____ *senescent* changes: (a) sorry (b) age-related (c) pain-induced (d) sudden

12. _____ accelerated *pace:* (a) foot (b) walk (c) rate (d) place

13. _____ a reasonable *analogy:* (a) situation (b) plan (c) comparison (d) feature

14. _____ *embodiment* of strength: (a) weariness (b) sign (c) hilt (d) model

15. _____ *prolong* life: (a) begin (b) end (c) shorten (d) extend

Charts for Measuring Speed of Reading

To find the speed at which a given selection is read, divide the total number of words (given at the end of each passage and on the charts below) by the number of seconds it took you to read the passage. Then multiply that figure by 60 in order to get the speed in words per minute (W.P.M.). For example: if you read Passage 1 in 90 seconds, or 1.5 minutes, you could calculate your speed in this way:

$$640 \div 90 = 7.1 \times 60 = 426 \text{ W.P.M.}$$

The charts below show how many words you read per minute depending on how long it takes to read the passage.

SECTION I

				SELECTIONS					
TIME IN MINS.	1	2	3	4	5	6	7	8	9
1	640	240	465	875	770	450	555	640	900
1.5	426	160	310	585	513	298	370	426	600
2	320	120	233	437	385	224	277	320	450
2.5	256	96	186	350	308	179	222	256	360
3	213	80	155	291	258	149	185	213	300
3.5	183	67	133	250	220	128	158	183	257
4	160	60	116	218	192	112	138	160	225
4.5	142	53	103	194	171	99	123	142	200
5	128	48	93	175	154	89	111	128	180
5.5	116	43	85	159	140	81	101	116	164
6	106	40	78	145	128	75	92	106	150
6.5	98	36	72	134	118	69	85	98	138
7	91	34	66	125	110	64	79	91	129
7.5	85	32	62	116	103	60	74	85	120

SELECTIONS

TIME IN MINS.	10	11	12	13	14	15	16	17	18	19
1	713	814	816	860	800	880	885	815	1120	1170
1.5	475	543	543	574	533	587	590	543	747	780
2	356	407	408	430	400	440	442	406	560	585
2.5	285	326	326	344	320	352	354	326	448	468
3	237	271	271	230	233	293	295	271	373	390
3.5	204	233	233	246	229	251	253	233	320	334
4	178	203	208	215	200	220	221	204	280	292
4.5	158	181	181	191	178	196	197	181	249	260
5	142	163	163	172	160	176	177	163	222	234
5.5	130	148	148	157	145	160	161	148	204	213
6	119	135	135	143	133	146	147	136	187	195
6.5	110	125	125	132	123	135	136	125	172	180
7	102	116	116	123	114	126	126	116	160	167
7.5	95	109	109	115	107	117	118	109	149	156
8	89	102	102	108	100	110	111	102	140	146
8.5	84	96	96	101	94	104	104	96	132	138
9	79	90	90	96	89	97	98	90	124	130
9.5	75	86	86	91	84	93	93	86	118	123
10	71	81	82	86	80	88	89	82	112	117
10.5	68	78	78	82	76	84	84	78	107	111

SELECTIONS

TIME IN MINS.	20	21	22	23	24	25	26
1	1240	1370	1150	1385	2180	1780	1800
1.5	827	913	767	923	1453	1187	1200
2	620	685	575	693	1090	890	900
2.5	496	548	460	554	872	712	720
3	413	457	383	462	727	593	600
3.5	354	391	329	396	623	509	514
4	310	343	288	346	545	445	450
4.5	276	304	256	308	484	396	400
5	248	274	230	277	436	356	360
5.5	225	249	209	252	396	324	327
6	207	228	192	231	363	297	300
6.5	191	211	177	213	335	274	277
7	177	195	164	198	311	254	257
7.5	165	183	153	185	291	237	240
8	155	171	144	173	273	223	225
8.5	146	161	135	163	256	209	212
9	138	152	128	154	242	198	200
9.5	131	144	121	146	229	187	189
10	124	137	115	139	218	178	180
10.5	118	130	110	132	208	170	171
11	113	125	105	126	198	162	164
11.5	108	119	100	120	190	155	157
12	103	114	96	115	182	148	150

SELECTIONS

TIME IN MINS.	27	28	29	30	31	32	33	34
1	1880	1400	1720	1800	1900	2200	1480	1910
1.5	1253	933	1147	1200	1267	1467	987	1273
2	940	700	806	900	950	1100	740	955
2.5	752	560	688	720	760	880	592	764
3	627	466	573	600	633	733	493	637
3.5	537	400	491	514	543	629	423	546
4	470	350	430	450	475	550	370	478
4.5	418	311	382	400	422	489	329	424
5	376	280	344	360	380	440	296	382
5.5	342	255	313	327	345	400	269	347
6	313	233	287	300	317	367	247	318
6.5	289	215	265	277	292	338	228	294
7	268	200	246	257	271	314	211	273
7.5	251	187	229	240	253	293	197	255
8	235	175	215	225	238	275	185	239
8.5	221	165	202	212	224	259	174	225
9	209	156	191	200	211	244	164	212
9.5	198	147	181	189	200	232	156	201
10	188	140	172	180	190	220	148	191
10.5	179	133	164	171	181	210	141	182
11	171	127	156	163	173	200	135	174
11.5	163	122	150	157	165	191	129	166
12	157	117	143	150	158	183	123	159
12.5	150	112	138	144	152	176	118	153

SELECTIONS

TIME IN MINS.	35	36	37	38	39	40
1	1360	1750	3650	2430	2310	3410
1.5	907	1167	2433	1620	1540	2273
2	680	875	1825	1215	1155	1705
2.5	544	700	1460	962	924	1364
3	453	583	1216	810	770	1170
3.5	389	500	1043	694	660	974
4	340	438	912	607	578	853
4.5	302	389	811	540	513	758
5	272	350	730	486	462	682
5.5	247	318	664	442	420	620
6	227	292	608	404	385	568
6.5	209	269	562	374	355	525
7	194	250	521	347	330	487
7.5	181	233	487	324	308	455
8	170	219	456	304	289	426
8.5	160	206	429	286	272	401
9	151	194	406	270	257	379
9.5	143	184	384	256	243	359
10	136	175	365	243	231	341
10.5	130	167	348	231	220	325
11	124	159	332	221	210	310
11.5	118	152	317	211	200	297
12	113	146	304	203	193	284
12.5	109	140	292	194	185	273
13	105	135	281	187	178	262
14			261	174		244
15			243	162		227

How to Measure Reading Efficiency

You may also wish to measure your efficiency in reading. This means simply that you may want to consider the speed by which you read a passage as a measurable function of your total score. In that case use the following formula:

Speed in W.P.M. × **total** score for passage expressed in percentage. The result will be a comparable figure you may use to measure your increase in speed even if your total score should decrease somewhat. An example will show how this works. Two people read the same passage and get the same total score, but one person takes much longer to do the reading. The difference can be measured in terms of efficiency as shown here:

> *Person A:* reads Passage 1 at the rate of 193 words per minute and scores 70 points. He computes his reading efficiency thus: 193 × .70 = 135 reading efficiency score.
>
> *Person B:* reads Passage 1 at the rate of 90 words per minute and scores 70 points. He computes his reading efficiency thus: 90 × .70 = 63 reading efficiency score.

Table of Reading Efficiency

Speed in W.P.M. × Point Score in Percentage = Reading Efficiency Score

SECTION I

1. _____ × _____ = _____

2. _____ × _____ = _____

3. _____ × _____ = _____

4. _____ × _____ = _____

5. _____ × _____ = _____

6. _____ × _____ = _____

7. _____ × _____ = _____

8. _____ × _____ = _____

SECTION II

9. _____ × _____ = _____

10. _____ × _____ = _____

11. _____ × _____ = _____

12. _____ × _____ = _____

13. _____ × _____ = _____

Speed in W.P.M. × Point Score in Percentage = Reading Efficiency Score

14. _____ × _____ = _____

15. _____ × _____ = _____

16. _____ × _____ = _____

17. _____ × _____ = _____

18. _____ × _____ = _____

SECTION III

19. _____ × _____ = _____

20. _____ × _____ = _____

21. _____ × _____ = _____

22. _____ × _____ = _____

23. _____ × _____ = _____

24. _____ × _____ = _____

25. _____ × _____ = _____

26. _____ × _____ = _____

SECTION IV

27. _____ × _____ = _____

28. _____ × _____ = _____

29. _____ × _____ = _____

30. _____ × _____ = _____

31. _____ × _____ = _____

32. _____ × _____ = _____

33. _____ × _____ = _____

34. _____ × _____ = _____

SECTION V

35. _____ × _____ = _____

36. _____ × _____ = _____

37. _____ × _____ = _____

38. _____ × _____ = _____

39. _____ × _____ = _____

40. _____ × _____ = _____

Graph for Measuring Progress in Retention

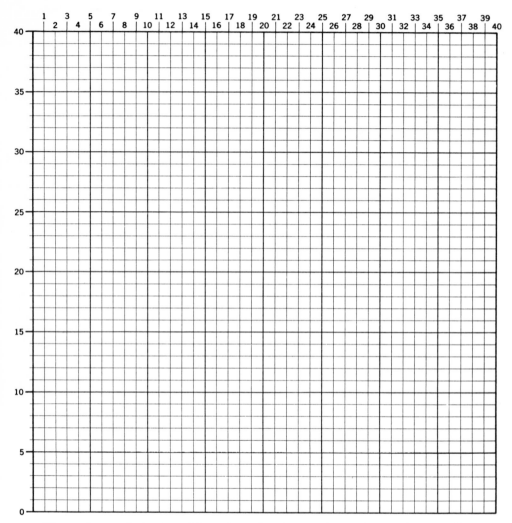

The numbers on the horizontal line refer to the selection; the numbers on the vertical line refer to the point score. Make a dot at your Retention score for each selection and connect the dots with a line.

Graph for Measuring Progress in Vocabulary Skill

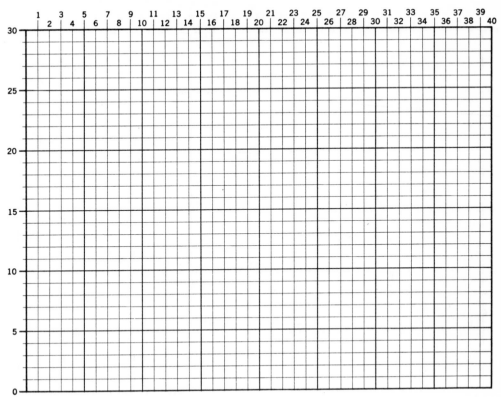

The numbers on the horizontal line refer to the selection; the numbers on the vertical line refer to the point score. Make a dot at your Definition score for each selection and connect the dots with a line.

Graph for Scores for Inferential and Completion Questions

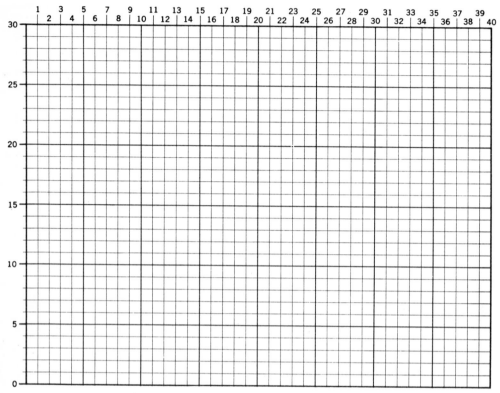

The numbers on the horizontal line refer to the selection; the numbers on the vertical line refer to the point score. Add the scores for Inference, Completion, Main Sentence, Generalities, and Purpose questions. Enter the total on the graph as a dot and connect the dots with a line.

Graph for Measuring Progress in Reading Speed in Words per Minute

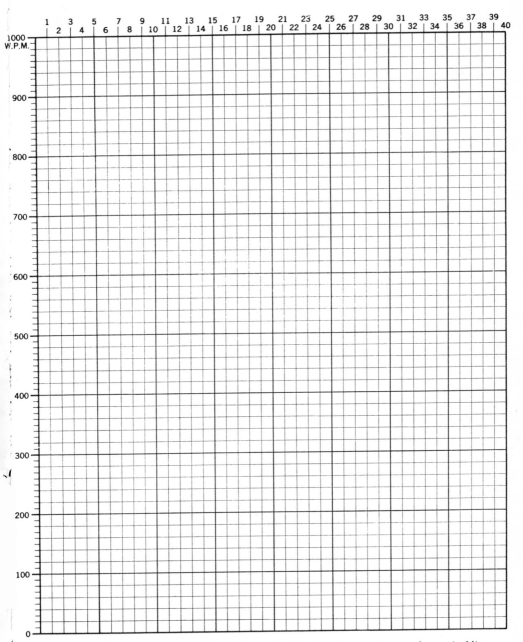

The numbers on the horizontal line refer to the selection; the numbers on the vertical line refer to reading speed in words per minute. Make a dot at your speed for each selection and connect the dots with a line.

Progress Chart

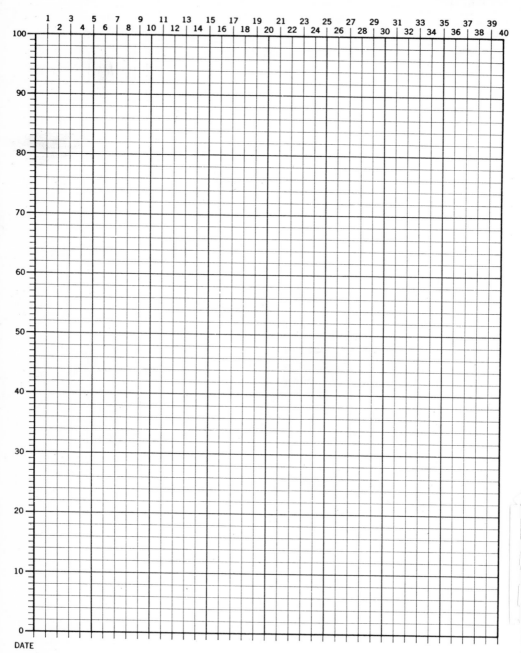

The numbers on the horizontal line refer to the selection; the numbers on the vertical line refer to the total point score of each selection. Make a dot at your score for each selection and connect the dots with a line. Put the date of each exercise on the lower part of the graph.